Yugoslavia

The Making of the 20th Century

David Armstrong, Lorna Lloyd and John Redmond, *From Versailles to Maastricht: International Organisation in the Twentieth Century*

V. R. Berghahn, *Germany and the Approach of War in 1914, 2nd edition*

Raymond F. Betts, *French Decolonisation, 1900–1960*

John Darwin, *Britain and Decolonisation: The Retreat from Empire in the Post-War World*

Ann Lane, *Yugoslavia: When Ideals Collide*

Robert Mallett, *Mussolini and the Origins of the Second World War, 1933–1940*

Sally Marks, *The Illusion of Peace: International Relations in Europe, 1918–1933, 2nd edition*

Philip Morgan, *Italian Fascism, 1919–1945*

A. J. Nicholls, *Weimar and the Rise of Hitler, 4th edition*

R. A. C. Parker, *Chamberlain and Appeasement: British Policy and the Coming of the Second World War*

Anita J. Prazmowska, *Eastern Europe and the Origins of the Second World War*

G. Roberts, *The Soviet Union and the Origins of the Second World War*

Alan Sharp, *The Versailles Settlement: Peacemaking in Paris, 1919*

Zara S. Steiner and Keith Neilson, *Britain and the Origins of the First World War, 2nd edition*

Samuel R. Williamson, *Austria–Hungary and the Origins of the First World War*

R. Young, *France and the Origins of the Second World War*

Yugoslavia: When Ideals Collide

Ann Lane

First published 2004 by
PALGRAVE MACMILLAN
Houndmills, Basingstoke, Hampshire RG21 6XS and
175 Fifth Avenue, New York, N.Y. 10010
Companies and representatives throughout the world

PALGRAVE MACMILLAN is the global academic imprint of the Palgrave Macmillan division of St. Martin's Press, LLC and of Palgrave Macmillan Ltd. Macmillan® is a registered trademark in the United States, United Kingdom and other countries. Palgrave is a registered trademark in the European Union and other countries.

ISBN 0–333–78662–9 hardback
ISBN 0–333 70663 7 paperback

This book is printed on paper suitable for recycling and made from fully managed and sustained forest sources.

A catalogue record for this book is available from the British Library.

A catalog record for this book is available from the Library of Congress.

10 9 8 7 6 5 4 3 2 1
13 12 11 10 09 08 07 06 05 04

Printed in China

Contents

List of Tables   vi

Acknowledgements   vii

Chronology   viii

Introduction   1

1   The Emergence of the South Slavs   7

2   The Collision of Ideals   35

3   Dictatorship and Compromise   57

4   Civil War and Communist Revolution   75

5   Stalinism and Heresy   94

6   Tito's Yugoslavia Consolidated   115

7   Market Socialism and the Resurgence of Nationalism   129

8   The End of Illusion   154

9   Nemesis   172

Conclusion   195

Notes   198

Glossary   210

Bibliographical Essay   211

Index   213

List of Tables

2.1	Yugoslavia's population in 1918	41
2.2	Parliamentary elections, 1920–27	49
4.1	War dead in Yugoslavia, 1941–45	78
7.1	Annual rates of inflation, 1961–80	145
7.2	National income per capita, 1947–78	147
8.1	Annual inflation increases, 1985–89	159
9.1	Yugoslavia's population, by nationality, 1981, 1991	173
9.2	Ethnic composition of officers in the Yugoslav People's Army (JNA)	175

Acknowledgements

The author would like to acknowledge the research leave provided by the Defence Studies Department, King's College London from teaching commitments at the Joint Services Command and Staff College over the winter of 2001–02 when much of this book was written, and for funds that have facilitated the necessary research. In this regard particular thanks are due to Geoffrey Till, Dean of Academic Studies and Director of Defence Education at the JSCSC. Thanks are also due to Chris Hobson and his staff at the JSCSC Library whose extensive knowledge of the collections has been invaluable. The staff of the Library of the School of Slavonic and East European Studies have been similarly helpful in providing guidance. Several individuals have given encouragement along the way: Geoffrey Warner, who first suggested that this book be written; Marcus Wheeler, Jera Vodušec-Starić and Dušan Biber have shared generously of their knowledge of the region at various times. Much was learnt about the politics of ethnic conflict through many conversations with Paul Mitchell, Robert Harmsen and Rick Wilford, former colleagues at The Queen's University, Belfast. Terka Acton and Sonya Barker at Palgrave Macmillan have skilfully steered the project to fruition. Any errors in the text are, of course, my own. Finally, this is an opportunity to acknowledge the MA students at the JSCSC and RCDS, many of whom have the practitioner's experience of the conflict which Yugoslavia's violent dissolution occasioned, but who remain humble enough to study the subject as part of their degree in order to learn more. It is to them that this volume is dedicated.

Great Bedwyn, January 2003

Chronology

1804		First Serbian uprising
1813		Second Serbian uprising
1814–15	October–June	Congress of Vienna
1848		Revolutionary disturbances in Europe
1867		*Ausgleich* – Dual Monarchy of Austria-Hungary created
1868		*Nagodba* – agreement granting Croatia autonomy as an 'adjacent territory' alongside Hungarian rule
1875	July	Outbreak of insurrection against Ottoman rule in Hercegovina and then Bosnia
1876	May–September	Insurrection in Bulgaria
1876	30 June	Serbia declares war on Turkey
1878	3 March	Treaty of San Stefano
1878	13 July	Treaty of Berlin
1881	28 June	Austro–Serb alliance
1885	13 November	Serbia declares war on Bulgaria
1886	3 March	Treaty of Bucharest between Serbia and Bulgaria
1903	10/11 June	Assassination of King Alexander I
1903	August	Illinden Uprising. Macedonia
1908	7 October	Austrian annexation of Bosnia triggers fresh crisis
1912	13 March	Serbo–Bulgarian Treaty
1912–13	October–May	First Balkan War
1913	June–August	Second Balkan War
1914	28 June	Gavrilo Princip assassinates Archduke Franz Ferdinand in Sarajevo
1914	28 July	Austria declares war on Serbia
1915	26 April	Treaty of London
1917	20 July	Corfu Declaration on creating a South Slav state
1917	July–August	Trial and execution of Black Hand leadership
1918	11 November	Armistice signed by Germany
1918	12 November	Austrian Emperor Charles abdicates
1918	1 December	Unified Kingdom of the Serbs, Croats and Slovenes proclaimed

1919	18 January	Peace Conference opens in Paris
1919	12 November	Treaty of Rapallo between Yugoslavia and Italy
1919	12 September	D'Annuzio seizes Fiume
1920–21		'Little Entente' concluded by various treaties between Yugoslavia, Czechoslovakia and Rumania
1921	28 June	'Vidovdan' Constitution adopted by Constituent Assembly
1922	20 October	Mussolini becomes prime minister in Italy
1928	20 June	Croatian deputies shot in Parliament
1929	6 January	King Alexander suspends the Constitution. The name of the state is changed to Yugoslavia
1931	20 June	US declares moratorium on foreign loans
1931	November	Balkan Pact signed in Athens
1933	30 January	Hitler becomes Chancellor of Germany
1933	3 September	King Alexander grants new constitution
1934	9 October	King Alexander assassinated in Marseille
1936–39	13 July–28 March	Spanish Civil War
1936	1 November	Mussolini proclaims Rome–Berlin Axis
1937		Tito appointed Secretary-General of the Yugoslav Communist Party
1938	13 March	Germany completes *Anschluss* with Austria
1939	29–30 September	Munich Conference
1939	23 August	Signature of Nazi–Soviet Pact
1939	26 August	Croatia granted regional autonomy under the *Sporazum*
1939	1–3 September	Nazi Germany invades Poland; Britain and France declare war on Germany
1941	25 March	Cincar-Marković signs Tripartite Pact in Vienna
1941	27 March	Coup d'état overthrows regency; Tripartite Pact denounced; King Peter II declared of age
1941	6 April	Yugoslavia invaded by Nazi Germany
1941	17 April	Yugoslavia signs armistice with Germany
1943	28 November–1 December	Teheran summit conference of Grand Alliance
1943	29 November	Declaration of Anti-Fascist Council of National Liberation of Yugoslavia, Jajce
1944	1–16 June	Tito and Šubašić meet on Viš
1944	10–12 October	Percentages agreement proposed to Stalin by Churchill in Moscow
1944	20 October	Belgrade liberated by Red Army and Yugoslav People's Liberation Army
1945	April–May	Yugoslav NLA disputes occupation of Trieste with British forces

1945	15 May	German forces surrender in Yugoslavia
1945	29 November	Federal People's Republic of Yugoslavia proclaimed
1946	31 January	First communist constitution adopted
1946	June–July	Trial and execution of Draža Mihailović
1948	28 June	Yugoslavia expelled from the Cominform
1950	25 June	Korean War begins
1952	November	Sixth Party Congress. Communist Party of Yugoslavia changes its name to the League of Communists of Yugoslavia
1953	13 January	Second communist constitution adopted
1953	5 March	Stalin dies
1954	January	Djilas disgraced
1954	5 October	London Agreement partition's Venezia Giulia, awarding city of Trieste to Italy
1955	9–11 May	Khrushchev visits Belgrade
1955	14 May	Warsaw Pact signed
1956	April	Cominform dissolved
1956	4 November	Soviet invasion of Hungary
1958	April	Seventh Party Congress, Llubjlana
1961	September	Belgrade Conference of Non-aligned States
1963	April	Third communist constitution adopted. State renamed Socialist Federal Republic of Yugoslavia
1964	December	Eighth Party Congress, Belgrade
1966	1 August	Ranković disgraced
1968	April	Student revolt in Kosovo
1968	June/July	Student revolt at Belgrade University; disorders throughout Yugoslavia
1968	21 August	Warsaw Pact invades Czechoslovakia
1971	1 December	Tito implements purges as part of repression of *masprok*
1974	January	Fourth communist constitution adopted. Tito becomes president for life
1975	August	Final Act of the Helsinki Conference on Security and Co-operation in Europe
1977	October	Belgrade conference to review Helsinki agreements opens. Concludes six months later with little accomplished
1978	11 June	Eleventh Party Congress. Collective leadership implemented
1980	4 May	President Tito dies
1981	March–April	Albanian student riots in Kosovo
1983	July	Stabilisation Plan adopted. First formal rescheduling of Yugoslavia's foreign debts
1985	March	Mikhail Gorbachev becomes President of the USSR
1986		Election of new leaderships in Serbia, Croatia and Slovenia

1987	Summer–Autumn	Agrokomerc financial scandal, Bosnia
1987	September	Milošević elected president of Serbia
1989	February	Trepča miners strike
1989	March	Autonomy of Kosovo and Vojvodina rescinded
1989	April	Contested elections to Slovenian Presidency
1989	October–November	Berlin Wall breached
1989	November	Macedonian Tenth Party Congress ousts communist leadership
1990	1 January	Marković's economic reform package implemented. Self-management abolished
1990	20–21 January	Fourteenth Party Congress, Belgrade
1990	22 January	LCY struck from Yugoslav Constitution
1990	8 and 22 April	Elections in Slovenia
1990	22 April, 6–7 May	Elections in Croatia
1990	1–2 July	Serbian referendum endorses Constitutional changes
1990	11 November	Elections in Macedonia
1990	18 November	Elections in Bosnia and Hercegovina
1990	December	Elections in Serbia and Montenegro
1991	January	Gulf War
1991	25 June–5 July	'Ten Day War', Slovenia
1991	7 July	Brioni Agreement
1991	27 August	Attempted coup against Gorbachev foiled by Yeltsin
1991	7 September	EC Conference on Yugoslavia convened at The Hague
1991	21 November	Macedonia declares its independence
1991	December	The USSR is dissolved and replaced by the Confederation of Independent States
1992	15 January	Slovenian and Croatian independence recognised by EC
1992	6 April	Bosnia and Hercegovina proclaim independence. War begins
1992	27 April	Federal Republic of Yugoslavia (Serbia and Montenegro) proclaimed
1992	August	London Conference on Former Yugoslavia
1993	January	Vance–Owen Peace Plan introduced (rejected in May)
1993	September	HMS *Invincible* talks
1993	December	Macedonian independence recognised
1994	February	Sarajevo market place massacre
1994	May	Contact Group Plan introduced (rejected in August)
1995	August	Operation Storm
1995	12 October	Ceasefire in Bosnian War
1995	1–21 November	Dayton peace talks

1995	14 December	Dayton peace agreement signed in Paris
1998	September	UNSC Resolution 1199 identifies Kosovo crisis as threat to international peace and security
1998	13 October	Holbrooke–Milošević talks secure Eleven Point plan on Kosovo
1999	February–March	Rambouillet peace talks
1999	24 April–9 June	Operation Allied Force

Introduction

BACKGROUND AND SUMMARY

Yugoslavia was a twentieth-century phenomenon. Proclaimed in December 1918, its history as a sovereign state spanned some seventy-three years of the most troubled and violent in Europe's history. Just as this period of turbulence in Europe could be said to have begun with the assassination of the Austrian Archduke Franz Ferdinand and his consort in Sarajevo on 28 June 1914, so too, the dawn of a new era of uncertainty and international instability coincided with the refocussing of world attention on the Bosnian capital, then engulfed in the violence which accompanied Yugoslavia's dissolution in 1991–92. The symbolism of these events was not lost on observers: the 'Sarajevo century' and the 'Short Twentieth Century' became metaphors for a distinct historical epoch the boundaries of which seemed to be delineated by conflict in the Balkans.[1] After the West's initial triumphalism occasioned by the collapse of the communist system in 1989, and the subsequent demise of the Soviet Union itself just two years later, the discovery that the post-Cold War world could spawn political violence in Europe on such a scale, and so quickly, was deeply shocking. On 28 June 1992, François Mitterrand, the octogenarian President of France, made an unannounced visit to Sarajevo to draw attention to the seriousness of the Bosnian crisis. Eric Hobsbawm refers to this event in the opening paragraphs of his study of the twentieth century, observing that for those educated in European history, 'the coincidence of date and place could only be a reminder of the catastrophic consequences of the political miscalculation by Europe's major powers which followed the assassination in 1914'.[2]

Until Yugoslavia's dissolution in the final European war of the twentieth century, the study of Yugoslavia outside the region was not accorded mainstream importance. This small, mountainous country bordering the eastern Adriatic was much frequented by Europeans, either on vacation, or in transit to more southerly destinations. But its history and people were little understood among the wider public. While the roads along its magnificent coastline provided a much remarked

1

drive, the interior remained inaccessible and little known, a function largely of the mountain ranges which lie parallel to its coast and make east–west communications habitually difficult. Of its politics and history, general knowledge was similarly superficial. The workings of its peculiar adaptation of the communist political system and economic structure, to say nothing of the complexities of its social relations, were the provenance of a narrow band of scholars and practitioners who engaged with the country through professional calling. For much of the twentieth century the Balkans in general, and Yugoslavia in particular, has all too often been perceived in the West as a region characterised primarily by deceit, blackmail and intrigue, which by implication defies rationalisation and political integrity. Such a conceptualisation has frequently been unhelpful in promoting a perception of Yugoslavia as a legitimate and functional European state.

It would be more accurate to say that Yugoslavia is deeply paradoxical.[3] In every direction, political, social, economic and even in its external relations, this state has been torn persistently by its own internal contradictions. The major powers, sometimes deliberately, sometimes inadvertently, have exacerbated these tensions. It is here that the cultures shaped by the three great religions have met, to work out their political and economic interests as power waxed and waned between imperial states. The result was a population of South Slavic peoples whose perceptions and outlook have been shaped by widely differing political, economic and social traditions in which apparently common interests are constantly subverted by communal hubris and insecurity rooted in the experiences of conflict and empire.

For the generation now reaching maturity the very concept of Yugoslavia requires some explanation. Yugoslavia was a twentieth-century creation, emerging from the ruins of two empires, one in terminal decline throughout the nineteenth century, the other going into sudden and voluntary dissolution at the end of the First World War. Yugoslavia was founded in 1918 on the basis of two ideals: those of national self-determination and, paradoxically, of South Slav Union. It was destroyed and dismantled by forces from outside its borders in 1941, only to be reincarnated through the will of its own inhabitants during 1944–45. Again, it was to be based on an ideal, this time one represented in the Soviet system in which the teleological goals of the classless society and social ownership of the means of production, as defined by Marxist–Leninist teaching, served as a device to give the idea of Yugoslavia meaning and ambition, while simultaneously subduing nationalist tensions by rationalising them away through theoretical explanation or, when all else failed, through the instruments of state coercion. The 'Long Peace' of the Cold War provided Yugoslavia with a stable international framework in which European boundaries seemed immutable. It is no coincidence that the Yugoslav state enjoyed its one sustained period of stability during this period and that its dissolution proceeded in tandem with the Cold War's ending.[4]

There are four principal strands in the explanations for Yugoslavia's dissolution. The first is the populist, but now largely discredited 'ancient hatreds' thesis, which holds that the struggle between the Serbs and Croats is historic, endemic and fundamentally irresolvable, and for this reason Yugoslavia was never viable. Certainly, Serbo–Croat struggle was responsible for the paralysis of the first attempt at building a united South Slav state between the two world wars, and resurfaced again in the latter stages of the Tito era.[5] But there is little evidence of such conflict prior to 1918. Rather, these ethnic identities have provided ready means of group identification when the Yugoslav authorities have failed to generate stable governance and economic well-being.

A second line of argument holds that a combination of economic weakness and strategically motivated international meddling has prevented the evolution of a viable unitary state. This thesis encompasses those of both the left wing economic determinist school which maintains that the rise of nationalist tensions is a direct product of economic disadvantages, and those of the realist balance of power persuasion who seek to explain Yugoslavia's demise in terms of the imbalances which arose in economic and political power between the most dominant ethnic groups.[6] Economic backwardness was a characteristic of this region at the time of unification and was compounded by the successive economic crises of the interwar years and the mismanagement of the economy during the Cold War, but it remains open to criticism from those who dispute the proposition that economics dictates political decision-making. Similarly, the arguments which emphasise the impact of the major powers frequently fail to give enough attention either to the connections between international and domestic politics or to the fact that the existence of external threats has often been an essential element in Yugoslav unity.

Another line of enquiry emphasises the cultural roots of the dispute and in particular the problem of ethnicity and its interaction with both democratic and communist forms of political organisation. Such explanations focus on the persistence of a variety of languages, religions and cultural identities which communist rule repressed but did not eliminate. A refinement of this argument holds that it was Yugoslavia's lack of a *staatsvolk*, a single culturally defined entity, around which the state could be organised which was the root cause of the problem. No single ethnic group has been sufficiently dominant to establish itself as the legitimate centre of gravity for Yugoslavia. Tito attempted to create just such a centre around himself, with 'Yugoslavia' as the only legitimate expression of the state's identity. This failed, for reasons which will be examined in Chapter 7.[7]

Indeed, Yugoslavia as an entity was recognised by the major powers in 1919 on the assumption that it would be able to evolve political, social and economic institutions such as those which characterised the Great Powers, that is the political infrastructure of a functioning nation-state. And yet, during the course of the next seventy years, not only the Yugoslavs, but the French, the British, the Germans, and the Spanish, to name a few, would all encounter major difficulties in sustaining a countrywide acceptance of the legitimacy of their respective states, even though these had evolved in an incremental manner. How much more difficult was this process of unification and legitimation likely to be in Yugoslavia where a diverse group of peoples, whose sense of national identity had been manufactured to counter imperialist pressures, were abruptly placed within a common boundary with little history of shared experience or even common ideals to act as a basis for their union. For this project to succeed, the peoples of Yugoslavia were required to swiftly evolve the habits of compromise, accommodation and mutual tolerance in the absence of agreed political institutions and infrastructure. While the notion that the South Slavs have always been at each others throats is a contemporary myth, it is nonetheless the case that the peoples who comprised Yugoslavia were singularly lacking a unitary vision of the state they hoped to create.

Since the end of the Cold War in 1989, and the consequent reunification of Germany in October 1990, the notion of the immutability of European boundaries has been broken. But the tension which lies between the founding pillars of the international order, those of sovereignty and self-determination remain unresolved. One of the most compelling arguments about Yugoslav unity made during its descent to dissolution at the end of the 1980s was that there was really no alternative, that Yugoslavia must exist and that its lack lay in its failure to evolve the practices of popular participation in politics.[8] Indeed, it is the contention of this book that Yugoslavia was not redundant, but that its political system was incapable of producing a new generation of leaders sufficiently above the political fray to carry the project beyond its communist formulation.

The dissolution of Yugoslavia was the response of a fractured community with little experience of the practice of pluralist politics to the rapid imposition of western democratic practices of government and the pressures on the economy and society arising from globalisation. The wars which accompanied this process were the product of contemporary changes but were fought with medieval methods. While it may be misleading to frame the Yugoslav conflict within the paradigm of predicted north–south conflict, it is nonetheless the case that it provides a startling example of the failure of the modern state to resolve intractable intracommunal differences, however these be defined. During the last decade of the twentieth century the legitimacy of the state itself as the primary organisational unit of society, has become the subject of mainstream social science debate. The dissolution of the Yugoslav state has provided a living context in which such debate could flourish.

THE APPROACH

Given that the very legitimacy of the Yugoslav state has been so long a source of contention among two or sometimes more of its subject peoples, the writing of Yugoslavia's history is characteristically prone to distortion in which even the known facts are the subject of bitter dispute. History's detractors are apt to remark that far from needing any further analysis of its history, Yugoslavia, in common with Ireland and Israel-Palestine, is a region which already has too much history and that it is only the process and mechanisms of conflict resolution that shape the future, which should matter. While this is a basis for argument, it overlooks one fundamental issue: that the failure to engage in the task of revision and re-evaluation, the proper tasks of the historian in any society, is to leave the way open for the exploitation of historical fact for furtherance of political agendas. It is the job of the historian to remember what others forget, and as such to keep a knowledge of history alive in order to better inform the decision-makers of the present. Yugoslavia has profound lessons to teach about the human condition in its widest sense, and the consequences of the breakdown of trust between peoples in particular, to the point where defence of parochial interests through outright aggression acquires a rationality of its own.

The process of examining exactly what did happen, why it happened and accounting for its significance, remains both necessary and constructive as a contribution to shaping the future.

The approach of this volume is therefore historical in so far as it neither adopts a framework for analysis, nor seeks to advance or challenge a particular theory. Rather it seeks to explain and understand, in the light of current scholarship, the history of Yugoslavia in its two incarnations, drawing on documentary as well as published sources to reconstruct the social and economic circumstances in which the political decisions which determined Yugoslavia's history were taken in order to achieve a synthesis, if incomplete, of the current knowledge of the subject. This is by no means an attempt to write a comprehensive history, which would run to many more pages. Rather it seeks to concentrate on specific themes and issues which appear central to an understanding of the forces which held Yugoslavia together for so long, and simultaneously made it so unstable. The structure of this volume, therefore, is chronological and within that thematic. It emphasises both domestic and international aspects to the history, since Yugoslavia as a minor European state has at times played a disproportionately important role in events, but conversely has been at the mercy of its more powerful neighbours at all of the most critical junctures of its short history. The point, however, is that this two-time experiment in state-building did not occur in an historical vacuum. The lands which constituted this unhappy state have been trampled upon all too often by the violent expressions of ideologically driven state-building on which their fellow Europeans have dared to embark. So this volume aims to consider Yugoslavia as a part of the history of Europe, rather than as an entity separate from it. After all, Yugoslavia's struggle has been primarily about the attempt to resolve the contradictions which the institutional conventions and practices of the European nation-state, as it has been understood during the twentieth century, impose on multi-ethnic communities.

CONVENTIONS USED

A multiplicity of languages and variety of spellings have been used in the past to provide certain differences which are significant to the interpretation intended. The intention here has been to use the most common and familiar forms and not to create an impression of ethnic bias. Diacritic marks are used with certain consonants to indicate sounds which have a separate sign in the Cyrillic alphabet. Spelling of personal names and place names is anglicised in cases where a commonly accepted form is used.

1 The Emergence of the South Slavs

Yugoslavia, as a sovereign state, was a purely twentieth-century phenomenon. However, the manner in which its constituent peoples emerged from imperial rule during the nineteenth century had a great influence on the course of Yugoslav history after 1918. This process drew strength from the past, particularly the histories of medieval statehood which were resurrected in this period to give legitimacy to the notion of South Slav identity as a distinct cultural and political entity. The primary motivation of South Slavs during the nineteenth century was to achieve and preserve a measure of autonomy if not always independence from powerful imperialist states. Such endeavours were necessarily defined by recourse to the language of national self-consciousness, precisely because European political discourse following the late eighteenth century revolutions determined that the coincidence of nation and state was the measure of political legitimacy. By demonstrating the existence of a nation, so the tribes of south-eastern Europe might also persuade the great powers to acknowledge their right to self-governance. Nationalism was therefore a means of achieving leverage over the strong by appealing to the very foundations from which European statehood drew its strength.

The most dominant elements in the nineteenth-century struggle of the South Slavs to attain recognition of distinct identity in the form of autonomy or independence had traditions of statehood which predated their submergence in the empires which dominated the region after the fourteenth century. Both the Croats and the Serbs had coalesced as medieval kingdoms around specific institutions and experienced sovereignty in their own right. Subsequently, the traditions and symbolism as well as the history of independence were carried in the institutions which survived their conquest; the Assembly, or *Sabor* and the office of governor or *Ban* in the case of Croatia; the autocephalous Serbian Orthodox Church for the Serbs. As for the other elements which composed Yugoslavia, Slovene national consciousness was acquired during the nineteenth century, and those of the Macedonians, the Montenegrins,

7

the Muslims of Bosnia-Hercegovina developed during the twentieth century as outgrowths of the South Slavic affinities.[1]

The South Slavs began arriving in the peninsula from the sixth century and acquired tribal identities which formed the basis for subsequent political organisation. These peoples were habitually migrant and their identities in this period were not closely tied to territory. The medieval model for political organisation in south-east Europe was that of loosely structured multi-ethnic empire, rather than a centralised state with strong nationalist identities. Both the Holy Roman Empire and that of Byzantium fitted this model. Communities defined their identity by religious affiliation and dialect; the political power of the church remained supreme until the evolution of native state structure in the nineteenth century.

During the early modern period, these great empires overlapped in what we know now as Bosnia-Hercegovina and Macedonia. The intermingling of communities speaking a variety of dialects derived from Slavic tongues and written variously in the Latin or Cyrillic scripts, as well as the cohabitation of a range of religious practices, from those of the Judaeo–Christian tradition to the Islamic faith, were features of this region. Despite the periodic changes in their imperial masters as the armies of the Ottoman Turks vied with those of the Habsburg dynasty for conquest and security, these communities thrived in the harsh mountainous terrain without inter communal strife. The militaristic and authoritarian dynasties which exercised a hegemony over them, offered protection in return for quiescence. This then was the *modus vivendi* in the Balkans for almost five hundred years.

At the beginning of the nineteenth century, the Balkan peninsula was educationally and economically the most backward of the European lands. Communications systems were primitive, the vast majority of the population was illiterate and disenfranchised. When, in the early nineteenth century, European nationalism permeated the region, it interacted with these tribal loyalties and feudal traditions to create aspirations and expectations which rivalled those of the great nationalist movements of the Germans, French and Italians, only without the social basis which made the building of cohesive states composed of multiple identities viable. The South Slavs lacked comparable economic and social foundations and were less able, therefore, to generate strong leadership with sufficient legitimacy to forge modern states on the European model. Instead, they produced societies divided within themselves, dependent upon authoritarian practices to achieve stable governance in which the currency of corruption and even assassination were tolerated above the practices of popular participation and parliamentary rule.

The restlessness of the South Slavs, particularly towards the end of the nineteenth century, was magnified by two overarching factors: the European states system and the impact of industrialisation. Following the restoration of the European order at the Congress of Vienna (October 1814–June 1815), the Great Powers sought to prevent an outbreak of conflict between themselves by balancing power through the device of alliances. Vienna represented the collective rejection of dominance of the Continent by any one individual power, and of the disturbances of warfare and revolution. The balance was held by France, Great Britain, Austria (Austria-Hungary after 1867), Prussia (Germany after 1871) and Russia. The Great Powers did fight one another, certainly, but these conflicts were fought for limited objectives and over localised issues. Elaborate steps were taken to avoid another European conflict out of awareness that such a war would bring destruction to them all. As the century progressed so this balance became ever more precarious, first because the unification of Italy and Germany brought new Great Powers to the equation, and second because of the inexorable decline of the Ottomans as a force in European politics which constantly threatened to destabilise European peace. The South Slavs were at the heart of the 'Eastern Question' as it affected Europe and the near conflict or actual wars which were waged here during the latter part of the nineteenth and early twentieth centuries generated a particular legacy which had deleterious consequences for Yugoslav statehood.[2]

Despite the skirmishes which punctuated the nineteenth century, the Concert of Europe succeeded in giving international relations an underlying stability which lent the century its defining character and provided the certainties which facilitated commercial expansion and industrial growth. Living standards across the whole of Europe rose steadily, with a commensurate rise in educational standards, methods of communication and popular participation in government. The Habsburg and Ottoman lands lagged far behind the rest of Europe in these processes: neither industrialisation nor road building reached the Balkan peninsula before the final quarter of the nineteenth century. Nevertheless, an improvement in literacy levels which began earlier in the century was accompanied by limited experimentation among the South Slavs with parliamentary government as a greater percentage of the population began to demand that their rulers provide better economic and social conditions in order to retain their power and privileges.[3]

This was the Europe in which the South Slav peoples defined and developed their ideas for South Slavic statehood. In its modern form, South Slavic nationalisms emerged as part of the wider process of state development which built on the ideas of the Enlightenment and the French Revolution, and in particular the abstract and misleading notions about the coincidence of the nation (people) and the state. Much has been written on the phenomenon of nationalism and the related concept of ethnicity which is outside the scope of this study.[4]

This chapter seeks to explain the history of the emergence of the South Slavs from imperial rule in the context of European development. To what extent were the nationalisms of the South Slavs compatible politically? What efforts if any did they make to compromise in order to achieve solidarity? How were their respective agendas shaped by the differing political, social and economic conditions which forged their societies? What legacies did the varying experiences of politics generate? To what extent did the activities of the Great Powers help or hinder the progress of South Slav independence?

THE HABSBURG SLAVS

The Habsburgs had replaced the Frankish feudal lords as Holy Roman Emperors in the fifteenth century. During the sixteenth century both the Ottoman heirs to the Byzantine empire in the south, and the Habsburgs themselves took steps to stabilise the frontier between their territorial possessions. During the early years of the century, the Ottomans created a military border in the northern Bosnian lands, an example, which the Habsburgs followed in 1538 as a result of repeated Ottoman incursions from Bosnia into Hungary. This military border, known as the *krajina*, was placed directly under the authority of Habsburg military headquarters in Vienna and manned by settled military colonists commanded by the local Croat aristocracy. Thus the Croat nobility received freedom from Hungarian control throughout the seventeenth century, and enjoyed an extension of the territory under its purview with the acquisition of Slavonia into the Vojvodina following the Treaty of Sremski Karlovci in 1699. In order to maintain the frontier troops, the Habsburgs settled an ethnic mixture of peoples as colonists including Croats, Germans, Serbs, Hungarians, Czechs, Slovaks, Italians and others. The largest ethnic group was the Orthodox Serb refugees who had come to the region to escape the Ottoman rule at the end of the seventeenth century and who settled in large enclaves in the Slavonian and Vojvodinan military border zones.[5] Under this régime, the Serb communities were permitted religious autonomy. In 1713 an independent Serbian archbishopric was established in Sremski Karlovci with jurisdiction over all Slavic-rite Orthodox believers in Vojvodina, Slavonia and Pannonian Hungary. The traditional role of the Orthodox Church in defining the intellectual, cultural and educational life of the community was permitted to continue, and was even reinforced by the grant of the right of Serbs to own land. The connections with Russian orthodoxy were strengthened in this period owing to Russian sponsorship of these communities through patronage of their schools and reading rooms. Consequently, the Serbs of the Croatian borderlands had developed by the end of the eighteenth century, a strongly pro-Russian outlook.

The Emergence of Croatian National Consciousness

Following the restoration of the Bourbon dynasty in France in 1815, the Austrian Habsburgs were concerned above all else with preservation of the Monarchy and its dominant role in the European system. The main supports of the régime were the aristocracy, the church, the army and bureaucracy, as well as the interests of the ruling classes in certain provinces which had both social standing and ethnic loyalties. In such an environment, the promotion of modernising tendencies was never a possibility and the rise of nationalist particularisms and the consequent demands on the Habsburg political system were a tiresome and unwelcome development.

Croatian nationalism emerged in the early nineteenth century in response to the pressures the process of moderating these potentially disturbing forces set in train. The Habsburgs attempted to manage their minorities through denationalisation of their subject populations. However, this policy proved counterproductive because it had the effect of posing a direct threat to the very existence of minority identities. The Croatian intelligentsia, which had preserved a record of Croatia's history as an independent medieval state, was stimulated by Vienna's policies to take active measures to ensure that the history of this period survived.[6] Moreover, at the end of the eighteenth century, the liberalisation which flowed from the Enlightenment, fostered greater stridency among the other nationalities of the empire, particularly the Austro-German, Hungarian and Italian identities, and this in turn encouraged the lesser minorities of the Habsburg lands to actively sustain their own cultural identity. In this sense, the emergence of modern Croatian nationalism was a direct consequence of the elevation of Hungarian national identity at the end of the eighteenth century. The brief experience of French Revolutionary ideas occasioned by Napoleonic conquest of the Adriatic coast as far south as Cattaro and inland along the River Sava contributed to this cultural awakening. The French had called its Balkan territories 'Les Provinces Illyriénnes', drawing on the legend of South Slavic descent from the Illyrians who had inhabited the region in ancient times. When Croatian national consciousness emerged during the 1820s and 1830s, this brief interlude in Habsburg rule provided the intelligentsia with an instructive precedent.

The Croats could trace their history as a distinct community to the seventh century and could claim to be Christian converts from the ninth century when their lands came under the suzerainty of the Holy Roman Emperor, Charlemagne. The relationship with Hungary began at the beginning of the twelfth century when Kalman, a Hungarian prince, was crowned king of Croatia and within a few years succeeded to the Hungarian throne. Subsequently, Croatia's boundaries fluctuated along with the extent of its autonomy, although the Croats maintained that their state was never formally absorbed into Hungary. It was in relation to Hungary that Croats began to define their South Slavism during the nineteenth century.[7]

During the 1820s and 1830s the appellation 'Croatian' implied not that a person subscribed to a distinct and separate identity but rather that they were a Magyarophile (*madjaroni*), the style set by the nobility who lived in the Croatian vendée.[8] Two institutions defined Croatian statehood and were central to the events which followed. These were the parliament (*Sabor*) and the governor (*Ban*). The subjugation of these to the influence of Hungary's Magyar nobility in this period is demonstrated by the parliament's introduction in 1827 of Hungarian as an obligatory subject in higher education, and the fact that governors, though appointed from Vienna, were often drawn from the Hungarian nobility.

Illyrianism was the name given to the programme of national unification which developed as a counter to the fear of what was called 'magyarisation'. The very name, which referred to the ancient peoples of this region, was chosen to reflect a broad South Slavic identity rather than a narrowly Croatian one. Accordingly, the principal aim was the ethnic, linguistic and cultural unity of all South Slavs, but some of its adherents soon began articulating their hope of eventual political unification and economic independence in a South Slav state. Surrounded variously by Austrians, Hungarians and Italians, the Habsburg Slavs were motivated to minimise their differences in order to co-operate in the furtherance of their immediate aims. The cornerstone of Illyrianism was to be a common language. Under the philatelist, Ljudevit Gaj, a group of scholars worked in the 1830s to produce a formal grammar, adopting as they did so the *štokavski* dialect which was spoken not only by Croats but also by Serbs. This was a deliberate choice and aimed to appeal to all South Slavs. Importantly, it required that the Croats forsake their well-developed literary tradition in the *kajkavski* and *čakavski* dialects. This development was reinforced in the 1830s by the establishment of a Chair in the Illyrian language at Zagreb's ancient University, while the launch in 1835 of the newspaper, *Illyrian Morning Star (Danica ilirska)* provided a forum for the wider discussion of South Slavic politics and culture. In practice, however, the Illyrian solutions were seen to be dependent on Croatian culture and traditions and consequently drew a cool response from the other South Slav identities. The Serbs were hostile, perceiving in this development a threat to their plans to extend the Slavic language promulgated by the Church and written in the Cyrillic script.[9]

Following the 1848 revolutions, which came close to ending Habsburg rule, several things happened which changed the character and outlook of nationalism in the Croatian lands. Firstly, Metternich, the Austrian Chancellor, exploited the Illyrian movement as part of his strategy for counter-balancing Hungarian nationalism. By so doing he weakened the Illyrian movement as a political force by legitimising its agenda, drawing it into mainstream politics and depriving it thereby of the cache of official opposition. To an extent the liberal Croat cleric, Josip Juraq Strossmayer, Bishop of Djakovo and leader of the Croatian Liberal Party, succeeded in capitalising on this development, by advancing an agenda which sought to bring about the union of all South Slavs through cultural integration on the Illyrian pattern.[10] However, this ambition was unrealistic. Serbian suspicions of Illyrianism were as deeply entrenched as ever and besides, Belgrade's ambitions had been focussed more narrowly on Serbian interests as a result of Garašanin's policies of the 1840s and 1850s. In 1866, Strossmayer proposed a direct connection with Serbia, but before this could be realised, his political career was cut short by the reform of the Habsburg empire.

Croatia and the Dual Monarchy, 1867–1914

The *Ausgleich* (or Compromise) of 1867 reincarnated the Habsburg empire as the Austro-Hungarian Dual Monarchy. Formerly, Croatia was permitted a special status in the empire being granted its own Diet and the right to use Croatian as an official language. However, the Hungarian–Croatian *Nagodba* (or Agreement) of 1868 placed Croatia firmly under the control of Budapest, a fact reflected in the imposition on Croatia of Hungarian flags and emblems. In every sense, Croatia was increasingly integrated into the Hungarian state apparatus, symbolised by the railway building which linked Zagreb with Budapest and Vienna, but not with the Slavic towns of Llubljana or Split. This process was completed in 1883 when Károly Khuen-Héderváry was appointed governor. Khuen-Héderváry handled the region's nationalities problem in classic imperial style – divide and rule. The Croats were played off ruthlessly against the Serbian minority in Slavonia which created for the first time the tensions which were to undermine the first attempt at creating a Yugoslav state. Minor concessions were granted to the Serbian minority with respect to the use of Cyrillic and local government, but served only to exacerbate these tensions. Anti-Serbian demonstrations occurred in Zagreb in 1902 which revealed the potential such a strategy had for destroying Croatia's social fabric.[11]

The more extreme Croatian nationalists were represented in the Party of Croatian Rights headed by Ante Starčević, a populist nationalist with strongly anti-Serbian ideas. The Party of Rights came to represent the Croat opposition to the 1867 compromise and the agreement with the Hungarians the following year. It also instilled a deep fear of Croat nationalism in the Serbian population, a process which the Croatian intellectual and political elites were not strong enough to resist. Starčević's ideas proved especially inspirational to the younger genera-tion of intellectuals and the emerging political leaderships of Dalmatia, Istria and Bosnia-Hercegovina. Instead of uniting with the Serbian pop-ulation against their occupiers in a common South Slav programme, the Party of the Right promulgated the notion that Serbs were in fact back-ward Croats, destined eventually to become Croats. While the majority of Croats remained persuaded of Illyrianism, this strand of extreme Croat nationalism had come to stay in Croatian politics.[12]

The Croatian–Serbian Coalition (*Hrvatska–srpska koalicija*) of 1905 was formed in response to perceptions of German expansionist ambitions which were seen as a threat to those of the South Slavs in the context of wider European politics. The coalition was an alliance of the Party of Croatian Rights and the Croatian Progressive Party (*Hrvatska napredna stranka*) with the Serbian People's Independent Party (*Srpska narodna samostalna stranka*) and the Serbian People's Radićal Party (*Srpska narodna radikalna stranka*). This brought together, for the first time, a large and representative group of Croatian and Serbian politicians united with a common political goal – the unification of the South Slavs. It was committed to liberal democratic political institutions and to the principal of national self-determination, as well as the separation of church and state. This coalition quickly developed a confrontational agenda as a result of the attempt by the new Hungarian government in 1907 to impose Magyarisation through educational reform and the enforced use of Hungarian as the official language on state railways.[13]

Within Croatia the economic boom enjoyed at the turn of the century exaggerated existing differences between the various elements which it comprised, principally those between Civil Croatia–Slavonia and the lands of the former Military Border which had been incorporated into both of them after 1881. This, when combined with the growing economic disparities between this and the other South Slav lands contributed to shaping the narrowness of the Coalition's political vision. The latter focussed increasingly on political union of Dalmatia with Croatia–Slavonia alone, with no acknowledgement of the broader South Slav agendas.[14]

Slovenia

Slovenia had never constituted an historic province and its claims to statehood, owing to its virtual absorption in the Habsburg administrative structure during the sixteenth century, were tenuous. Until the eighteenth century there had been no single Slovene entity in the region; the vast majority of Slovenes inhabited Carinola, but they were also living in Styria, Gorizia, Istria and Gradisa.[15] The unifying factor was language, the distinct identity of which was promoted first in the late eighteenth century by Tomas Linhart who managed to destroy the notion that the Slovenes were ethnically Germans (a legacy from their governance by the Frankish feudal lords during the Middle Ages). Thus began a cultural movement which sought to advance the Slovenian language in education, culture and administration. A Slovene grammar was produced by Vuk Karadžić during the Napoleonic period, but the emergence of national consciousness was then halted, firstly by the Illyrian insistence on the abandonment of Slovene as a separate language, and then by its re-incorporation in the Habsburg empire at the Treaty of Vienna.

Slovene Radićals called for the unification of Slovenia during the revolutionary year of 1848, but generally the Slovenes were loyal to the Habsburgs. The Slovene Society (*Slovenska Matica*) was founded in 1864 but after the *Ausgleich* of 1867, which solved Slovene fears of being submerged in Croatian culture by assigning Slovenia to the western (Austrian) half of the empire and Croatia to the eastern (Hungarian) half, Slovene politics turned inwards, not to re-emerge until the require-ments of its booming economy in the early twentieth century stimulated the peoples of this region to seek greater political leverage. Prior to the First World War their national movement was much more preoccupied with economic and cultural issues rather than with the more overtly political goals of the Serbs and Croats.[16]

Slovenia's geographic location on the economic crossroads between the Mediterranean and central Europe, combined with its Adriatic coastline, gave it certain natural advantages in developing a thriving economy. The opening of the railway connections between Slovenia's greatest centre of urban population at Laibach (Ljubljana in Slovene) and the commercial port of Trieste and Vienna opened up great possi-bilities for entrepreneurial activity. Slovenia's population, hitherto landowning peasant farmers, began to gravitate to the towns, with one-fifth of the population urbanised by 1912, and industrial production four times that of Serbia measured in per capita terms. Lacking an indige-nous nobility, it was the entrepreneurs, the bourgeoisie and the intellec-tuals which filled the ranks of the leaders. By the early twentieth century, then, the Slovenes were economically and socially the most advanced of all the South Slav peoples.[17]

THE OTTOMAN SLAVS

The Balkan peninsula had been conquered progressively during the fourteenth and fifteenth centuries by the Ottoman Turks. At its greatest extent, the Islamic Ottoman empire stretched as far north as Vienna, boasting an efficient bureaucracy and flourishing mercantilist economy as well as a greatly respected army. After the middle of the sixteenth century, however, changes in western Europe in trade patterns and tactics of warfare had a destabilising effect on the conservative Ottoman society which proved too slow in adapting to these developments. Pressures to increase state revenues led to an increasingly venal culture in which high offices, formerly staffed on the basis of ability alone, were sold increasingly to wealthy born Muslim subjects, a practice which progressively undermined the Sultan's absolute authority over the military and government. The economy stagnated and living standards declined, and Europeans began the long process of driving the Ottomans from Europe. Belgrade was captured by the Habsburg armies in 1717, only to be re-conquered by the Turks in 1736.

During the nineteenth century, the instability in the Balkans which developed as a consequence of the declining authority of the Ottoman empire became a central part of what is generally referred to as the 'Eastern Question'. Nationalist concepts had spread to Ottoman Serb subjects as a result of emigration from the Habsburg lands of Slavonia and Vojvodina. Rebellion broke out in Belgrade in 1804, stimulated by grievances arising from high taxation, and the attempt by the Porte (the Turkish Sultan's staff) to re-centralise the collection process. This rebellion was led by Djordje Petrović, a pig dealer and outlaw nick-named Karadjordje. Fierce fighting met with equally fierce reprisals which were instrumental in reviving in Serbian minds the destruction of their thriving medieval kingdom by the Turks, a process memorialised by their defeat at the battle of Kosovo Polje in 1398, and concluded seventy years later at Smerderevo.[18] The Serbs of the military frontier region sent volunteers to assist, and later attempted to establish a military alliance with Russia which in 1806 made war on the Ottomans. However, when the Turks and Ottomans signed an armistice the following year, the Serbs were at Constantinople's mercy. Napoleonic victories on Russian soil in 1812 diverted Russian attention totally from their Balkan ambitions, leaving the Serbs without great power support. The Turks reinvaded and Karadjordje fled. But a second uprising occurred along the Military Frontier in 1813–14, led this time by Miloš Obrenović. This succeeded in achieving the autonomy for which the Serbs craved and taken with the struggle since 1804 could be said to mark the beginnings of the contemporary Serb problem, establishing in Serb minds the imperative of Serbian self-government. The fact of Serbian autonomy was recognised by the Ottomans in 1817 and Obrenović continued to press Constantinople for concessions, adopting the tactics of accommodation rather than confrontation with the Porte. When Karadjordje returned from exile, he was immediately critical of this approach. However, he did not live long enough to press his case for Obrenović organised his assassination in 1818, thereby beginning a bitter rivalry between these two families which punctuated Serbian politics until the beginning of the twentieth century.

The Ottoman period had a deep impact on the outlook of the Balkan peoples and generated a legacy which contributed to shaping the twentieth-century conflict. This stems in the first instance from the fact that the Ottoman empire was defined in religious rather than secular or nationalistic terms. During the period of imperial expansion, non-Muslim subjects greatly outnumbered Muslims and in view of the primacy of the Islamic religious authorities expressed in the Sacred Law (*Şeriat*) in the governance of the empire, such a high incidence of non-Muslims within Ottoman jurisdiction generated an administrative problem. The solution was found in the *Millet* system, introduced in 1454 which provided a means of integrating the non-Muslims. The subjects were divided into nations (*millets*) defined by religious beliefs. Like the Muslims, the non-Muslims were to be governed by their own religious authorities, and accordingly received considerable autonomy within the empire as a reward for ordering their administrative affairs, including collection of taxes, in accordance with the interests of the Ottoman state. The sense of community, of nation, was rooted thereby in religious rather than ethnic or territorial considerations. For Orthodox Serbs, the Orthodox Church, based on the Patriarchate of Peć, became the custodian of Serbian history and literature, as well as the principal administrative authority.[19]

However, this system also denied access to the privileges of society to those who were not of the Muslim faith. Only by conversion to Islam, could non-Muslims achieve influence and high office, and during the sixteenth and seventeeth centuries, many of the Ottoman's Balkan subjects did precisely that. These people gave rise to thriving towns which developed in Bosnia and Hercegovina creating a two tier social structure in which Allah-worshipping Slavs led a privileged existence while the Christian Slavs, both Orthodox and Catholic, along with the Jewish population, were destined to remain peripheral.[20]

The Development of Serbian Nationalism

Between 1817 and the formal recognition of Serbia as a sovereign state in 1878, the Serbian agenda as an expansionist force in the Balkans was defined. The first step in this direction was taken during the 1820s by the Serbian literary reformer, Vuk Karadžić who recognised the political weaknesses for the Serbs of total reliance on the Orthodox Church as the sole national institution. In order to extend the boundaries of Serb nationhood, Karadžić sought to broaden the definition of Serbdom through the device of language. He introduced the idea that the appellation 'Serb' should include all those who spoke the *štokavian* dialect, regardless of religion, which would permit both Muslims and Catholics of Croatia and Bosnia to be included in the Serbian state-building project.[21] Despite the continued presence of a Turkish garrison in Belgrade, Serbia steadily evolved the institutions of a modern state, looking towards England and more especially to France for its inspiration. The first peaceful transference of power was accomplished between 1839–42 when Obrenović abdicated in favour of his son who was succeeded in 1842 by Karadjordje's son, Alexander. In practice Alexander was a weak monarch and for much of the next twenty years, Serbian politics was dominated by the Prime Minister, Ilija Garašanin.

This was to prove a defining period for Garašanin was an authoritarian figure who saw little practical value in promoting free speech and other trappings of democracy in a society composed of a largely illiterate populace. Instead, he concentrated on building an internal political programme around the Ottoman model of hierarchy and centralised administrative structure in which authority was reinforced by the existence of a standing army.[22] To justify this militaristic and centralising programme, Garašanin only had to point to Serbia's encirclement and lack of total freedom. Such preoccupations, together with eschatological fears of national destruction, were deeply ingrained in the Serbian psyche as a consequence of centuries of demonstrably alien rule, and would surface to unify the community with little provocation.

It is during this period that the Serbian belief in their legitimacy as the natural leaders of the South Slav struggle against imperialism emerged. The notion was articulated for the first time in the secret memorandum known as the *Nacertanije* (Outline), which was prepared by Garašanin in 1844. This memorandum contains a definition of the aims of Serbian foreign policy as first the achievement of complete independence from the Ottoman empire, and second the unification of all Serbs and South Slavs.[23] While Garašanin accepted Karadžić's linguistic definitions of 'Serbdom', he nevertheless discounted for any practical purposes the interests of South Slavs outside those of the territory of Serbia as it then existed.

The Serb agenda to extend its territory in the Balkans identified it as a possible thorn in the flesh of the Ottoman empire and thus it had value to other Great Powers seeking to further their own empires at Ottoman expense. During the middle of the nineteenth century, the Russians became increasingly interested in the assertiveness of the Ottoman Slavs, and Tsar Nicholas I actively encouraged the South Slavs to pursue their demands for unification and independence. Russia, he claimed, was the natural protector of Slavic interests in the widest sense. However, Garašanin was sufficiently shrewd to recognise that while Russian influence was useful to Belgrade in its pursuit of Serbian interests, over-reliance on Russian patronage would open the way to eventual partition of the Balkans between Russia and Austria. Rather than being a Russian client, Serbia had to gain wider international legitimacy through independent statehood. It was this which caused Garašanin to focus Serbian attention on the Turkish patrimony of Bosnia and Hercegovina. By making the creation of a greater Serbia by acquisition of Bosnia and Hercegovina the goal of his foreign ambitions, he not only avoided the danger of challenging both the Ottoman and Habsburg interests at the same time, but also would improve the chances of replacing Turkish hegemony with that of Serbia.[24]

The Balkan Wars, 1875–76

During the 1870s two territorial issues were to emerge which have remained at the heart of Balkan instability ever since. These involved first the lands of Bosnia and Hercegovina and second those of the less clearly defined provinces of Macedonia.

Bosnia had been the scene of periodic unrest for much of the nineteenth century and, as we have seen, had become the focal point for Serbian expansionism. While neighbouring Serbia and the tiny principality of Montenegro had managed to develop along the path of independent statehood, Bosnia remained firmly under the Ottoman yoke. Its population of some 60,000 farmed in small mountain villages, exporting nothing but livestock and linked to the outside world by only the most primitive system of communications. Its outlook was clannish and highly parochial. The example of Montenegro's war with the Turks in 1858 and again in 1862 fuelled the impetus to rebel. The old feudal order, and more immediately an attempt by the Ottomans to revive the power of the state through imposition of ever more burdensome taxation, created an environment of incipient rebellion which exploded into open conflict, first in Hercegovina, then in Bosnia also. Turkish efforts to suppress the revolt failed and the fighting provoked a substantial refugee crisis as refugees entered the neighbouring states.

The impact of this on British and Russian strategic interests provoked both to enter the arena. The Russians perceived an opportunity to further their ambition towards acquisition of a warm water port. The British, for whom the Mediterranean was a vital route to the Suez Canal and Indian Ocean, were determined that they should not succeed. Austria-Hungary was also interested in the outcome of this struggle, owing to its desire for southern expansion following its expulsion from German affairs by Prussia in 1866. If the insurgents were successful in their aim of uniting Bosnia and Hercegovina with Serbia and Montenegro, then by default, Russian designs on the peninsula would have been given a major advance.

Serbian participation in the war was domestically divisive, and left a deep psychological scar. In 1876, the Serbian Government joined forces with the independent principality of Montenegro to fight in support of the Bosnian rebels with the aid of Russia. Somewhat unexpectedly, the Serbs were defeated in October by the recently modernised Ottoman forces which, but for the Russian ultimatum demanding a ceasefire, would have occupied Belgrade. The Serbs sustained 15,000 casualties, but worse was to follow when the British organised a conference with Russia in Istanbul at which they devised an agreement uniting Bosnia and Hercegovina into a single province, and creating two autonomous Bulgarian provinces.

Unsatisfied, Russia launched a direct war against the Turks in April 1877. The diplomatic ground had been carefully prepared, Russia having negotiated Austro-Hungarian neutrality in the case of Russian hostilities with the Ottomans, on the basis that a Russian presence in the peninsula would be accepted in return for Austro-Hungarian occupation of Bosnia-Hercegovina. Britain, meanwhile, had desisted in its support for the Ottomans following the rumours of Ottoman Muslim atrocities against Christians during the brief rebellion which had taken place in the Bulgarian lands in May 1876. After an uncertain beginning, Russia succeeded in driving the Turks back to Istanbul, provoking the startled British to send a fleet to the Straits with orders to intervene should Russia take the city. The Russians bowed to international pressure and imposed the Treaty of San Stefano in March 1878 which awarded nearly all of the central Balkans to Bulgaria, including Macedonia and part of what is now Albania. International uproar ensued once the contents of this Treaty became known. The Balkan states (with the exception of the satiated Bulgarians), together with the European Great Powers were horrified by this act of *force majeure*.[25]

The Congress of Berlin, 1878

The crisis was settled at the Congress of the European Great Powers held at Berlin at the invitation of the German Chancellor, Otto von Bismarck, who was anxious to use the opportunity to underline Germany's arrival as a member of the Concert of Europe. The small states were not represented and the Ottomans were little more than observers. The resultant Treaty of Berlin, signed on 13 July 1878, dismantled Greater Bulgaria, returning Macedonia to Ottoman administration. Serbia received the long-awaited recognition of its independence, a status which it had enjoyed de facto since the withdrawal of the Ottoman garrison from Belgrade in 1867. But it was also disappointed to discover that the Treaty provided for Austro-Hungarian occupation of Bosnia-Hercegovina and the Sandjak of Novi Pazar, an Ottoman province that separated Serbia from Montenegro. This prevented the unification of these two into a single state.

The two great achievements of the Congress of Berlin – resolution of the sovereignty of the provinces of Bosnia-Hercegovina and Macedonia – both contained the seeds of future disaster.[26] Antagonism between the Muslims and Serbs had developed in the decades prior to the Balkan Wars of the 1870s and were sharpened as a direct result of the transfer of sovereignty to Austria-Hungary.[27] In 1879, the population of Bosnia-Hercegovina was 43 per cent Orthodox, 38 per cent Muslim and 18 per cent Catholic. Both the Serbs and the Croats sought to claim the Muslims while the administrative arrangements attempted to promote the Bosnian identity. Austria-Hungary failed to modernise the state, leaving the Muslim controlled landholding régime in place which meant in practical terms that a small number of Muslims, owning large estates, wielded enormous power over the vast numbers of Christian peasants. Failure to modernise the agricultural system, on which the Bosnian economy depended, meant that the vast majority of the population remained poor and increasingly restless.[28]

More broadly, the residual sense of outright betrayal provided the impetus for the radicalisation of Balkan politics which proved a persistently disruptive force up to the First World War. The nationalist ambitions of both the Bulgarians and the Serbs had been raised to tremendous heights during the recent conflict, and both had their aspirations dashed without consultation. The Serbs in particular, considered that their great Slavic ally had betrayed them utterly, firstly in choosing to reward Bulgaria rather than Serbia under San Stefano, and then by permitting Austria-Hungary to succeed the defeated Ottomans in the ruling territories the Serbs had come to see as theirs by right. The arrangements had created spheres of influence in which the Serbs found themselves dependent on Vienna with whom they had to make some accommodation if they were to be free to deal with the rivalry of Bulgaria over the territories in the south.[29] Recognising their bargaining power, Vienna agreed to advance Serbian aims, but demanded that the Serbs accept a political treaty in 1881 which made of Serbia a satellite, both politically and economically. This reality was covered in 1882 by the device of elevating Serbia to the status of a kingdom.

The Beginnings of the Macedonian Problem

Macedonia lacked a distinctive national character at the time of the Berlin Treaty, and because of this, or perhaps inspite of it, the region formed the subject of a triangular dispute between Bulgaria, Greece and Serbia in which all parties claimed just entitlement to sovereignty, motivated not least by the desire to recover face after the humiliations of Berlin. During the mid-fourteenth century, when the Serbian kingdom had been at its greatest influence, the Macedonian lands had been at the heart of Serbia and Skopje had served as the capital. Denied its ambition to occupy Bosnia-Hercegovina the Serbian government fastened on Macedonia as the next legitimate goal in pursuit of the recreation of Greater Serbia. Bitter rivalry with the Bulgarians followed, since the latter could claim sovereignty over Macedonia at an even earlier date, and much greater linguistic similarity to the dialect spoken in Macedonia than could the Serbs. When in 1870, the Ottoman authorities permitted the new Bulgarian Exarchate to open Orthodox churches and schools across northern Macedonia, the struggle was joined by officially supported groups in Serbia and Greece which set up their own schools and sought to persuade the Slav Macedonians that they were Serbs or Greeks rather than Bulgarians. To this conglomeration was added the claims of the Greeks whose nationalistic drive led them to demand recreation of the Byzantine Empire as a natural Greek nation-state. Outright war between Serbia and Bulgaria in 1885–86 failed to resolve the question and the conflict degenerated into a three-sided terrorist struggle waged by armed bands.[30]

The Macedonian province was particularly vulnerable to guerrilla warfare, lacking in either legitimate political organisation, or a functioning economy. In 1883 the Macedonian Slavs formed the Internal Macedonian Revolutionary Organisation (IMRO), a nationalist movement which demanded for the first time a 'Macedonia for the Macedonians'. This organisation sparked the abortive Illinden Uprising against Ottoman suzerainty in August 1903 which once more drew the western Great Powers into the Balkans to restore order and uprooted vast numbers of peoples who fled to south western Bulgaria where they established a substantial minority and became a disruptive force in Bulgarian politics.

The Principality of Montenegro

Montenegro's population was also Serb but this tiny principality had differed from Serbia largely because its mountainous terrain made it inaccessible and thus it had been able to retain its independence of Turkey. Formal recognition of this status had been made by the Sultan of Turkey in 1799. This was lost only briefly following the incursion by the Turkish army in 1861 led by the Croatian convert to Islam, Omar Pasha, when it became legally part of the Ottoman empire. Following the Balkan wars of 1875–76, the Russians sponsored recognition of its independence at San Stefano with border changes which doubled its population to 117,000. Montenegro kept this status at Berlin, but with some territorial losses including its valuable coastline which was handed to Austria-Hungary.

Serbian Expansionism, 1903–08

The twentieth century began violently in Serbia. The ruling Obrenović dynasty which had lost support domestically owing to its determination to compromise with the Dual Monarchy, was finally extinguished. On the night of 10/11 June, a group of disaffected army officers broke into the royal palace and murdered the monarch together with his consort and family. Alexander was replaced by Peter Karadjordjević, formerly an officer in the French army who had been living quietly in exile in

Switzerland. King Peter differed from his predecessor in recognising the value of government by parliamentary majority and accepted the limitations the Skupština placed on his powers through its modifications to the 1888 constitution.

Abroad, the coup had a detrimental impact on European opinion. The constant war fighting, and the savagery which accompanied it, had formed the impression in western European political circles that this region as a whole was barbaric, uncivilised and not amenable to rationalisation through normal political process. The regicide could only reinforce this impression in a Europe where the predominant form of government was hereditary monarchy. It was in this period the adjective 'balkan' acquired the pejorative connotations which it has never shaken off. The British even went as far as to break off diplomatic relations, a luxury that neither Austria-Hungary nor Russia could indulge. The cynicism of the Austro-Hungarian Minister, Constantine Dumba, who observed that ethical questions had to 'take a back seat' because of the great interests which the Dual Monarchy had in Serbia, captured the mood of the times.[31] For Vienna and St Petersburg, the question of who ruled was of little interest, so long as they were pliant supplicants of great power machinations.[32]

Domestically, Serbia's self-confidence was on the rise, and Serbian apologists are quick to note that the low tax threshold meant that at 20 per cent the franchise was higher than anywhere in Europe at this time bar France and Switzerland.[33] This period was one of accelerating economic growth and political unrest across Europe. Communications were improving, both through the medium of the popular press, and trade and travel. The most dominant politician in this period was the veteran leader of the Serb Radical Party, Nikola Pašić, who was either prime minister or foreign minister almost continuously between 1904 and 1918. Pašić was a consummate politician who excelled in the black arts of playing his rivals off against one another. The prevailing habit of publicly ambiguous and largely secret dealings between states suited his approach to the diplomatic game and enabled him to further advance Serbia's international standing.[34] Along with King Peter, Pašić felt an instinctive attachment to Russia and both disregarded the limitations imposed on Serbian ambitions by the agreements with Austria-Hungary which had bound Belgrade's foreign policy with that of Vienna. Within two years of the coup, Belgrade defied the Austrians by signing up to a customs union with Bulgaria. Thus began a chain of events which was to lead to the First World War. The government in Vienna retaliated, implementing a veterinary ban against Serbian livestock. A tariff war, known as the 'Pig War' owing to the fact that pigs were Serbia's principal export, ensued which continued from 1906 until 1911, in the middle of which, and as a direct consequence of Serbia's reaction against the tariff war, a fresh international crisis arose over Bosnia.

The Bosnian Crisis, 1908

The event which triggered the crisis was the annexation of Bosnia by Austria-Hungary on 7 October 1908. Opposition to the Dual Monarchy's occupation of Bosnia-Hercegovina after Berlin, had come not only from Serbia, but also from within the Empire itself.[35] Hungarians and liberal Germans were anxious lest this acquisition of territory would exacerbate existing tensions arising from the status of Slavs within the Dual Monarchy. However, Austrian assertiveness in the Balkans in the early twentieth century, was widely supported by the Germans, and besides, Pašić's increasingly aggressive stance over Bosnia, where Serbian nationalists were receiving support from Belgrade to clamour for reform, convinced Aerenthal, the Austrian foreign minister, that Vienna must act lest the Serbs be tempted to seize Bosnia by force. It was axiomatic in the eyes of the Austrians that Serb influence and power must be contained and that they should be prevented from accomplishing their goal of securing a port on the Adriatic.[36]

The Bosnian crisis proved deeply divisive within Serbia because it blocked one route for the building of greater Serbia. The response on the part of Belgrade was to threaten to make war, a move in which it was supported by Montenegro. But in the absence of backing from Russia, neither could do anything other than bluster. The fait accompli was recognised by Turkey in December and by the rest of Europe the following year.[37] Crippled economically by the dependence on Austria for trade, the Bosnian crisis confirmed in Serb minds the imperative for access to the sea. Thus, they renewed their interest in Macedonia. Domestically, the crisis impacted badly on the embryonic party system which had begun to emerge since 1903. In particular, it led to the exclusion of the Independent Radical Party which was the one force in Serbian politics which was in contact with the Croatian–Serbian Coalition in the Zagreb Sabor.

The Coalition viewed the annexation as a catastrophe, fearing in particular that it would enhance the ambitions of Croat nationalists who were pursuing the agenda of Greater Croatia. During this period the Archduke Franz Ferdinand, heir to the Habsburg Monarchy, had made it known that once he acceded he wished to restructure the Empire, giving the same measure of political autonomy to the Czechs and also, possibly, to the Croats as enjoyed by Hungary. Under this vision of trial-ism the Slavs would be the third great force, an idea which had wide appeal not just for Croats, but for Slovenes also, who were too few in number to bid for an independent state, but who saw alignment under a Slav identity as the best course for advancing their political status.

THE BALKAN WARS, 1912–13

The combination of impotence in the face of Austria-Hungary's arbitrary actions, combined with their own burgeoning ambitions for territorial expansion and the weakness of the Ottoman presence in the peninsula, left the small Balkan states vulnerable to manipulation by the Great Powers. Serbia's sworn enemy was Austria-Hungary, but recog-nising the futility of attempting to take the Austrians on under present circumstances, Pašić and his foreign minister, Gueshov, refocussed their attention on the Ottoman lands to the south. During 1911–12, the Serbs even entered a period of co-operation with their Balkan neighbours in their efforts to undermine Ottoman authority, but with the ulterior motive of seeking Bulgarian help to deal with the Austrians once the Turks had been driven from the peninsula. With Russian backing, a for-mal Serbo–Bulgarian Treaty was signed on 13 March 1913 which com-prised a plan for a three-way division of Macedonian territory still under Ottoman rule, including recognition of Greek claims to southern Macedonia, to roughly the present border. To its north, Serbia would receive the north-west triangle, and Bulgaria the south-east as far as Ohrid. Russian mediators would decide the fate of the section in between including Skopje.[38] The Serbs sought to capture all Turkish territory on the Adriatic while the Bulgarians hoped to overrun Thrace and even take on Constantinople. Greece soon joined this alliance in the hope of gaining Salonica or even Constantinople.

In practice, none of the Triple Entente did anything to prevent the pending Balkan war. Of the Triple Alliance, Italy, which had been engaged in a war with the Turks in 1911 over Tripoli, welcomed the impending conflict. The Germans believed that they could benefit if Balkan nationalism were to drive the Ottomans out, while the Austrian

Chancellor, Berchtold, regarded Balkan developments as lamentable but beyond remedial action. An Austro-Russian note presented on 8 October warned that the Powers would not accept a change in the status quo, but Montenegro was impatient and despite Russian calls for restraint, declared war on Turkey. By the end of the month every Turkish army in Europe had been defeated and the Balkan League concluded an armistice on 3 December without seeking Great Power endorsement. The British Foreign Secretary, Sir Edward Grey, promptly moved to re-impose the presence of the Great Powers on the situation by calling a peace conference which resulted in the Treaty of London in May 1913 which formally ended the first Balkan war and brought Albania into existence.

After a brief interlude, the fighting resumed. While the Bulgarians had been preoccupied with their struggle to win Adrianople, the Serbs had not only occupied the whole of Macedonia but insisted on keeping it, in flagrant violation of the Serbo–Bulgarian Treaty. This destroyed the Balkan League and resulted in a second Balkan war which began when Bulgaria attacked Greece and Serbia without warning on 29 June 1913. This misfired. Rumania now joined in on the side of the defenders in order to occupy the Dobrudja. Peace was made at Bucharest in August when Bulgaria lost Dobrudja to Rumania, Adrianople to Turkey, and the bulk of Macedonia to Serbia with the remainder going to Greece. Immediately prior to the First World War, then, the Balkan states had established their independence and the borders defined in 1913 for Bulgaria and Greece remained relatively stable throughout the twentieth century.

THE FIRST WORLD WAR, 1914–18

Writing in January 1913, the British Ambassador in Vienna, Sir Fairfax Cartwright observed that 'Serbia will some day set Europe by the ears and bring about a universal war on the continent.'[39] The Russians, he advised, were encouraging this 'little country' to antagonise Austria to the point of exasperation. But the Russians were not the only factor in the growing tension. The Serbian victory proved deeply disturbing for the complex but hitherto peaceful relationship between the three tribes of Bosnia. The impetus generated for Serbian nationalist sentiment by their military successes was particularly unsettling for the Muslim inhabitants. The Croat population of Bosnia, much like the Croat population within the Empire, was even more deeply divided on the subject than hitherto. To this was added the behaviour of the Austro-Hungarian authorities within the province since 1908.[40] Shortly after the annexation, there emerged a new Bosnian Serb movement, known as 'Young Bosnia', a widespread association created around a nucleus of younger Bosnian Serbs, poor and unemployed, but educated and deeply imbued with a hatred of the Austro-Hungarians whose opposition to Serbian expansionism they deeply resented. 'Young Bosnia' was disinterested in the tactics of political persuasion, and under the influence of the more politically radical of the Russians, adopted the strategy of terror and martyrdom as means to further their goal of achieving independent Bosnian Serb statehood.

Their strategy brought them into contact with the ultra-nationalist elements in Serbia itself, in particular the proscribed revolutionary organisation, Union or Death (*Ujedinjenje ili Smrt* or more popularly, *crna ruka* – 'The Black Hand'). This latter had emerged in 1911 and was deeply disapproved of in official circles not least because it was headed by one of the regicide conspirators of 1903, Colonel Dragutin Dimitrijević (Apis). It was also regarded with deep suspicion because it required its members to take an oath which contradicted the duties of a Serbian military officer.[41] Its outlook was influenced by German militarism as much as by the political ideas of Italian nationalism, and it also had close links through Dimitrijević (who in 1913 was appointed Chief of Intelligence of the Serbian General Staff) with the Russian General Staff. The membership of the Black Hand overlapped with another secret organisation which had a critical bearing on Serbian politics at this time, namely *Narodna Odbrana* (National Defence), founded in December 1908 to develop a network of agents in South Slav lands. Together these organisations constituted a challenge to the authority of Pašić. This crisis, which centred on the control of the military, was preoccupying the Serbian government during the spring and early summer of 1914 when the assassination of the Archduke and his Consort by the Young Bosnia activist, Gavrilo Princip, in Sarajevo, sparked the First World War.[42]

Bosnia, as we have seen, was a deeply disturbed community in the summer of 1914. The choice of *Vidovdan*, or St Vitus' Day (28 June) which Serbs morbidly celebrate as the anniversary of their defeat in 1398 at the hands of the Turks, for the Archduke's visit was either naïve or else exceptionally arrogant in view of the violence being propagated by the activities of Young Bosnia and the aggressively nationalistic and anti-Austrian tone of Belgrade's foreign policy. Following the assassination, Austria-Hungary wanted to crush Serbian nationalism in a localised war and issued an ultimatum to Belgrade in such a manner that its rejection was virtually predetermined. Once the Austro-Hungarian armies began their invasion of Serbia on 29 July, the network of great power alliances drew the major powers into the long avoided all-out conflict.

When the war began, the general expectation was that Serbia would be quickly defeated. This was not the case. The Battle of Cer in August resulted in a heavy defeat for the Austrian-Hungarian army, but this success was then wiped out as an offensive in October resulted in the fall of Belgrade. A Serbian counter-offensive launched on 3 December drove the Austro-Hungarian armies out and they were not to return for almost a year. In the interim, the French set about reconstituting the Serbian army, and re-equipping it to create a fighting force of some 115,000 soldiers who then served on the Salonika front under French command.

War Aims: Serbia

The first task for the Serbian Government was to articulate formal war aims. Serbia had not only a reasonably effective army, but also considerable diplomatic leverage in view of the strategic importance of the Balkans and the various war aims of the major players. The notion of Greater Serbia as it had evolved by 1914, was based on the objective of acquiring the lands which had historic connections with Serbia proper or which had once been under the jurisdiction of the Orthodox Church. However, in the definition of war aims drawn up during the autumn of 1914, the idea of Greater Serbia was quietly set aside in favour of a vague concept of a 'Yugoslav' state which was the logical concomitant of the liberation of all of South Slavic ethnicity. The theoretical underpinnings for this aim were drawn from the work of the eminent geographer, Jovan Cvijic, who was leader of a school of thought which maintained that the three ethnic groups, Serb, Croat and Slovene, were simply tribes of the same people. Adoption of this approach was strengthened by its acceptance by Montenegro and the borders of the new state were accordingly envisaged as including territories within the Dual Monarchy. The programme was formally declared at Niš, to which the Serbian Government had retreated following the loss of Belgrade, on 7 December 1914. It is best seen as a defensive document intended to attract wartime support from the Habsburg South Slavs by projecting both territorial and political aims which appeared, on the surface at least, to be similar to those of the Slovenian and Croatian émigré politicians who had taken refuge in Florence.[43]

War Aims: Habsburg Slavs

Slavic opinion within the Monarchy represented several sets of aspirations, some of which were in direct conflict with one another. Ante Starčević and his close friend, the lawyer Josip Frank, led the narrowly nationalistic Croats. These men were interested primarily in creating a Croat state, to include Dalmatia, Slavonia and Bosnia-Hercegovina, as a federal unit on an equal footing with Austria-Hungary. This was Croatian nationalism of the Right at its most extreme, vested in the Roman Catholic Church which in turn contributed to sustaining antagonism towards the Orthodox elements within the community. But this, as we have seen, was not the only or necessarily the most influential strand in Croatian politics.

The Croatian–Serbian Coalition was composed of parties with no single programme but firmly committed to the principal of co-operation. Like the Croats, they sought a reformation of their status within the monarchy.[44] Finally, there was a group of Dalmatian émigrés who had taken refuge in Florence and were determined to work for a solution which would place the Slavs outside the Austro-Hungarian empire. At the heart of this group were three individuals – Ante Trumbić, a Zagreb lawyer, Frano Supilo, editor of the Rijeka newspaper, *Novi List*, and a sculptor, Ivan Mestrović. In November 1914 they formed the Yugoslav Committee which had the remit to work towards creation of a united Yugoslav (possibly Serbo–Croat) state by informing leading circles and by publicity activity. However, their project was largely an abstraction because it could not bear fruit without the destruction of the Dual Monarchy, and for this there was no plan among the Great Powers. Recognising that they required the support of others with a vested interest in dismantlement of the Monarchy, the Yugoslav Committee sought and succeeded in obtaining the adherence of Pašić. Realistically, this was probably the best that Trumbić could have hoped for but the Yugoslav Committee's position remained weak relative to the Serbian Government. Serbia was not a mere partner in this arrangement, but rather saw itself as the liberator to whom the other Slavs should look.

Macedonia and Montenegro were both defined as Serb in Pašić's eyes, and he was prepared to concede to them a vision of a Yugoslav state in which they could keep their own national emblems, alphabet, religion and possibly even political organisation. The power to grant or withhold such rights, however, would be reserved to the Serbs.[45]

The Treaty of London, 1915

In April 1915, these war aims brought the Yugoslav Committee into direct conflict with Italy, the other state with a vested interest in the political settlement of the Dual Monarchy, and thereby with the Great Powers themselves. Under the Treaty of London, signed on 26 April 1915, Italy was bribed to declare war on Austria-Hungary by the promise of Dalmatia in the post-war settlement. Italy's national war aims were extensive. Approximately 800,000 Italian speakers were under Habsburg rule, mostly in the Trentino and around Trieste. The irony was that while the war had begun, ostensibly at least to save Serbia, the use of Habsburg territory by the allies to bribe Italy would deny Serbia its principal war aim, namely the acquisition of a piece of the Adriatic coast. Trumbić and Supilo reacted to this by moving the headquarters of the Yugoslav Committee to London and in May, it produced a memorandum, which countered Italian claims. Thus, by mid-1915 both the Yugoslav Committee and the Serbian Government had proclaimed war aims which would challenge the pre-1914 order.[46]

The Corfu Declaration, 1917

The relationship between the agendas of the Serbian Government and the Yugoslav Committee developed a stage further in 1917 when in May, their attention was focussed by an apparent challenge from deputies of the Croatian Sabor and South Slav members of the Austrian parliament who met as a Yugoslav Parliamentary Group under the chairmanship of the Slovenian clerical leader, Anton Korošec. This group represented the views of those who wanted unification of the Habsburg lands of the Slovenes, Croats and Serbs into a state of the Habsburg dynasty based on the nationality principle and on the rights of the Croatian state. Trumbić and Pašić responded by signing the Corfu Declaration on 20 July 1917 which called for creation of a democratic, constitutional Kingdom of Serbs, Croats and Slovenes under the Karadjordjević dynasty in which cultural and religious rights of all three peoples would be preserved. A constitutional assembly would be held after liberation to determine the future government.

The Corfu Declaration of 20 July 1917, while successful in combining the war aims of the leading protagonists at the expense of the supporters of Trialism (the elevation of the Croats to the same status as the Austrians and Hungarians) did nothing towards addressing the differences in the agendas of the two key players. Pašić had come to the negotiations in a position significantly weakened by two factors. First he was seeking to reserve the role of the Serbian Army, on which he was now deeply dependent for support which it had achieved, in large part, simply for surviving despite appalling hardship. Over the winter of 1915–16 it had been driven back to the Adriatic Coast and eventually to Corfu, traversing a country rife with typhus leaving behind battlefields and villages littered with lightly buried dead and the streams polluted with the detritus of war.[47] The Serbian army thereby became a significant factor in the balance of power between Pašić and the Yugoslav Committee which explains why he was able to negotiate an agreement with the Yugoslav Committee to recognise the Serbian Army as the Yugoslav army, in preference to their own proposal that there should be an Adriatic Legion. This, however, was to be used subsequently as an example of Serbianisation of the Yugoslav project and it contrasts with the Czech experience where Thomas Masaryck was able to use the Czech Legion, a combined force of Czechs and Slovaks, as a key pillar in the state-building process.

In July 1917, Pašić finally moved to rid the army of its disloyal elements and in particular the ringleaders of the Black Hand. This latter represented a centre of independent power in Serbia which had proved so disruptive before the war and had close links with opposition elements. In order to eradicate Dimitrijević and his collaborators, a show trial was staged in Salonika which condemned the Black Hand leadership to death.

Creation of Yugoslavia

The creation of Yugoslavia just three weeks after the armistice which ended the First World War was possible only because the Austro-Hungarian empire had gone into voluntary dissolution several months earlier. The abrupt disappearance of this entity created a political vacuum in which the minorities of Eastern Europe were at liberty to reorganise themselves into the most effective political and economic units they could conceive. This process was encouraged further by the evidence of Italian ambitions for expansion into Habsburg lands as a reward for their participation on the Allied side. The French supported the initiative, being keen to promote the break up of the monarchy while seeking to prevent Italy from acquiring sovereignty over the Adriatic Coast. The Slovenes and the Croats saw advantage in joining the Serbs, whose army was one of the few among the Balkans to emerge from the struggle victorious, and who might offer greater opportunity for self-determination than they would expect under Italian colonisation. Indeed, it is arguable that without such an army, the Serbian government could not have convened Slovene and Croat representatives in Belgrade on 1 December at which meeting the new kingdom, of which the Serbian King was the focal point, was proclaimed. Since the Serbs were triumphant in the war, the Slovenes and Croats were in the position of suppliants where the Serbs were all too eager to assert themselves in furthering the extension of Serbian frontiers. In 1918, only Serbia was strong enough to provide a focal point around which the South Slav peoples would organise.[48]

The new state was named the Kingdom of Serbs, Croats and Slovenes, adopting the name of Yugoslavia a decade later. It united in one political entity three distinct but nevertheless ethnically related peoples. It consisted of the pre-war kingdoms of Serbia and Macedonia and the South Slav parts of Austria-Hungary (Slovenia, Croatia, Dalmatia, Bosnia-Hercegovina and Vojvodina). The adoption of such a cumbersome appellation was just one manifestation of the fact that here was created a state which was not greater than the sum of its parts. The histories of these three peoples, while interwoven, is at the same time separate and the experiences which each brought to the state-building project which came to be known as Yugoslavia, had forged peoples of differing outlooks and expectations. This new state was not, therefore, the product of one community's search for national self-determination, nor the unification of a diaspora which could trace and agree upon a common heritage; nor was it the outcome of a series of disparate peoples' struggles against a common foe. Rather, it was a solution constructed in the power vacuum created by the collapse of both the Ottoman and Habsburg empires, combined with the determination on the part of the victors that the justification for enforced dismantlement of the defeated empires would be application of the principle of self-determination.

2 The Collision of Ideals

What sort of state had the South Slavs proclaimed on 1 December 1918? Even the key players would have found it difficult to answer this question directly. From the outset, the Kingdom which eventually came to be known as Yugoslavia (South Slav) was characterised by imbalance and paradox. The Serbs turned to the state-building process full of hopeful expectation. They had fought gallantly on the winning side during the war, emerging with international respect, and had been granted their now century-old ambition of the unity of at least a proportion of South Slavic peoples within a common frontier. What they could offer to the state-building process was expressed in their existing institutional structures – the monarchy, the army and the bureaucracy – together with a clear conception of political organisation. Their primary demand was that Serbian identity be protected.

The Croats and Slovenes, the other major elements in this enterprise, were less well orientated to the circumstances in which they found themselves. The wartime negotiations of the Yugoslav Committee had proceeded on the assumption that Austria-Hungary was a given of the post-war order. The South Slav subjects of the empire could be forgiven if they felt a little bemused by the sudden withdrawal of the protection and infrastructure which this unwieldy but economically effective empire had provided. Having been on the losing side in the war, a war which had been sparked by Vienna's determination to bring Serbia to heel, the Croats and Slovenes found themselves in a weak position relative to their partners in state formation. Their political experience was altogether different from that of the Serbs, and indeed the other South Slavs who were included in the Kingdom, and their expectations for the future did not include the submergence of their identities in a unitary state.

These, then, were the foundations on which the Yugoslav peoples were to build a multi-ethnic state. What united them was a desire for stability – a common denominator across Europe following the cataclysmic war in which so many of the old certainties had been destroyed – and security, defined in terms of the preservation of cultural identities within the state, and protection against external predators who might cast envious eyes on these strategically important lands. To achieve these ends the South Slavs required strong government which could accomplish the process of post-war reconstruction and lay the foundations for a modern economy and rising living standards.

The post-war order was founded on the principle of collective security, a more formal system of international security than the Concert of Europe, designed to prevent the occurrence of further armed conflict. However, the punitive nature of the peace settlement, combined with the failure to translate the ideals of Versailles into workable institutional arrangements, produced a climate of ongoing uncertainty in which the revisionist ambitions of the resentful losers of the recent conflict were ever present to unsettle the status quo which the winners were determined to impose. To this was added the emergence of radical new ideological challenges to the existing assumptions about the ordering of social relations. The triumph of Bolshevism in Russia and then the rise of fascism in Italy, unleashed forces as yet untested into European politics. Within this international framework of uncertainty, the South Slav peoples were left to build a new state to act as a common homeland for peoples who had little shared history and fewer mutual values.

THE PARIS PEACE SETTLEMENT, 1919–20

The new SCS Kingdom bore the name of the three principal ethnic communities it comprised. This choice acknowledged the founding principle of national self-determination, but more ominously reflected the inability of the participants to compromise on a collective noun. The régime's first tasks were to achieve the related objectives of international recognition as a political entity together with the negotiation of territorial boundaries.

The attitudes of the Great Powers towards the Kingdom varied. All were cautiously accepting of the eventual dissolution of the Habsburg monarchy, but the French alone, who wanted both the destruction of the Dual Monarchy and the containment of Italian expansionism, had actively pursued the creation of a South Slav state which they saw as the means to achieve both of these ends simultaneously. The United States was the first to recognise the Kingdom, doing so in February 1919. President Woodrow Wilson had been convinced by the arguments of his Secretary of State, Robert Lansing, who believed that the South Slav idea was valid because it was in line with the principle of self-determination for the peoples of the Habsburg and Ottoman empires to be accorded the 'freest opportunities for autonomous development' within frontiers drawn 'along historically established lines of allegiance and nationality'.[1] The pivotal assumption of United States' policy towards the settlement was that nationalism was the underlying cause of pre-war instability and that if the nation-state, which in Wilson's mind was linked with notions of popular sovereignty, were permitted to triumph over nineteenth-century imperialism and great power politics, then stability would return. What he failed to take into account was that popular sovereignty required a consensus among the participants about the legitimacy of the state to govern its subject peoples. While the South Slavs might see an advantage in co-operating within a single state, they did share common conceptions about the legitimacy of one form of government over another.

This preoccupation with national self-determination raised another difficulty for the peacemakers because there was inherent conflict between the principles of self-determination and those which arose as a result of the punitive nature of the peace settlement. Permitting self-determination in a given territory at the expense of a vanquished state fitted this policy well, but it became a problem when those who were supposed to be self-determining wished to remain with the vanquished at the expense of the victors, or where there was a dispute between subjects of two or more of the victors. Above all, adoption of the principle of self-determination suited the policy of a punitive peace in so far as it was used as a means of justifying the harshness of the Allies' judgement about reparations and territorial concessions, but it also made any attempt at addressing the fact of a marginal victory through promotion of conciliation among the warring nations virtually impossible. The recognition of Yugoslavia by the British and French half way through 1919 was a reflection of these dilemmas.[2]

The old players of great power politics were initially suspicious of this new state and prevaricated. But their manoeuvring ability was restricted by the secret treaties concluded with junior allies by reason of political expediency during the course of the conflict. In this regard, recognition of Yugoslavia raised embarrassing problems as a consequence of the Treaty of London of April 1915 which promised territorial concessions to Italy at the expense of Austria. In 1919, these territories were the subject of a counter claim by Yugoslavia itself. However, the British and French were pressured by the requirement for Serbia's signature on the Versailles Treaty which concluded the war with Germany; the latter had already recognised Yugoslavia. By June both the western powers had given in. This also resolved the anomalous position of the new Kingdom at the peace conference where the Serbs, by virtue of fighting on the side of the victors as a national entity were alone admitted as a delegation. Initially they had been obliged to represent the new Kingdom until a protest succeeded in obtaining a third seat, thereby permitting the Croats and Slovenes to send delegates also. Ante Trumbić and Anton Korošeć respectively joined Pašić as full delegates in Paris.

Defining the Territorial Limits of Yugoslav Sovereignty

Yugoslavia's interwar problems, both domestic and international, were in every sense a reflection of the post-war political settlement. The first great test of the cohesion of the leadership of the new Kingdom was encountered as it tackled the task of negotiating residual border disputes and minority issues. The region's armies had determined the boundaries in the Balkans and these now formed the foundation for the post-war settlement. Indeed, the major powers sensed pressure from the east European peoples to recognise this fact: Lansing alluded to this when he confided to his diary on 22 January 1919 that 'all the races of Central Europe and the Balkans in fact are actually fighting or about to fight with one another ... the Great War seems to have split up into a lot of little wars'.[3] So, it was the detail rather than the substance of the Kingdom which was discussed at the Peace Conference which sat in Paris between 18 January 1919 and 21 January 1920.

Nikola Pašić came to the peace conference determined to impose Belgrade's centralising influence on the new state. To that end he was prepared to sacrifice the territorial objectives of the Croats and Slovenes for sovereignty over disputed territories in the northwest, the better to barter for Serbian expansion at the expense of Albania and Macedonia in the south. Clearly, this compromised the bargaining position of the Yugoslav delegation because the resulting division between the territorial interests of Pašić, Korošeć and Trumbić was open to exploitation by their adversaries.

The most protracted border disputes were those with Italy, which had cultivated an appetite for territorial expansion during the nineteenth-century struggles for unification. Their exuberance at being able to attend the peace conference as a victor only added to their hunger to extract what they believed to be just dues from their erstwhile enemies.

The Treaty of London had promised them much including the city of Trieste, its industrial hinterland, and the Dalmatian coast. With the exception of the city, recognition of this so-called 'London line' for the boundary would leave a majority of ethnic Slavs under Italian sovereignty. Woodrow Wilson, who refused to recognise the clauses of the secret treaties, was determined that the London line would not be sustained. The Americans proposed an alternative which would bisect the Istrian peninsula from north to south and leave all of Dalmatia except the port of Zara (Zadar) to the Yugoslavs. While the Yugoslavs relinquished the moral high ground in this argument by demanding sovereignty over the predominantly Italian speaking city of Trieste, the government in Rome was also compromised by its demands for sovereignty over the old Venetian stronghold of Fiume (now called Rijeka), which in more recent times had served as the naval base of the Austro-Hungarian empire. Its population in 1919 was predominantly Italian. When this claim was rejected by the Paris conference in September 1919, the Italian Government weakened its case still further by tacit connivance at occupation of Fiume by an irregular army led by the irredentist writer, Gabriele D'Annunzio. The great powers promptly washed their hands of the whole business, leaving the Italians and Yugoslavs to deal with each other directly. The issue was resolved by the Treaty of Rapallo of 12 November 1920 which drew the border between the London line and the line of advance of the Italian troops; Fiume became a free city and Italy obtained sovereignty over Zara.[4] The agreement left over half a million Slovenes and Croats in Italian territory.[5]

More ominously, however, the march on Fiume in 1919 had inspired the Italian fascist leader, Benito Mussolini, who emulated this manoeuvre by marching on Rome the following year, overthrowing the government and installing a fascist dictatorship. For the next twenty years, Mussolini pursued his ambition to make Italy the dominant power in the Adriatic. He condemned the new Yugoslav state as an absurdity, arguing that it should be dismantled in order to facilitate Italy's penetration of the Balkans. Emboldened by Mussolini's revisionist ideas, D'Annunzio repeated his adventure in September 1923 and the final settlement, signed in Rome on 27 January 1924, awarded Fiume to Italy and confirmed Italian possession of Zara while recognising the Yugoslav claim to the Dalmatian coast.[6]

This was not all. The Treaty of London had promised Italy possession of the Albanian port of Valona and control over the conduct of Albania's foreign relations in the post-war period. The very prospect of such an arrangement united the governments in Belgrade and Tirana against the Italians, but the Italians pressured the major powers to compensate it by recognising a 'special status' for Italy in Albanian affairs. The matter was resolved by the Ambassadors' Conference which succeeded the Supreme Council as the organ of the Allied Governments in Paris. In November 1921, it passed a resolution declaring that in the event of a threat to the independence of Albania, the British, French and Japanese governments would propose, through the League of Nations, that Italy should be appointed to ensure Albanian independence. The irony at the heart of this diplomatic fudge was that the principal and probably only threat to Albanian independence in this period came from Italy itself. Moreover, the apparent ineffectiveness of the Italian government in furthering Italian interests in Paris contributed to the ease with which Mussolini was able to seize power in October 1922.

Yugoslavia and Italy were also engaged in a triangular dispute with Austria over the province of Carinthia which contained a substantial proportion of Slovenes. The Austrian frontier and the voluntary secession of Slovenia from Austria was dealt with in the Treaty of St Germain-en-Laye of 10 September 1919, but the issue of Carinthia was complicated by the presence of German minorities in the key towns and by the important railway links between Austria and the coast of Trieste and Fiume which the Italians argued should not pass through Yugoslav territory. Accordingly, they maintained that the frontier between Austria and Yugoslavia should follow the line of the Karawanken mountains, or even, in the case of Assling, a line to the south. Italy also had a counterclaim to part of Carniola. The issue was decided by plebiscite on 10 October 1920 and despite the fact the proposed arrangements favoured Yugoslavia, the majority voted to remain within Austria. Elsewhere the Yugoslavs gained most of Carinola and lower Styria, and (under the Treaty of Rapallo) Assling and Tarvis with special arrangements for railway traffic between Austria and Italy.[7]

Regarding the Hungarian frontier with Croatia, the secession of Croatia was formalised in the Treaty of Trianon of 4 June 1920. There was no natural dividing line between the Vojvodina and the Danubian lands of Hungary, nor did a clear ethnic division suggest itself. The line which was drawn favoured the victor and in practice gave to Yugoslavia an addition of some three quarters of a million of non-Slavs.

Issues arising from the frontier with Bulgaria were dealt with under the Treaty of Neuilly-sur-Seine of 27 November 1919. This confirmed

Bulgaria's losses under the treaty which ended the Second Balkan War in 1913, to which was added a further modification of the frontier with Serbia in the latter's favour. But the most significant and sore of Bulgaria's losses was Macedonia which had been promised to Bulgaria (by the Serbs) in return for its participation in the First Balkan War. At Paris, the Serbs refused to recognise either the non-Serb majority in Bulgaria or the legitimacy of the one in Kosovo. The 1919 settlement succeeded in perpetuating for subsequent generations the controversy about the racial identities of the Macedonians.

Yugoslavia was established with a population of just over 12 million, and contained three major ethnic components. The ethnic minorities amounted to approximately two million (some 17 per cent of the total population). Serbo–Croat speakers constituted some 74 per cent of the population, with just over 8 per cent speaking Slovene. In terms of religious affiliation, 46 per cent were Orthodox, 39 per cent were Roman Catholic, and 11 per cent were Muslim. Some 720,000 South Slavs remained outside Yugoslavia's borders (Table 2.1).[8]

Table 2.1 Yugoslavia's population in 1918

Nationality	Number	Per cent
Serbs	4,665,851	38.83
Croats	2,856,551	23.77
Slovenes	1,024,761	8.53
Bosnian Muslims	727,650	6.05
Macedonians or Bulgars	585,558	4.87
Other Slavic	174,466	1.45
Germans	513,472	4.27
Hungarians	472,409	3.93
Albanians	441,740	3.68
Romanians, Vlachs and Cincars	229,398	1.91
Turks	168,404	1.40
Jews	64,159	0.53
Italians	12,825	0.11
Others	80,079	0.67
Total	12,017,323	100.00

Source: Banac, *The Nationalities Question in Yugoslavia*, p. 58.

POLITICS, 1919–29

Provisional Government and Vidovdan Constitution

During the interim, that is between 10 December 1918 and 28 October 1920, Yugoslavia was administered by a provisional government with a joint cabinet composed initially of representatives of the Zagreb Parliament (*Narodno Vijece*) and the Serbian government. Representatives of the other republics were added gradually. To prepare elections to the Constituent Assembly, an Interim National Parliament (*Privremeno narodno predstavništvo* – PNP) was set up in March 1919 which was really the Serbian parliament (*Skupština*) by another name. In November 1920, this body was replaced by a Constitutional Assembly (*Ustavotivarna Skupština*) that had 416 members with the authority to act as a legislature in addition to its role as debating chamber for the constitutional drafts. This body was subsequently transformed into the National Assembly once the new constitution was ratified. Debate within the Constitutional Assembly revolved around four issues: the name of the state, the recognition of religious freedoms, the need for a legislative chamber and the nature of local administration.

The French had encouraged the Serbs to develop their vision of a unitary state after the Italian or Polish model. The arguments used to support this viewpoint were rooted in the assumption that a federal model would leave the new state vulnerable to external attack, a weighty argument given the predatory nature of several of its neighbours. However, this approach had vociferous detractors among the international advisors to the Kingdom in this period. Chief among these were Henry Wickham Steed and the British Slavophile scholar, R.W. Seton Watson. Both men were keen to impress upon the Serbs the state's need, as they saw it, for the Kingdom to acquire a federal character with real power devolved to the Croats. Failure to adopt this approach would jeopardise any chance of the Kingdom's survival. Although the result, a constitutional, parliamentary monarchy, resembled in many ways the pre-war Serbian experiment with democratic forms, to say that this was solely a reflection of the existing balance of power is not entirely fair.[9]

The principal source of coherent opposition to the Serbs in this period was provided by the Croat Peasant Party (*Hrvatska seljačka stranka* – HSS) of Stejpan Radić. Founded in 1905, the HSS stood for the aspirations for independent statehood of the newly liberated Croatian peasantry. In this formative period, Radić shied away from the politics of conciliation and co-operation, choosing instead the tactics of obstruction. In February 1919, just over two months after the state's creation, he wrote to President Wilson, appealing to the United States to recognise a Croatian Republic. In order to underline the point, he had the word 'Republican' added to the Party name. A decision by the radical–democrat alliance to back the government decision that the constitution be passed by a simple majority rather than a qualified majority vote provided the excuse for the HSS to boycott the Assembly. Probably, the real problem for Radić was that he had anticipated that the Central Powers would emerge from the war victorious and when the Dual Monarchy collapsed, he and his party were unprepared. They sought to shape the future with reference to the familiar federalist structure of the Dual Monarchy, envisaging for themselves a role in the new Kingdom commensurate with that of Hungary in the Austro-Hungarian empire. In doing so they were conveniently forgetting the problems which the experiment with Dualism had generated. Their political experience dictated that a federal structure was the solution to multi-ethnicity and thus they chose to forget the decades of conflict with their overbearing Magyar neighbours and sought to replicate the Dualist model of the Habsburgs. This, and the subsequent boycott by the Croats of the Assembly, left them open to the charge of disloyalty to the new state, while from a practical point of view, it left the Serbs and the Serbs from the former Habsburg lands, to fashion the state as they chose.

Radić's choice of the tactics of abstention was influenced partly by the example of Sinn Fein in Ireland. He concluded that by holding aloof from the central parliament he would be able to dictate the final form of the constitutional settlement. Politically, it was deeply unwise because it absented the Croat deputies during the most crucial period of state formation. With no opposition in the Constituent Assembly, Pašić was able to model the new state on the pre-war Serbian model so that the 1921 constitution can be said to represent the culminating point of the pan-Serb tendency. The Serbs believed they had every right to dominate the new polity. Their reasoning was rooted in Serbia's successful maintenance of autonomy since 1804, and their distinctive contribution to furthering – or leading even – the movement for South Slav unification. Wartime casualties were also significant: if the two Balkan Wars of 1912–13 are included, these amounted to some 1.9 million of whom 900,000 were military.[10] The brunt had been borne by the Serbs and the Macedonians (whom the Serbs counted as fellow Serbs) and thus it was the Serbian monarchy, army and institutions which were advanced as the founding institutions of the new state.

The Serbs were lacking in neither strength nor determination in providing the necessary leadership; but they did not have the legitimacy in the new Kingdom's population as a whole to assume the role of the *staatsvolk* of the new Yugoslavia. They believed that once they had granted religious freedom as a constitutional right, then this should be the end of all dispute among the constituent peoples and that the centralised model could be made to work after the French example thereafter. Among the non-Serb populations it was the Croats who reacted most aggressively to Serbian hegemony. To this conflict of political organisation was added a conflict about extension of hegemony within Yugoslavia: both the Serbs and the Croats aspired to domination of Bosnia. Often this conflict has been described as one between the conflicting notions of centralism and federalism, but it would be more precise to argue, as some scholars do, that the issue was a conflict between Serbian unitarism and Habsburg dualism.[11]

Institutionally, the central role was given to the unicameral parliament of 312 members, elected by a system of proportional representation. Theoretically, the monarchy and parliament were designed to balance each other since both had responsibility for legislation. In practice, the real power lay with the monarch who appointed both the Council of Ministers and senior civil servants. Consequently the government was heavily dependent upon royal patronage which reinforced the tendency towards the centralisation and Serbianisation that was so antithetical to the other nationalities. The ministries were very powerful in relation to the legislature in which the various political parties were so badly divided within themselves that effective debate on legislation was impossible. There was neither a second chamber, nor a constitutional court to act as checks and balances on the executive.

Opinion is divided as to what exactly was created. Was it synonymous with the Kingdom of Serbia or had Serbia disappeared to be replaced by something new?[12] Serbia's critics condemn it as being in fact the Greater Serbia envisaged by Belgrade's war aims. Certainly, Serbia had succeeded in swallowing Macedonia and Montenegro and was in a position to dominate Bosnia-Hercegovina. It was Serbia's monarchy, army and civil service which were at the centre of the new state which also adopted Serbia's system of treaties and agreements, a legacy from the pre-war year. At the same time, the bureaucratic structures in place in the former Habsburg lands, along with their military, were dissolved.

The new government in Belgrade moved swiftly to Serbianise the gendarmerie. These factors then provided the basis for non-Serbs to claim that the new state was in fact an extension of the old Serb kingdom.

However, when viewed from the perspective of the Constitutional Assembly, the picture is less clear. The Assembly behaved much like a revolutionary committee, ignoring all that was past and genuinely seeking a constitution to meet the novel circumstances. The struggle over the issue of state's name was itself interesting because the name Yugoslavia was selected and accepted by all the parties except the Radićals and the Democrats who were accused of being the most centralist. In fact what the Serbs wanted was to protect Serbian identity, rather than to subjugate the Slovenes and Croats. Nevertheless, these latter who stood for the autonomy of their respective provinces on the basis of ethnic identity, and demanded a single name which did not mention their individual ethnicities.[13]

Political Struggles, 1921–28

Strong government and radical (if not revolutionary) ideas were required to establish this new state in its formative years. Neither was present in the SCS Kingdom during the 1920s. In Yugoslavia, as elsewhere in Europe, the bloodletting of the First World War ensured the dominant element among the political class was drawn from the same generation which had held political power in the pre-war period. Between January 1921 and April 1926 the governments, of which there were ten, were headed by the aged Nikola Pašić, leader of the Serbian Radićal Party. In its post-war incarnation, the Radićals were anything but radical, having achieved their revolutionary aims when the new Kingdom was proclaimed. Between the adoption of the Vidovdan Constitution and his death in early 1926, Pašić's sole achievement was to retain power despite the bitter atmosphere of intrigue, corruption and dishonesty which characterised the political environment in Belgrade at this time. Undoubtedly, Pašić enjoyed enormous prestige, the consequence of his successful leadership of Serbia during the Balkan and First World Wars. In his younger days, he had demonstrated an awareness of the inherent conflict in the aims of Serbian nationalism and Yugoslavism as expressed by the Croats, observing in the early 1880s that the 'road to unification of the Serbo–Croat people under the leadership of Serbia runs in a completely opposite direction to the road of unification under the leadership of the Triune Kingdom'.[14] However, by the time the Kingdom came into being he was too inflexible, or else too little of a statesman to attempt to build political institutions that would bridge this void.

Moreover, the Radićals were insufficiently powerful to achieve effective governance alone. They were a minority Party from the outset and in such a heterogeneous environment were incapable of forming a sustainable majority. Their principal ally in this period was the Serbian Democratic Party, which had been formed in Sarajevo in February 1919 under Ljuba Davidović. Initially, the Democrats hoped to unite both the Slovene liberals with the Habsburg Serbs and others opposed to Pašić. In the Constituent Assembly of 1920 they had 92 seats, one more than the Radićals, but they went into decline after this, losing many supporters in the 1923 elections. Part of the reason for this was the rift in the Party between Davidović, the compromiser, and the Serb Svetozar Pribičević, a pre-war member of the Croatian parliament and Croatian representative in the Hungarian Parliament. During the war he had worked closely with Supilo and other Croat leaders to further the Yugoslav cause.[15]

Under the new régime, Pribičević was leader of the Croat–Serb Coalition. Pribičević and his political associates were revolted by the strident nationalism of Radić, and joined initially with the Democrats. However, he soon fell out with the latter and created the Serbian Independence Party in 1924 which became the champion of Serbian centralisation. Apologists for Pribičević argue that his commitment to Serbian nationalism was tempered by a genuine enthusiasm for the wider cause of Yugoslav unity. This may have become true towards the end of the decade, by which time he had recognised the extent to which the Radićals had used him to sustain their pre-eminence, but the evidence from the early part of this period indicates that he was a convinced advocate of the unitarist principle. He fully accepted the Serbian belief in the requirement for a centralised constitution, while his tenure as Minister of the Interior in the Provisional Government saw the Serbianisation of the gendarmerie and local administration in the former Habsburg lands. Indeed, some argue that it was Pribičević rather than Pašić who enforced rigid centralisation, as opposed to simply a centralised constitution, citing his authorship of the single system of secular schools in place of existing religious networks of which the Roman Catholic was the largest.[16]

Apart from the alliance of Serbian interests, Yugoslav politics contained two further forces, the communists and the Croats. The Communists had

58 seats in the Constitutional Assembly, and could boast support from all over the country, particularly from the Macedonian tobacco workers and the railway-men in the poorer southern areas as well as from former prisoners of war. The Yugoslav Communist Party (*Komunistička partija Jugoslavije* – KPJ) was formed in April 1919 and gained much inspiration from the example of Bela Kun in Hungary. Tactically, the communists were unsophisticated at this time, relying on terror rather than the political process. Their assassination of Minister of the Interior, Milorad Drasković, on 2 August 1921, was completely counterproductive, succeeding only in increasing existing public hostility towards the communist movement in general and leading to the party being outlawed. From this point onwards its importance in pre-war Yugoslav history is generally greatly exaggerated, a product of the official 'revision' of history during the Tito period. For the most part the Yugoslav communists spent the interwar years wrestling with increasing radicalism from within their own ranks, as well as the hostility towards the Yugoslav idea from the Communist International (Comintern), which at its conference in July 1924, proposed that the Balkan states should be reorganised into a federation of worker-peasant republics including Bulgaria, Serbia and Macedonia. The Comintern's interpretation of Marx and Lenin led its leaders to adopt the view that Yugoslavia was an imperialist project created through territorial enlargement of Serbia at Versailles and as such was deemed an illegitimate entity to be dismembered at the earliest opportunity.[17]

The other potentially powerful force in Yugoslav politics was centred on the Croat Peasant Party (HSS) which, with 70 seats in the Skupština in 1923 represented a substantial voting bloc which it used to sustain itself as the most consistent and united party of opposition. Deeply critical of Serbian domination of parliament, the effectiveness of its protest was blunted by the determination with which its leaders boycotted the Assembly, thereby ensuring that they were outside the political debate rather an integral part of it. Stejpan Radić, its irascible and demagogic leader, was a remarkable man by any standard who had risen from an illiterate peasant background, educating himself, to be one of the most active and powerful forces in Croatian politics before the First World War. Throughout his long political career, Radić remained loyal to his ancestry through steadfast and passionate advocacy of radical land reform. He believed simultaneously in the establishment of Croat sovereignty as well as agreement with the Serbs, but his fiery reputation and notorious predisposition to unpredictable outbursts did much to discourage his adversaries from attempting compromise and negotiation. His hyperbolic likening of Yugoslavia to 'a Serbian Bastille' on 14 July 1923 captured his rhetorical flourish as well as the uncompromising and oppressive behaviour of the Serbian politicians.[18]

In the summer of 1925, King Alexander attempted to use Radić (who had been imprisoned for his alleged connections with the Bolsheviks) in an attempt to break the political paralysis. Using an intermediary, the King urged Radić to deal with the Radicals, and on his release, the Croat became Minister of Education in a new Cabinet formed in July. By return, the word 'republican' was dropped from the Croat Peasant Party name. Reciprocating the move, King Alexander and Queen Mignon visited Zagreb in August to participate in the celebrations of one thousand years since the establishment of the Croat medieval monarchy. This co-operative spirit was short-lived however, and in 1926, Radić and a deeply disillusioned Pribičević, were reconciled. Bitterness, always a distorting motive, united these old adversaries as they fulminated at Belgrade's centralising tendencies. Politically this was detrimental because it confused the public, undermining the status of parliament in public opinion still further, ultimately creating conditions in which the monarchy could appeal to the people over the heads of the political process, and abrogating all vestiges of the constitutional process.[19]

The political struggles resulted in stagnation: legislation which should have been introduced to effect the unification of taxation, the judiciary and various branches of local administration had been neglected owing to the petty squabbling and centralist influences. Croat complaints as to the inequality of the taxation system were largely justified, but their indignation at the corruption and inaction of government departments was shared fully by the Serbs. The King, who appears genuinely to have wanted to achieve a compromise with the Croats and Slovenes, was in a very difficult position. If he went too far in conceding to the Croats, he would lose ground in Serbia. Above all, the singular absence of disinterested advisers or statesmen of real ability and vision disadvantaged him. The civil service was inefficient and rife with corruption. Almost one half of the junior ranks of the old Serbian civil service had been killed in the war and it had proven impossible in a country with such high levels of illiteracy to find sufficient numbers of trained and responsible officials to administer the enlarged kingdom, at least long enough for the post-war university intake to reach maturity.

The defining issue had been Croat dissatisfaction with the centralised Serbian dominated state and the total denial of their alternative vision. However this interpretation of the political failure of this decade is perhaps overly simplistic. Although the Croats were certainly the most vocal critics, they were unconvincing in action and failed to produce one practical statesman who could lead them into constructive collaboration with the other elements in the Kingdom. Nor is it the case that the Croats alone had grievances: the Slovenes regarded the Croats with even more suspicion than the Serbs in this period. The Serbs, meanwhile, were clearly divided between themselves and as such cannot be accused of acting as a monolithic bloc motivated by a determination to oppress the Croats. Indeed, the many cabinets constructed during this period contained politicians from all over the country and representing a wide cross-section of ethnic, social and economic views. To some extent they must share the blame for what transpired (Table 2.2).

A series of assassinations within the Skupština on 20 June 1928 brought this first period of attempted state building to a close. The casualties included Radić, although he was not the intended target. Hospitalised with wounds from which he would die six weeks later, Radić presciently declared that 'nothing is left but the King and people'.[20]

Table 2.2   Parliamentary elections, 1920–27 (number of seats won)

Political party	1920	1923	1925	1927
Democrats	92	51	37	6
Independent Democrats (SDS)	—	—	21	22
Radićals	91	108	143	112
Communists (KPJ)	59	—		—
Croatian Republican Peasant (HRSS)	50	70	67	61
Agrarian Union	39	11	3	9
Slovenia People's Party (SLS)	27	24	21	21
Yugoslav Muslim Organisation (JMO)	24	18	15	17
Social Democrats	10	—	—	1
Germans	—	8	5	6
Montenegrin Federalists	—	2	3	1
Other	27	21	—	—
Total mandates	419	313	315	315

Source: *Enciklopedia Jugoslavkje*, v, III (Zagreb: Jugoslavenski leksikogvafski zavod, 1983), p. 269, quoted in Lampe, *Yugoslavia as History*, p. 135.

Society, 1921–29

Although the union of the South Slavs obliged Zagreb to give up its status as a capital city, it continued to grow apace with Belgrade throughout this decade. Much was written about the differences to be found between Belgrade and Zagreb in this period, particularly in the physical manifestation of each societies' cultural aspirations. While Belgrade is frequently reported as dishevelled and disorderly, Zagreb appears in contemporary accounts as a Teutonic counterpoint with imposing public buildings and paved streets more in keeping with the ambience of central Europe than the more southerly regions of the state of which it had become a part. Similarly, differences could be discerned in the intellectual pretensions of each, the Croats being ever ready to accuse the Serbs of being uncultured. In fact, the differences were more those of experience derived from social origin since the Croatian intelligentsia was drawn not from its rough-hewn peasantry but from the middle classes and even the nobility, while the Serbian intellectual was generally of peasant extraction and more in touch with society in its widest sense. Nevertheless, cultural communications between these two cities as well as with Ljubljana flourished. Cafés became the centre of a thriving cosmopolitan life which included women whose numbers among the student body at Belgrade University rose to 25 per cent in 1928. Zagreb had a long-established university and an excellent library as well as a lively artistic community. In Ljubljana, a new university was established while Bosnia and Hercegovina developed a creative rivalry in intellectual and cultural matters.[21]

During the 1920s literacy levels across the Kingdom varied widely from over 90 per cent in Slovenia to less than 20 per cent in Bosnia and Hercegovina. Nevertheless, evidence that a civil society did emerge in this period can be found in the degree to which newspapers and publishing houses flourished. More significantly, the Radical paper, *Vreme*, did not enjoy the circulation of the largely independent *Politika*, indicating that public opinion was formed independently of the party of government. Of all institutions in the Kingdom, it was the Army alone which received wide popular respect. Predominantly Serb in this period, it was seen to be hard working, efficient and free from the corruption which characterised much of the rest of the state. However, it was also very Prussian in its outlook, and still influenced by the White Hand which clung with dogmatic determination to the inviolability of Greater Serbia.

The Economy, 1921–29

One of the principal criticisms of the First World War settlement in Eastern Europe is that it destroyed the region's economic organisation. The extensiveness of the Dual Monarchy had facilitated the construction of a complex web of industrial development, communications and trade, centred around the Danube River which crossed central Europe from the Alps to drain into the Black Sea on the coast of Rumania. The creation of so many successor states effectively dislocated this economy: raw materials were spread among the successor states, while river navigation, the heart of regional trade, was subject to customs posts from no less than five new riparian states. The peace settlement attempted to forestall such difficulties by making provision for a substantial measure of economic integration among the successors, but this did not ameliorate the difficulties which arose from the political rivalries and insecurities which beset the region in the absence of a unifying power, and the disruption of economic life persisted throughout the interwar period.

The SCS Kingdom was an excellent example of the problems raised by this political reorganisation. Before 1914, the territory it controlled was traversed by four separate rail networks. Under the new régime, one of the earliest tasks was to link these networks so as to integrate the country rather than reinforce the existing connections with external states. Much of the pre-war rail network had been destroyed during the war and in any case the Austro-Hungarian authorities had directed the railway building with purely strategic interests in mind, or with a view to centralising all traffic on Vienna and Buda, or Trieste and Fiume. With slender resources and indifferent materials obtained through German reparations and elsewhere the Pašić government commenced a project to link the country by rail. The problems were two fold: geography, in particular the karst mountains which run parallel with the coast from Trieste to Montenegro, were an immediate barrier to communications between the narrow coastal strip and the interior which required vast amounts of expensive tunnelling to overcome, as well as an elaborate system by which water could be pumped up to the building sites owing to the absence of nearby river systems. The second problem arose from the poor construction practices, which meant that on the main line between Belgrade and Zagreb, nineteen different types of rails were used, and the majority were too light or too short for the heavy traffic which passed on that route.

The achievement of proper economic integration was hampered by the pre-unification trading networks which focussed on peripheral states rather than with other members of the Kingdom. Industry, such as it was, concentrated on the northern plains of Croatia and Slovenia, so that in the mid-1920s, these regions had 60 per cent of the total industry and 45 per cent of the total employment in manufacturing with exports going predominantly to central Europe. Industry made an early recovery after the war, with some 63 per cent of foreign trade going to Austria and Italy.[22]

This was mirrored by rapid recovery of the financial sector centred in Zagreb. By 1924–25, the revival of shipping and tourism in particular, together with French loans and armaments, as a consequence of Yugoslav membership of the Little Entente, fostered relative prosperity which was reflected in a favourable trade balance; war debts were paid by 1926, at which point the dinar was stabilised, and France and Britain began programmes of investment which resulted in their ownership of almost half of the Yugoslav mining industry by 1939. However, this prosperity concentrated as it was in the northern provinces, appeared to reinforce the political differences between Zagreb and Belgrade, heightening the rivalry between these twin focal points of power within the state and contributed to undermining the centralist tendencies of the Vidovdan Constitution. For a brief interval the Zagreb commercial banks even refused to participate in the new Kingdom's central bank in Belgrade.[23]

The predominant source of employment in this period, across the Kingdom, was agriculture. During the First World War, the principal demand of the peasant soldier was fulfilment of their ideal, ownership of the land. The Serbian government promised that land would be distributed as early as 1912, and in 1917 it had encouraged the co-operation of South Slav volunteers from the Habsburg monarchy by offering land to them also. The National Council in Zagreb made similar promises. In practice, land reform, which affected all estates over 100 hectares, was carried out piecemeal and not fully settled until early 1930. The owners were compensated in state bonds which the beneficiaries would repay to the state over thirty years, except in the case of veterans who had served with the Allies; the Slav peasants were advanced at the expense of the minorities. The process was extended to uncultivated land also. The plan was short-sighted because it permitted the creation of holdings under five hectares, which were uneconomic. By the 1930s, then, the land was providing a living for too many people and this fragmentation was then exacerbated by the consequences of inheritance. Part of the solution was to cultivate lands abandoned by the Muslims and others who had migrated during the wars. Legislation encouraged land reclamation and peasants from the mountains of Montenegro and Hercegovina migrated to the plains of Kosovo and Morava–Vardar corridor in Macedonia, quite knowingly reversing the Muslim Albanian expansions of the Ottoman period. One consequence of this was the widening of the gap between the Serbs and Albanians in Kosovo. Overall, it was a successful strategy for distracting the peasants from the attractions of Bolshevism which emphasised collectivisation in this period, but it built in severe structural weaknesses which subsequently required draconian solutions.

Regional Security, 1921–29

Internally divided, the SCS Kingdom derived strong incentives for unity from the revisionist aspirations of its immediate neighbours. Given its strategic location it was immediately a factor in the calculations of the Great Powers as they responded to their disillusionment with the post-war settlement by either resisting or promoting revisionist aspirations.

Immediately after the Peace settlement, both Yugoslavia and Czechoslovakia were concerned that the Hungarians might seek to restore the Habsburg crown. Minorities in the ceded territories of both Croatia and Slovakia were known to be nursing residual loyalty to the monarchy which was considered by the governments in Prague and Belgrade as potentially destabilising for the new states. Despite its republican status, Hungary was, in constitutional form, a monarchy and this encouraged the deposed King Karl IV to persist with the self-delusion that popular sentiment favoured his restoration. Indeed, he tested this proposition on several occasions in 1921, returning from exile in Switzerland unannounced in the expectation that the country would rise in his support. He was disappointed on each occasion and simply succeeded in embarrassing the new government. But it had the by-product of cementing an alliance between Czechoslovakia, Bulgaria, Rumania and Yugoslavia, known as the Little Entente, by confirming that their security fears were well founded.

This alliance was then strengthened by its success in attracting a guarantor from among the Great Powers. French preoccupation with ensuring its security and its determination to block any attempts to revise the Paris settlement dominated European affairs throughout the interwar period.[24] Two factors drove the French to revert to their pre-war policy of seeking security through creation of military alliances. The first was the failure of the United States Senate to ratify the Paris Treaty in March 1920, resulting in its absence from the League of Nations which called into question the very notion of collective security on which the new peace in Europe was founded. This combined with the second factor, namely the more general reluctance of Great Britain to commit itself to guarantee European (that is, French) security. Accordingly, France traded on the prestige of her victorious army and the bartering power which derived from her possession of vast stocks of munitions. The inherent instability and insecurity of the interwar international environment, provided the context in which France could exploit these advantages to build a security bulwark. In return for French support against Hungary and Italy, their immediate predators, the Little Entente tacitly agreed to assist France in maintaining the Versailles settlement. The consequence of this was that French security interests were thereby extended beyond the Versailles Treaty with Germany to the whole European settlement including the revisionist claims of Bulgaria and Italy against the various successor states in the Balkans. During the entire interwar period, France as the champion of the Versailles Settlement and the sworn enemy of revisionism was directly concerned as a matter of national interest, to protect Yugoslavia against the revisionist claims of both Bulgaria and Italy.

The Bulgarians, as we have seen, never accepted the loss of Macedonia to Yugoslavia and border raids organised by IMRO along the Serbia–Bulgarian frontier, as well as those along Bulgaria's frontier with Greece, continued until 1923 as a source of irritation and potential instability. After this, Bulgaria remained a safe haven and training ground for irredentists and separatists until the late 1930s. The government in Belgrade refused even to acknowledge the existence of a Bulgarian minority, even though from a linguistic point of view, these peoples had more in common with the Bulgarians than the Serbs. Officially, they were called Southern Slavs, and the region was regarded as a part of Greater Serbia. In practice, the Macedonia Slavs cared little as to who ruled. Their communities were poor and almost totally dependent on the limited agricultural employment which centred on the cultivation of tobacco. The central government invested in the region in terms of opening up communications, but in the towns its constructional efforts tended to focus on the wrong things: for example, at Skoplje, the first public buildings to be erected were the theatre and officer's club; similarly in Bitolj where a theatre was built while schools and hospitals and other public facilities were noticeably absent. In general, discontent, such as it was in this period, was rooted in economics and the lack of trade, rather than political affiliations. The Macedonian Slavs in the contested zone were forced to contribute to the IMRO in Sofia under the nose of the Serb gendarmerie through agents in Macedonia. If they defaulted they were liable to pay with their property and lives.

The more destabilising event, in this period, arose from Italian revisionist claims on the Adriatic coast. Mussolini's promise to destroy the new Balkan state, which he saw as the principal obstacle in the way of Italian ambitions to establish itself as the Balkan hegemon, was necessarily a constant source of preoccupation for the government in Belgrade during this period. Albania, in which Belgrade had no direct interest, except in its determination that the Italians be kept out, provided the focal point for these tensions. During 1925, the Italians tried to tempt Belgrade to permit it the extension of Italian influence into the peninsula by suggesting that Italy and Yugoslavia partition Albania between them. The Yugoslav government turned immediately to Britain and France to seek help to prevent any non-Balkan actors from extending their spheres into the region.

CONCLUSION

During this period, the SCS Kingdom made some evolutionary progress, adopting a responsible and considered attitude towards its external problems from which it drew much of the rationale for its existence in the first place. To this was added a measure of economic advance and the foundations for integration through development of internal communications. The granting of land ownership fulfilled the basic demands of the peasants and these still constituted over three quarters of the population.

These achievements have to be weighed against the stagnation which resulted from the inability of the central political leadership to co-operate in the building of a viable and popularly acceptable (legitimate) state. This struggle, waged essentially between the Serbian and Croatian elements, dominated the decade to the extent that the Kingdom's tangible achievements are often overlooked. In this predominantly illiterate society, with its absence of deeply rooted democratic traditions or political sophistication, it is to the three most commanding political leaders, Pašić, Radić and Pribičević, that history apportions the largest share of the blame for the failure of the constitutional monarchy. Pašić, by virtue of his political stature, was perhaps the one man who could have led the Serbs to accept compromise but his method of government encouraged the many abuses which led to the eventual suspension of parliament. He took everything from a narrowly Serbian angle, tempered by slavish devotion to Tsarist Russia. The suspension of the Vidovdan Constitution less than three years after his death, was testimony to his abject failure to construct a viable political system. Radić, for his part, had been consistent only in his determination to obstruct. The holder, simultaneously, of pacifist and nationalist ideas, he was unwise enough to attempt to use Bolshevism as a lever against the régime in a climate which was profoundly anti-communist. He then compounded the widespread suspicion of his motivations through his insincerity when agreeing to reconcile with the Serbs in 1925.[25] Pribičević was arguably the most culpable. As leader of a coalition of interests which held the power balance, he demonstrated lack of political wisdom or sense of vision in first aligning so closely with the Radićals when he might have used his political power to negotiate with Pašić towards a compromise, and then by compounding the mistake through an about-turn through alignment with the HSS which left him isolated and distrusted by the remaining sources of authority in the state.

The legacy of the 1920s, which was reinforced during the following decade was the perception that the Serbs and Croats could not live together. However, this is not entirely accurate since it suggests that Croatian and Serbian opinion was neatly divided along ethnic lines. This was not the case. It also suggests that there were no other grievances among the other populations, which is also erroneous. External threat provided a powerful incentive to unity but it did not compensate for the absence of common values or a consensus about political organisation. The Serbs provided the leadership because they alone were in a position to do so in 1918, but they were not strong enough in relation to the rest of the population to organise the state without coming up against powerful opposition. In short they did not have the legitimacy to act as the central authority and precisely because it was their institutions and monarchy which formed the backbone of the state, it was towards them that all blame for the Kingdom's shortcomings was directed.

3 Dictatorship and Compromise

The Kingdom of the Serbs, Croats and Slovenes had proven, in effect, ungovernable owing to the failure of its politicians to accept the necessity for compromise and concession implicit in parliamentary government in an environment characterised by a series of strongly held cultural identities. Despairing of the politicians, King Alexander saw the solution in an autocratic government, appealing to the people over the heads of the political process as the one source of power with sufficient legitimacy in the wider community to command the ordering of the state. What the 1920s had demonstrated was that Yugoslavia was viable as an economic unit but that it lacked any one group with sufficient legitimacy in the population as a whole to function as the focal point around which the state could be organised. The principal element giving it cohesion was the threat of external enemies who saw the South Slav state as the factor in the way of dominance of the Balkan peninsula. This combined with the economic crisis which afflicted the world economy at the end of the 1920s to drive the monarch to adopt more autocratic methods of government. Retrogressive though this solution was, it was in keeping with the general tendency in the region in this period towards stronger royalist influence, which resulted from disappointments with early experiments with democracy that had been made difficult by the international uncertainties both political and economic which threatened to worsen the already weak condition of the south-east European domestic economies.

In 1929, Yugoslavia entered a new phase in its development in which the difficulties were suppressed rather than addressed. Although this proved temporarily stabilising, and may even have been essential owing to the onset of worldwide economic depression, it did nothing towards solving the underlying problems which had been created with the union of the Serbs, Croats and Slovenes. The use of coercion left the most deeply disaffected elements at the extremes of the political spectrum with little recourse but to adopt illegal and covert activities, often organised from outside Yugoslavia's borders. These cells of political dissidents became tools of the great ideological movements which fought for political control of the region during the Second World War.

Monarchical Autocracy, 1929–31

Throughout the 1920s, King Alexander had attempted to remain above the factionalism of his politicians. Genuinely eager to create a Yugoslav state rather than an enlarged Serbia, he had attempted to achieve this goal through constant urgings of compromise and conciliation. When the assassinations of June 1928 convinced him that reliance on the methods of parliamentary democracy could not succeed, his temperament and training led him to resort to authoritarian methods. The King was himself a military man, and had spent his formative years in Tsarist Russia. Naturally suspicious of people, he relied on a group of trusted advisers rather than seek the ideas of less known but intellectually original thinkers. His solution to Yugoslavia's problems was consistent with this upbringing and outlook.

On 6 January 1929, under conditions of great secrecy, the King abrogated the Vidovdan Constitution. Using royal prerogative, which he expressed in the first person rather than the conventional royal 'we', he identified himself in the most personal way with this essentially illegal act which transferred all legislative power to the Crown.[1] Recognising the need for fusing the various elements in order to establish a single identity, the state was renamed 'Yugoslavia' and vested entirely for the time being, in the person of the monarch. A new law was promulgated on the defence of the state under which any and every activity against the new régime carried the risk of arbitrary arrest. Political parties were effectively abolished, since they could only exist if authorised by the Crown, and any activity which was based in sectional interests was banned. Even the army, the one unifying element still remaining and on which the monarch depended for support, was required to modify in order to recognise the emphasis on Yugoslav identity. Accordingly it abandoned its prized emblems which were associated with Serbian traditions rather than with those of the South Slav community in its widest sense.

The centrality of the military was manifest in the King's choice of General Peter Živković as Prime Minister. Živković's loyalty, having once been a leader of the White Hand, was unquestioned and since the war he had served as commander of the Royal Guard as well as being Alexander's closest adviser. The remainder of the King's cabinet were Serb, with the exception of the redoubtable Slovene, Anton Korošeć.

The military, then, were used to stabilise the state, but Alexander and Živković used the police to impose order. All sources of opposition were forcibly repressed, which had the effect of driving the more extreme elements abroad where they regrouped under the patronage of foreign sponsors who recognised their future utility as *agents provocateur* in any attempt to revise the peace settlement at Yugoslavia's expense. Among these exiles were the most extreme of the Croat nationalists who found a welcome in both Italy and Hungary. The KPJ elements still within Yugoslavia were progressively imprisoned. Their harsh encounters there with the state police proved formative in driving the Yugoslav communists towards formulation of a coherent agenda and effective organisation which stood them in good stead once the opportunity to impose their programme finally arrived.

Mainstream politicians were not immune to these draconian measures. Vlatko Maček, Radić's successor as leader of the HSS, was among those who were rounded up. Maček was charged with inciting the Croats to secessionist violence but acquitted, but many others served prison sentences. Pribičević was arrested in May for publicly expressing his dissent from the régime. He was detained without trial until August 1931 when the personal intervention of Masaryk resulted in his exile in Czechoslovakia.

The wider reaction to the King's initiative was initially surprisingly favourable. The Croats saw it as a sign that their grievances would now be addressed, while the Serbs were relieved because it signalled an end to the infighting which they recognised as a threat to the very existence of the state. Both parties, in their different ways, were to be disappointed by the subsequent course of events. The suspension of democratic politics meant that all elements in Yugoslavia lost their freedom, not least among them the Serbs who saw themselves as having to surrender rights for which they had fought. In practice, the squabbling had ceased, but the underlying problems remained and it is probably fair to conclude that over a period of two and a half years, the absolutist solution actually multiplied existing problems. Its impact was to drive the disputes below the surface and to bring together disaffected elements in prison cells where the brutal conditions they faced enabled them to bury their doctrinal squabbling and unite, unshakeably, to intrigue against a régime they had come to hate. The practices of clandestine organisation and the refinement of subversive ideas which served both the forces of right and left so well were honed under these conditions.

This notwithstanding, the pacification measures paid off in the short run. Eighteen months passed quietly and thus on 3 September 1931,

Alexander signalled a retreat from dictatorship by introduction of a new constitution which permitted a partial return to parliamentary government. A bicameral parliament was set up, consisting of a senate of royal appointees and indirectly elected provincial representatives and an assembly elected by universal male suffrage. The government was responsible to the monarch alone who remained the 'guardian of the unity of the nation and of the integrity of the state'.[2] In the interests of promoting integration, the original thirty-three provinces established under the Vidovdan Constitution were replaced by nine units of which river valleys were the focal point. These were called 'banovinas', reflecting superficially the Croatian tradition but the demography of the Serbian communities meant that in reality this development reinforced the Serbian hegemony because ethnic Serbs constituted a majority in six out of the nine.

Despite these modifications, the régime remained inherently centralised, as the prerogative of the King continued to reside on the loyalty of the army and the bureaucracy. Of course, it was precisely this centralism which discontented elements so vehemently opposed. Moreover, by abrogating parliamentary government and ministerial responsibility, the King was weakening his own position, leaving himself without a buffer between government and public opinion. Since criticism could not be tolerated, there would be silence. This was a strategy which gave the forces of opposition and extremism the very focal point they required to organise against.[3]

EXTERNAL AFFAIRS, 1929–34

The Great Depression

The world economic crisis of the late 1920s and early 1930s impacted as severely on Yugoslavia as elsewhere. Its downward spiral began in the autumn of 1929 when the United States declared that it was discontinuing its loans to Europe. This was rapidly followed by the drying up of purchasing power all over the world leading to a general and catastrophic fall in prices. The European debtor countries were doubly hit because they could no longer borrow dollars nor generate commodities of sufficient value to pay in kind. The only way out of the trap was to transfer their gold which in turn exacerbated the problem by making this commodity scarce. This eventuality depressed prices still further.

The major European states responded in 1931 by prohibiting the export of gold, and by adoption of every other possible remedy – tariffs, import restrictions, quotas, export subsidies and exchange restrictions amounting eventually to state control over foreign trade. Unemployment rose everywhere. European states were all either already bankrupt or under the threat of bankruptcy.

The Great Depression, as this event became known, took longer to have an impact in Yugoslavia than in some other parts of Europe.[4] This was a function in part of the variation in Yugoslav agricultural exports and partly because the government initially implemented liberal measures to deal with the depression through Belgrade based institutions. However, the Hoover Moratorium which ended German war reparations, enforced on Yugoslavia the loss of an annual $16 million. When Britain left the gold standard in September 1931, the convertibility that Yugoslavia had coveted for so long became of much less worth.

Despite the inventiveness of the régime, the impact of these catastrophic events could not be staved off indefinitely. Prices began falling in 1929 and by 1932–33 the grain was worth between one-third and one-half its value in 1929. Already the peasants were deeply in debt and by the 1930s they could not meet these debts let alone pay their dues to the state. The consequence was a progressive deterioration. In 1929–30, the average annual income was $330 compared with $1368 in the United States. The unevenness of economic development throughout Yugoslavia meant that the depression impacted harder in some areas than others. For example, while the government could intervene to compensate Serbian peasant farmers, it could do nothing to help the Croatian banks. Endemic regional jealousies were therefore even more deeply entrenched as a result. The great collapse finally came as a result of the long winter and the poor fodder crop of 1933.

The Rise of Fascism and its Impact on Yugoslavia

The world economic crisis altered fundamentally the economic circumstances in which the Yugoslav state functioned. Throughout Europe, domestic discontent followed on economic hardship and created the conditions in which authoritarian parties, which promised to use strong leadership and discipline to create order amid the chaos, could build an electoral base. Fascism was the reactionary form of authoritarianism, having much in common with nineteenth-century forms of government

in which religion was institutionalised in the service of a paternalistic
monarchy. Once that had been achieved, the fascist régimes were driven
in pursuit of conquest and revolutionary change, supported by romantic
notions of strength through conquest.[5]

The election of Hitler as Reich Chancellor at the end of January 1933
and the implementation of the National Socialist (Nazi) programme had
an impact on European relations which was to have profound consequences for Yugoslav politics. Hitler's assertiveness abroad produced
quite quickly a shift in the balance of forces in Europe, especially in the
relationship between Italy and France, which in turn had implications
for Yugoslavia's security arrangements. During the winter of 1933–34,
Hitler's interest in closer ties with Austria led to a cooling in relations
between Rome and Berlin. Mussolini moved to block Hitler's path by
establishing a quasi-protectorate over Austria and by seeking a rapprochement with France. Before this could happen, however, the existing
pattern of alliances, and in particular the Little Entente for which France
was the guarantor, required that the various client states had to be
persuaded to accept the change.

Since 1929, the Yugoslavs had been drawn increasingly into a Balkan
Pact which had formed following a Greek initiative to organise an
annual Balkan Conference tasked to study questions of common interest within the region. Although the conference deliberated on the possibility of furthering trading connections, it was the more pressing
concerns relating to the need to secure frontiers, that received the greatest share of attention. In November 1933, Greece, Rumania and
Yugoslavia took steps to translate the conference into a more formal
regional grouping. A pact was signed in Athens in February 1934
between these three and Turkey. This effectively extended the principle
of regional security which underpinned the Little Entente. However, this
proved to be the only subject on which these allies could agree and
after Athens the annual conference was postponed indefinitely. The
Bulgarians, whose disaffection with the First World War settlement continued unabated, declined the offer to join the Pact on the grounds that
the Entente was designed to protect frontiers which the government in
Sofia had always regarded as unjust. Albania, the other potential source
of regional unrest, was firmly excluded. In any case, the Entente's potential for acting in its signatories' common interests was undermined by the
specific constraints under which each was operating. The Yugoslavs had
joined because they wanted protection from the perennial attentions of
the Italians. From their perspective, the Pact was flawed from the outset

because the Greeks refused to become involved in hostilities with any non-Balkan power essentially because Greece was militarily unable to risk conflict with the Italian navy.

Yugoslavia's foreign policy objectives in 1933–34 can be summed up as twofold: first, to sustain the status quo and prevent an outbreak of hostilities in the region; second, to prevent any external interference in the Balkans. Ideally, the Yugoslav government preferred complete independence from all the major powers. In practice, however, circumstances mitigated against such a stance. Belgrade had joined the Little Entente with Rumania and Czechoslovakia in order to guarantee its security against Italy. In this aim, the Entente was supported by France. But, whereas the Czechs and Rumanians were each only fearful of one major enemy, (Germany and Italy respectively), the Yugoslavs were watchful not just of Italian machinations, but of those of Germany and the Soviet Union. The latter pursued, until 1935, a policy seeking Yugoslavia's dismantlement and Yugoslavia remained one of the few states in Europe not to have recognised the Soviet government as legitimate. The threat to Balkan stability posed by each of these three, reinforced Yugoslavia's rationale for sustaining its alliance with France. This posed a dilemma, however, because such an association carried potential to draw the hostility of any one of its major enemies. Rapprochement between France and Italy which began in the late winter of 1934 required that Yugoslavia too find some means of moderating its anti-Italian stance.

The Assassination of King Alexander

During the spring and summer of 1934, the French foreign minister, Louis Barthou, visited Belgrade and Bucharest in an effort to persuade the Balkan allies to adjust their stance towards Italy. It was in this connection that King Alexander paid his fateful visit to France, landing at Marseilles on 9 October 1934. Shortly after being met by Barthou, both men were assassinated as they were driven from the port. The principal culprits were Croat fascists (*Ustaša*), the exiles of 1931 who had organised themselves into terrorist cells in Hungary and Italy, under the leadership of Ante Pavelić. While it was difficult to prove the complicity of either host state in this assassination, the Yugoslav government was determined to protest formally to the League of Nations.

The French and Italians were equally determined that Yugoslav indignation would not be permitted to damage their rapprochement.

Accordingly, Pierre Laval with the support of the British foreign
secretary, Anthony Eden, actively discouraged Yugoslavia from pressing
its charges at the League of Nations. Overpowered by these representa-
tions, the Yugoslav government was obliged to accept a compromise in
which the alleged Italian connection would not be mentioned. Hungary
took the full weight of international censure, against which it had little
defence in view of the absence of Italian support, which satisfied
Yugoslav indignation without prejudicing the efforts of the French and
British to contain Germany through a friendship with Italy.

The lasting impact of this episode was a further increase in
Yugoslavia's distrust of Italy since the ominous link had been made
between the Croat fascists and the wider issue of Italo–Yugoslav antagonism. Relations between Belgrade and Paris cooled significantly, a
move for which Belgrade compensated by developing the pro-German
stance which had begun during the last six months of Alexander's reign.
The Little Entente, its loyalties already strained by French overtures to
Italy, was torn still further.

REGENCY AND THE APPROACH OF WAR

Alexander left the Yugoslav crown to his son, Peter, still only eleven
years old, for whom he appointed his cousin, Prince Paul, the senior of
three regents until the heir came of age. The other Regents were
the Dalmatian, Iva Perović, former Ban of Primorska, and Radenko
Stanković, a Serb from the Vojvodina who had practised medicine in
Zagreb before being Minister of Education in 1932. Neither enjoyed
wide popularity and had had little experience of politics in Belgrade.
The Prince Regent had never played an active role in politics either,
which was an advantage since he was untainted with earlier political
struggles, but also a handicap because he lacked experience in managing
the intrigue and conflict which remained characteristic of Belgrade
political life. Potentially more serious was his lack of military credentials.
He had never served as a soldier. Under Alexander the army had been
both a national unifier and a willing servant of the Crown but should it
ever lose respect for the monarchy, its potential for replacing the Crown
with military dictatorship was all too evident. This danger was recognised and dealt with early by Prince Paul through the re-appointment of
Živković to the cabinet as minister of war and marine, thereby giving the
old Serb elements among the military and peasantry direct representation through a ministry which could underpin the authority of the state.

On the other hand, the fact that the Prince Regent was widely recognised as a cultured man made him more acceptable than his predecessor to the Croats. Throughout this period they persisted, hubristically, in professing themselves as inherently more cultured than the Serbs, and indeed focussed much of their resentment towards Serb dominance of the political life on exactly this issue. Overall, however, Prince Paul inherited from Alexander a state more aware of its need for unity and of its vulnerability as a consequence of the King's death. The Yugoslav people and government recognised that they must remain as a single entity, or disintegrate in a bloodbath. Dissolution was unthinkable.

Initially, a cabinet was assembled under the prime ministership of Bogoljub Jevtić in December 1934. His failure to reconcile the competing interests within Yugoslav politics led to the holding of fresh elections (the first of the Regency) in May 1935. Despite Živković's efforts to discredit Vladko Maček, to the extent of claiming that he had been party to the King's assassination, it was the HSS with the backing of Serb Agrarians, the Democrats and the Bosnian Muslims, which emerged as the strongest force. Prince Paul, whose English education inclined him to seek the advice of the British Ambassador in Belgrade, Sir Nevile Henderson, appointed the latter's choice as prime minister, the Serbian Radical, Milan Stojadinović. The latter had been an effective minister of finance when his liberalisation of the Yugoslav economy resulted in substantial progress towards economic recovery during 1934. Following his appointment, he proclaimed a new government party in August 1935, the Yugoslav Radical Union (*Jugoslovenska Radikalna Zajednica*), which claimed to stand for 'one state, one people, one king'. He relaxed the strict censorship imposed by Alexander and Živković, and attempted a measure of conciliation by granting amnesty to over 1000 political prisoners. He also broadened the cabinet membership to include a Bosnian Muslim, Mehmed Spaho, who joined Korošec as the non-Serb representative. Stojadinović also signed a concordant with the Vatican promising authority for church schools, although this was left for the Skupština to ratify.[6] The reality was not quite as clear-cut, however. On one occasion he told the British Ambassador, Ronald Campbell, that he had no ambition to become 'either a Chamberlain or a Mussolini', but would rather continue to 'crow on his Balkan dung heap'.[7] As the decade wore on, this modesty increasingly deserted him as his flamboyant and authoritarian style enabled him to fully indulge a lately acquired taste for acting on the European stage.

Just as Radić had boycotted the Constitutional Assembly, so Maček was unprepared to participate in the Skupština without constitutional reform. The political storms of the second half of the 1930s were more easily weathered than in the 1920s, however, primarily because the economy had improved. Similarly, the threatening international climate promoted a greater sense of collective need in time of crisis which had the effect of driving the Serbs and Croats to seek some form of détente within the existing framework: by the autumn of 1936, even the Serbs were prepared to admit that the royal dictatorship was bankrupt and that rather than breaking the resistance of the Serbs it had served only to undermine the old established Serbian parties. By October 1936, it was difficult to find anyone in Belgrade who did not freely admit the existence of the Croat question and the complete solidarity of all Croats and Serbs of the former Habsburg monarchy under Maček.[8]

Despite Stojadinović's claims to be a liberaliser and conciliator, his style in government was more authoritarian than democratic to the extent that he was suspected of harbouring fascist sympathies. Moreover, the government's majority was insecure because it depended upon the tactical support of the Slovenes and Bosnian Muslims. Political patronage held the coalition together, but the indissoluble nature of the Croat problem remained a source of internal weakness and external vulnerability. Even within Serbia support for Stojadinović was fragile owing to his arbitrary style and pro-German sympathies. The concordat crisis of 1937, in which the parliament had refused to ratify the concordat after the Serb Orthodox Church threatened to excommunicate any Serb who voted for it, gave his opponents considerable opportunity to undermine his majority. Elections in December 1938 revealed the extent to which Stojadinović's policies had become unpopular and so Prince Paul appointed the more conciliatory Dragiša Čvetković, his minister of social policy and public health, as prime minister, tasking him to negotiate with Maček appropriate terms for Croatian autonomy.

Economic Recovery, 1934–39

The general upturn in 1935 of the east European economies arrived at just the right time to assist the Stojadinović government in weathering the ongoing political storms. Indeed, the Yugoslav economy had begun to rally while Stojadinović was still minister of finance, when his programme to confront the depression was implemented, gearing the economy to international trade, while granting considerable tax concessions to both business and the peasantry, and generating employment by commencing an ambitious programme of public works.

To support initiatives in agriculture and industry, Belgrade looked increasingly towards Germany as Yugoslavia's principal trading partner in preference to France and the Little Entente. This shift had its origins in Yugoslav observance of the League of Nations' trade embargo against Italy which was implemented following Mussolini's conquest of Ethiopia in 1935, and it fitted in with Yugoslavia's implacable resistance to anything which might further Italian interests. The trade embargo impacted badly on the Croatian economy because the Croats were heavily engaged in the export to Italy of Dalmatian cement as well as timber. When the French subsequently failed to reward Yugoslavia for its observance of the boycott by a relaxation of protectionist tariffs, Yugoslavia was driven ever more towards its eager German customer. Hjalmar Schacht, the Reich's finance minister, was greatly admired by the German educated Stojadinović and the two men were on good terms. However, this was a risky enterprise for the Yugoslav government and it could only pay off so long as the Nazi régime was prepared to conduct its business by peaceful means.[9]

Between 1936 and 1939, metallurgy and mining, which received foreign backing particularly from Germany, led in boosting industrial production by 31 per cent. At the same time, the British and French provided much of the capital which backed the processing of non-ferrous materials through the device of joint-stock companies. Nevertheless, industry remained a small employer for the Yugoslav peoples in comparison to the agricultural sector which at the end of the 1930s absorbed over 75 per cent of the working population. This figure had changed little from the early 1920s. Furthermore, the rise in population of over 20 per cent since 1918, combined with the consequences of the redistribution of land in the early 1920s, meant that increasing numbers of peasants were making a living from smallholdings which were unproductive. Pressure on land was on the increase, while industrialisation was too modest in this period to tempt a significant proportion of the population to seek employment in the towns. Yugoslavia remained conservative, in places almost feudal in outlook, a country in which the bulk of the population held sharply defined prejudices which had yet to be softened through mass education.

External Relations, 1934–39

Yugoslavia's foreign policy under Stojadinović took a new direction during the second half of the 1930s. Two developments facilitated this. The first was the set back to Italian policy in the Balkans achieved through signature of the Balkan Pact in 1931. Following the assassination of Alexander, the French had forced the latter to compromise with the Yugoslavs by modifying the worst of its repressive measures towards the Yugoslavs in Venezia-Guilia, and discontinuing their support of the Croat Ustaše terrorists. The second was the election in Sofia in 1935 of a government with pro-Yugoslav sympathies which signalled that for the first time since the war, Bulgaria was no longer an agent of Italian ambitions in the peninsula. The Bulgarian government even took firm steps to deny further hospitality to the Macedonian terrorist bands which still infested the Yugoslav–Bulgarian frontier. At the same time the Balkan states were increasingly concerned about the possibility of a revival of Germany's *Drang nach Osten*, the expansion of German interests into the region through economic agreements, as well as their more insidious interest in the Balkan *volksdeutsche* populations. These fears became even more acute when Hitler accomplished his ambition to achieve the *Anschluss* with Austria in March 1938. Bulgaria now moved to make peace with the Balkan Entente, while Hungary, for similar reasons, finally came to terms with the Little Entente.

The 1938 Munich agreement, which permitted Germany a free hand in Czechoslovakia, finally opened Prince Paul's eyes to the danger which the machinations of Adolf Hitler portended. By the spring of 1939, the Yugoslav policy of making friends on every hand had collapsed like a pack of cards under the stress of the international crisis. Having attempted to steer a middle course between all the protagonists, Prince Paul's foreign policy succeeded primarily in making Yugoslavia the object of suspicion or patronage by all. The only possible friend on whom Prince Paul could call was Great Britain. All Europeans were conscious in the spring of 1939 of standing once more on the edge of the abyss which the post-war settlement had been designed to avoid. The arrival of German troops in Prague in the early hours of 15 March 1939 was the boldest yet of Hitler's ventures abroad, the action was echoed by Italy in April which took advantage of the collective paralysis of the major powers by seizing Albania. Prince Paul was invited to Berlin in June where he was treated to a display of the Third Reich's military power. So impressed was he that on his return to Belgrade he instructed his government to despatch Yugoslavia's gold reserves to New York forthwith.

The Čvetkovič–Maček Agreement

Domestically, Yugoslavia's greatest weakness lay in the apparently intractable Serbo–Croat conflict. During the summer of 1939, under the pressure generated by the gathering international crisis, the Serbs and Croats finally came to an agreement to compromise. Čvetkovič and Maček finally achieved agreement on 20 August. This compromise (*Sporazum*), which was passed by the Skupština six days later, recognised Croatia as an autonomous state (*Banovina*) within Yugoslav frontiers. Its territory was defined as encompassing most of the historic units of Croatia–Slavonia and Dalmatia, to which were added some of the Croatian speaking areas of Vojvodina, Srem and Bosnia. This gave Croatia governance over almost 30 per cent of the territory of Yugoslavia with a population of 4.4 million which represented a third of the total. This confederal state was to have its own elected parliament (*Sabor*) and a governor (*Ban*) appointed by the monarchy. Although the central government in Belgrade retained control over foreign affairs, trade and defence policy, in matters of domestic organisation the Banovina had considerable discretion to raise revenue and direct domestic affairs in areas such as forestry, agriculture and commerce as well as education. Similar schemes were under discussion for Serbia and Slovenia.

This development was in some sense a double tragedy for the Yugoslav peoples. It was tragedy because the attempt to solve the conflict through a confederal solution had not been attempted much sooner, thereby generating a history of conflict where little had previously existed. It was also a tragedy because it occurred at the very moment that Hitler was moving forward with his expansionist ambitions which plummeted Europe into total war, destroying the social, economic and political assumptions on which the first Yugoslavia had been built. On 1 September, Hitler's armies invaded Poland, thus provoking Britain and France to renew war with Germany once again.

ROYALIST YUGOSLAVIA ON THE BRINK OF WAR

Yugoslavia's only hope in 1939 was that it could stay out of the war. Between September 1939 and the Axis invasion of the Balkans in April 1941, Prince Paul trod a tightrope between the protagonists, dependent on Germany for trade, but looking to the British and French to guarantee Yugoslav security. Secret military discussions were conducted with the western allies over the winter and early spring of 1940, but the effectiveness of Blitzkreig in subduing the French and driving the British from north-west Europe combined with Italy's declaration of war in June 1940 revealed the effectiveness of Hitler's armies and the vulnerability of the Balkans to the machinations of Hitler and Mussolini.

The Emergence of the Yugoslav Communist Party

During this period, Prince Paul was finally persuaded to bury his deep hostility towards the Soviet Union. While the Wehrmacht was overrunning France, diplomatic relations with Moscow were reopened on 10 June. This was rather a token gesture, however, since the Russians promised only vaguely to oppose Italian ambitions in the Balkans, while the Yugoslavs were similarly circumspect in their talk of trade. But it was symptomatic of the underlying shift in the Soviet Union's stance which had begun in the mid-1930s when the Communist International was directed to abandon its policy of seeking dismantlement of 'colonial states' such as Yugoslavia in favour of unity with the national Popular Fronts against fascism. For such purposes an alliance with the two 'bourgeois' democratic states of Britain and France, was the foundation. This changed on the eve of war when the Soviet Union concluded a pact with its fascist enemy in August. From then on Stalin rebranded the western democracies as imperialists in the same manner as Nazi Germany. Up till the German invasion of the Soviet Union in June 1941 he attempted to play the two imperialist worlds off against one another in a desperate bid to keep the Soviet Union out of the conflict.[10]

The Yugoslav Communist Party re-emerged in this context. Although it remained a clandestine organisation, it nonetheless was able to function effectively within Yugoslavia as a consequence of the political disarray at the end of the 1930s, where it seized every opportunity to exploit the state's internal divisions. This suited Moscow which recognised the strategic value of Yugoslavia to the Soviet Union in the context of the Nazi–Soviet Pact.

Shortly before the war, the leadership of the KPJ had been passed to Josip Broz, also known by the nickname 'Tito'.[11] Broz was a native of the Croatian borderlands, born in the village of Kumrovec in May 1892 of mixed Croat–Slovene parentage. He had adopted communism while a prisoner of war behind the Russian lines during the First World War and as a party activist had spent much of the interwar period either inside Yugoslav gaols or else in exile. In 1936 he was in Moscow, working in the Comintern's Balkan secretariat and later operating from Paris from where he organised the despatch of volunteers to fight with the Republican Brigades in the Spanish Civil War. It was his good fortune that he never held high office in the Comintern. During the late 1930s, Stalin's purging of this organisation decimated its leadership. His appointment as caretaker leader of the officially suspended Yugoslav Communist Party between 1938 and 1939 was propitious because it enabled him to relaunch the Party on his own initiative and – crucially – to accomplish this independently of Moscow's financial patronage. Here then was the basis for an indigenous communist movement which became increasingly active during the final days of Royalist Yugoslavia where the internal divisions of the society provided exactly the conditions in which his clandestine organisation could flourish. Returning to Yugoslavia on Moscow's direction in 1940, Tito's organisation was instrumental in the strikes which occurred in Split during the autumn which prompted a very nervous government to close down the trade union organisation there.[12]

The war moved a step closer at the end of October 1940 when Mussolini set out to make his ambitions to control the Balkans a reality by declaring war on Greece and deploying his forces in Albania. The decision by both the Rumanian and Bulgarian governments to move closer to the Axis reinforced Belgrade's sense of isolation. By the autumn of 1940, Yugoslavia was surrounded by Axis or pro-Axis states on all but its southern flank.

Mussolini's adventure succeeded only in opening up a second front. The Greek Army drove the Italian forces back into Albania, and involved Britain directly in the conflict. Initially Britain supplied aid to the Greeks, but in March 1941, this was followed up with the arrival of troops and, more worryingly for the Axis leadership, squadrons of British bombers. These had sufficient range to enable them to threaten the Rumanian oil fields on which Nazi Germany was dependent. Italian adventurism was thereby jeopardising German interests and in March, Hitler resolved to take control of the region himself. The first move was to achieve an agreement with Yugoslavia so that the German army could subdue Greece by crossing Yugoslav territory. Ribbentrop was despatched to Belgrade to bully the Čvetković–Maček government into signing the Tripartite Pact, and he bribed the Yugoslavs with the offer of sovereignty over Salonika (a prize which had also been held out to the Bulgarian government in its alliance with Germany).

Meanwhile, both the British and Americans set about persuading Prince Paul to abandon neutrality. The British Secret Intelligence Service (SIS) and the newly created Special Operations Executive (SOE) had been busy in Yugoslavia for months establishing networks among the not inconsiderable numbers who dissented from the Regent's pro-Axis policy. Principal sources of potential agents were the Serb Peasant Party, the Independent Democrat Party and the Narodna Odbrana. Indeed, there had been plans afoot since the early summer of 1940 to remove Prince Paul and his government by violence if necessary.[13] During February and March 1941, King George VI wrote to Prince Paul, pointing out that British military planning hinged to some extent on Yugoslavia's intentions; at the same time, the United States' President, Franklin Roosevelt, passed a personal message to the Regent through his envoy William Donovan who visited Belgrade during the third week of March. This warned that the American government would be much more sympathetic to a state which mounted resistance to an invasion force than one which permitted itself to stand by tamely.[14]

This brutal but timely missive touched on the dilemma of all the small states of Europe in defining their policy towards the Nazi menace: to treat with the Berlin government was dangerous and distasteful in equal measure; but to defy Hitler openly was to court imminent destruction. As Churchill had noted in January, Prince Paul's attitude was 'that of an unfortunate man in a cage with a tiger, hoping not to provoke him while steadily dinner-time approaches'.[15] Prince Paul, for his part, responded to Roosevelt that the big nations were 'hard' for while they 'talked of honour', they were 'far away'.[16] Even while Donovan was in Belgrade, Cincar-Marković was on his way to Vienna to sign the Tripartite Pact.

The announcement of the Pact's signature on 25 March was deeply controversial within Yugoslavia. Demonstrations broke out in Belgrade and other cities. The communists retrospectively claimed the credit for their organisation. Then, on the night of 26/27 March 1941, Prince Paul and his government were overthrown in a coup d'état instigated by two air force officers, General Dušan Simović and Brigadier-General Bora Mirković. The British were aware of their plans and offered encouragement, but the coup was essentially an internal affair which removed the Regent and his cabinet and brought a reluctant Peter Karadjordje to the throne, still six months short of his eighteenth birthday. King Peter II's first cabinet, which lasted just three weeks, was headed by Simović, and included the Croat Dr Juraj Šutej, formerly finance minister in the Čvetković cabinet, and, with some degree of reservation, Vladko Maček.

Just as the signature of the Pact had divided opinion, so did the coup. The commitment of the Croats, Slovenes and Bosnian Muslims at a popular level to the new government was not as clear-cut as in Serbia; the Croats viewed the coup d'état as a purely Serbian affair and they felt no allegiance to the Simović government. Shrewdly, the Germans attempted to exploit this disunity by offering Maček the leadership of independent Croatia under German protection. But on 4 April, Maček accepted the office of Joint-Vice Premier with the eminent Serbian historian, Dr Slobodan Jovanović. That same day, Simović signed a Treaty of Friendship and Non-Aggression with the Soviet Union.[17]

Hitler's reaction to all this was to unleash a military campaign of vengeance. The Serbs were now branded as traitors, a label which stuck to them in Berlin's eyes for the remainder of the war. On 6 April, Germany invaded, intent on the state's dismantlement. The Italians marched into Slovenia and Dalmatia while the Germans, with help from their Balkan allies, pushed south taking Macedonia before going on into Greece. Belgrade fell on 12 April at which point the King and cabinet were flown to Athens, leaving behind no one with the authority to sign the act of unconditional surrender. This was resolved four days later when Cincar-Marković and General Radivoje Janković were flown from Pale, where they had taken refuge, to Belgrade to sign the armistice. Within a month both Yugoslavia and Greece had been completely overrun and their British sponsors forced off the mainland. King Peter and his government went into exile, first in Cairo, and later in London. Prince Paul, who had no wish to return to the Balkans, took refuge in Kenya from whence he lamented to his brother-in-law, the Duke of Kent, how he had been at the end of his physical strength when the March events took place, that the regency had been 'a dog's existence', and that he had hated his job: 'the last thing I wish is to have anything to do with Yugoslav politics!'[18]

CONCLUSION

The history of Yugoslavia is littered with ironies, and none so tragic as that of the late 1930s. International crisis generated the pressure required to focus the attention of the Serbs and Croats on the need for reform within Yugoslavia on the assumption that cohabitation within a single state was better than the divisive and potentially destructive

continuation of internal strife. The international crisis consequent on
the renewal of war was also at a single stroke responsible for destroying
this attempt at co-operation.

Yugoslavia's leaders were caught in a dilemma. While a strong government was essential in order to override the internal dissent, the tactics of
beating the population into submission were only ever going to be effective
for a relatively short time, after which the old questions of legitimacy and
popular grievance would resurface afresh. The royal dictatorship, which
imposed order by force in an environment of crisis which extended
well beyond Yugoslavia's frontiers, succeeded in imposing calm, but
achieved little in the direction of resolving the sources of conflict which
riddled Yugoslav politics. Alexander's assassination in 1934 was widely
perceived at the time as a tragedy which had deprived the Yugoslavs of the
one man of vision who could promote Yugoslav unity. Its effect was to
point to the deepening crisis occasioned by the link between Croatian
nationalism and problems in the relationship with Italy as well as providing
a sharp stimulus to redouble efforts to resolve the domestic antagonisms.

Yugoslavia was caught between too many competing interests, both
domestically and internationally. It is not possible to point to one single
factor as an explanation of its unsatisfactory interwar history. Certainly
the struggle between the attempt to impose the unitary Serbian model on
substantial minorities which had expectations of greater autonomy
within the South Slav state, is the pivotal question on which the rest turns,
but it is too simplistic – even erroneous – to define the conflict as exclusively Serbo–Croatian. Neither the Serbs nor the Croats could be seen as
a monolithic group, and there were other elements within the state which
had strong grievances which did not gain the same level of publicity.
Nevertheless, the direction of political debate was undoubtedly conditioned by the pre-war experiences of shaping 'South Slav' agendas in an
environment where they were in permanent opposition. These habits,
together with the politicians which had led both Serbian and Habsburg
Slav parties prior to 1914, engrained certain behaviours which were
never abandoned. These parties or politicians' formative experience was
that of dominating or confronting entrenched opponents.

Had the Second World War not broken out that summer, Yugoslavia
might have evolved a workable system of political organisation. But its
fate was determined by decisions being taken in other European capitals.
Yugoslavia, like post-1918 Europe, had begun the interwar period
with visionary hopes, only to be brought down to grim despair, or as
E.H. Carr once wrote, 'from a utopia that took little account of reality to
a reality from which every element of utopia was rigorously excluded'.[19]

4 Civil War and Communist Revolution

The invasion and partition of Yugoslavia in April 1941 began three and half years of harsh occupation which destroyed the embryonic political structures established during the latter years of Prince Paul's regency. During this period elements among the Yugoslav peoples openly fought one another, leaving a legacy of violence and bitterness which festered beneath the surface of the post-war régime. Two principal and paradoxical impressions of the occupation emerge. The first, and more conventional view is that German rule was a colonial conquest sustained by dismemberment together with an active policy of ruthless suppression in a manner designed to keep the country divided and at war against itself. The second view is that the Reich's interest in this region was its use as a thoroughfare and that what the Germans wanted to achieve primarily was the pacification of the Balkans so that it would not be a drain on German manpower resources. The truth, as so often, was a mixture of the two. Initially, the occupiers parcelled out land to parties aggrieved by the First World War settlement. They also sought to appease disaffected elements within Yugoslavia itself, the Croats being the most notable example of this strategy in action. However, this proved unworkable, for reasons arising from the behaviour of the assortment of quisling and fascist Yugoslavs who were placed between the occupation authorities and the people, and as a result of the shortcomings in the relationship between the Italians and the Germans in the region. In short, the lands of Yugoslavia were to provide a constant source of concern to the Third Reich, driving them to implement a progressively more punitive occupation with deleterious results both for the occupiers and for the Yugoslavs themselves.

The war for Yugoslavia's liberation was a conflict fought at several different levels each with more than two sides. At the level of high policy, Yugoslavia's importance to all sides was geostrategic. Only in 1943, after the western powers had made their choices about the re-entry to continental Europe, did its importance diminish to that of a sideshow in which the occupiers were subjected to a wearying war of movement and attrition which drained the reserves of the Reich away from the major theatres of conflict. At a more parochial level, the war was fought by many sides: by curious coalitions of occupation and resistance forces against the Partisan guerrillas, by the Partisans against the Serbian loyalists and the fascist Ustaša and eventually by the Germans against everyone. In what ways did the course of this most Balkan of conflicts shape the history of the post-war Yugoslav state?

PARTITION AND OCCUPATION

The immediate impression of the 1941 partition is that the Axis used their territorial spoils in the Balkans to oppress their enemies and reward their allies. Thus, Bulgaria received most of Macedonia, while Hungary re-acquired its pre-1919 territories of Bačka and Barana together with some other small areas. The remainder of the Vojvodina, the Banat, was put under the control of its German minority. In the north and west, Italy took most of the Dalmatian coast and the Adriatic islands, and imposed direct rule in Albania, the Kosovo region, part of western Macedonia and Montenegro. Slovenia was divided between Germany and Italy. Anything that remained was organised into Serbian, Croatian and Montenegrin political authorities, under the supervision of Germany and Italy. Montenegro's experience of war was turbulent. At first the Italians tried to establish a puppet kingdom. Their officials sought to win the allegiance of a small group of separatists and to exploit the fact that the Queen of Italy was the daughter of the pre-war ruler of the province. This proved disastrous, however, and by July 1941 the Montenegrin units who had been permitted to keep their armaments were using their supplies to fuel open revolt. Italian troops retook the region by June 1942 whereupon they imposed themselves firmly through harsh reprisals, which merely fomented further rebellion.[1]

Of the larger entities, Serbia, by virtue of being Slavic, was branded the perpetual enemy of Germany and consequently took the brunt of Hitler's vengeance for its 'betrayal' of the Tripartite Pact in March. After a brief spell of direct German rule, a puppet régime was established in August 1941, headed by General Milan Nedić, formerly a minister in both the Stojadinović and Cvetković governments. This administration was quisling rather than fascist, and functioned largely in the role of caretaker. A small military force of some 3600 men was set up, under the direction of the fascist Dimitrije Ljotić and entrusted with the task of assisting the *Wehrmacht* in its policing function.[2]

Independent State of Croatia

The most controversial element of the new Balkan order was the supposedly Independent State of Croatia (*Nezavisna Država Hrvatska* – NDH) which over the course of the war was to generate the deepest disruption to the Axis occupation. Formed on 10 April, the day before Zagreb fell, it was technically an independent fascist ally on the same footing as Bulgaria, Romania, Hungary and Slovakia. In order to appease Croatian nationalist sentiment, the occupiers awarded it sovereignty over most of Bosnia and Hercegovina. This generated another problem, however, because it brought to Croatia a multi-ethnic community. Out of a population of 6.3 million, only 3.4 million were Croatian, the rest being composed of 1.9 million Serbs, 700,000 Muslims, 150,000 Germans, 18,000 Jews, and some Italians. In practice, the NDH was divided into two halves: the western section bordering the Adriatic was controlled by Italy for obvious strategic and political reasons, the eastern half was, in reality, under German supervision.

Mussolini was permitted by Hitler to nominate the leadership and naturally chose the man he once described as 'our only pawn in the Balkan chessboard', Ante Pavelić.[3] At the same time, Croatia's dependence on Italy was underlined in May 1941 when the state was proclaimed a monarchy and, at Italian instigation, Prince Amione of Savoy, the Duke of Spoleto, accepted the crown, taking the name Tomislav II. Persistent rumours of plots to assassinate him should he have the temerity to set foot in Zagreb help explain why he never visited his kingdom.[4]

The relationship between Pavelić and Mussolini had been, and remained, one of mutual exploitation. Each hoped to use the other to satisfy their not wholly compatible aspirations. In Chapter 3 we saw how Mussolini had nurtured Pavelić and his followers since their exile from Yugoslavia, anticipating that he could use the Ustaša to initiate a break-up of Yugoslavia in order to achieve the extension of Italian influence in the Balkans. For his part, Pavelić required Italian sponsorship to sustain the independence of the NDH. During earlier times the Ustaša had enjoyed wide support among the Croats, but by 1941 this peculiar brand of fascism was a marginal force in Croatian politics. The new régime was dedicated to the preservation of Croatian national culture and identity, to which end the Serb took the place of the Jew in Nazism, as the principal subject of the official demonology. In that sense the Ustaša demonology was distinct among the fascist movements for its emphasis on the enemy within Croatian society, rather than the more typical antagonism towards an element outside.[5]

Pavelić returned to Zagreb in April 1941 with just a few hundred of his followers who had little if any experience of government or administration. Initially, both Maček and Archbishop Stepinać, the highest Croatian Catholic prelate, urged the population to support the new state, but later Maček retired to his farm and was subsequently interned, while Stepinać became increasingly uneasy at the methods of the proto-fascist régime which ruled under Italian tutelage and German supervision. Power was placed exclusively in the hands of fascist fanatics and in the more remote parts of Croatia, anarchy broke out. The Pavelić régime then added to the mayhem by pursuing a policy of annihilating the Jews in deference to Nazi and fascist anti-semitism, and the Serbs in the name of Catholicism; Muslims, who generally tried to remain outside the Serbo–Croat strife, found themselves motivated by this policy to join forces with the Croats. Chaos and civil war ensued as the Serb villagers retaliated. The Italian army gave this conflict further impetus by occasionally aiding the Serbs, some 350,000 of whom were killed at this time.[6] Camps in the areas of Gospić as well as the death camps of Jasenovac and Stara Gradiška became monuments to this element of fratricidal strife (Table 4.1).

The defining relationship in this region during the first three years of the war was that between Italy and Germany. Many *Wehrmacht* officers were horrified by the Ustaša's persecution of the Serbs and by 1942 these concerns were being articulated in Berlin by the German Plenipotentiary General in Zagreb, Edmund Glaise von Horstenau, whose utter distaste for the methods of the NDH régime was well known. Only the German minister in Zagreb, Siegfried Kasche, remained uncritical of Pavelić. What concerned the Germans most, however, was not so much the scale of the bloodletting as the impact

Table 4.1   War dead in Yugoslavia, 1941–45

	Numbers	**Per cent of total**
Serbs	487,000	6.9
Croats	207,000	—
Muslim Slavs	86,000	6.7
Jews	60,000	77.9
Montenegrins	50,000	10.4

Source: C. Bennett, *Yugoslavia's Bloody Collapse*, p. 45.

this was having on the stability and security in this strategically vital area. The German objective in partitioning the region was pacification rather than incitement to civil unrest, and this is implicit in the fact that some of the reorganisation did address the interwar grievances of various potentially disruptive parties. The Balkans was strategically vital to Axis lines of communication to the Eastern Front and Mediterranean. The region was also a source of raw materials and human resources required to sustain the war economy. German concerns to retain their grip on the region were also rooted in their belief in the possibility of an Allied landing on the Adriatic coast which in 1942 and 1943 seemed to German minds a real danger.

Accordingly the Germans took steps in 1942 to shore up their settlement in the Balkans. One element in this strategy was the strengthening of the military arm of the state through utilisation of locals for certain security tasks. German officers were prominent in Zagreb from the outset, particularly in the economic sphere and progressively extending their presence in the domain of state security. In Croatia they encouraged the creation of the Home Guard or *Domobranci*, and even trained some of its members in Germany. The *Domobranci* were utilised in the battles against the resistance movement, particularly against the Partisans, but remained a rather undisciplined and unreliable conscript army.

RESISTANCE

The mountainous terrain, and steep wooded valleys which run parallel to the Adriatic coast provide the ideal environment for waging guerrilla warfare. For centuries the remoteness, and lack of water were barriers to conquest of Montenegro or Bosnia-Hercegovina. Although it is difficult to speak of the existence of an organised and coherent resistance movement in Yugoslavia before the end of 1942, armed resistance bands were being formed in the mountains of Serbia and Croatia within months of the surrender. Early recruitment was stimulated partly by an upsurge of enthusiasm for Britain and her allies at the time of Hitler's attack on the Soviet Union on 21 June 1941, and later by the outbreak of a general revolt in Serbia at the end of July.

Resistance in Yugoslavia was multifaceted. Conventionally it was directed against enemy occupation, against nazism and fascism. But resistance was also evidence of opposition to the various quisling forces which the occupiers had ensnared to control the state apparatus.

And then there was the motivation of simple vengeance, of bloodletting for its own sake. And finally there was resistance motivated by political objectives for the post-war order.[7]

The Četniks

By the autumn of 1941, resistance movements were being organised around two distinct focal points. In Ravna Gora, a high plateau in western Serbia, the remnants of the royalist forces who chose to stay and fight rather than flee into exile, had gathered around the leadership of Colonel Dragoljub (Draža) Mihailović, an officer in the Royal Yugoslav Army. These bandits adopted the Četnik identity following the Serbian guerrilla traditions of resistance to the Ottomans. Mihailović sought to assert the legitimacy of the Četniks by seeking recognition from the government-in-exile in London. Utilising secret radio links, Mihailović succeeded in getting word to England of his activities in August 1941 where this news was received with some enthusiasm as the first sign that some vestiges of clandestine organisation had survived the invasion and that, however slender, Britain did still have contacts behind the Nazi lines. Mihailović's position was strengthened further through his promotion to the rank of general and appointment as Minister of War in King Peter's cabinet. In the months that followed the BBC world service built up Mihailović as the hero of European resistance, thus creating a hostage to fortune which the western allies would come to rue as the war progressed.

Četnik strategy was to lie low and consolidate their strength in the expectation that the Allies would mount a large-scale invasion in the Balkans, just as they had done during the First World War, at which point the Četniks would lead a mass rising against the occupiers. The strategy was conservative, designed to avoid self-destruction in the absence of outside assistance as well as the danger of provoking reprisals against the local population. Četnik officers were encouraged to conceal their identity by returning to their communities and even enlisting in Serbian quisling forces until the time came to assist the Allied landings.[8] In effect, Mihailović was operating what amounted to an informal understanding with the Nedić régime, which was justified by the need to preserve the non-combatant Serbian population from reprisals. This suited the Germans who realised that the joint efforts of Mihailović and Nedić would keep the communists out of Serbia.

Politically, Mihailović was constrained by his pan Serb programme which envisaged the purging of 'Serb lands' including Bosnia and Hercegovina and large parts of Croatia of non-Serbs. Nonetheless, the Četniks were joined by some Serbs from Croatia especially in the Italian occupied areas in the south around Knin. Here, the Italian authorities financed and armed them as auxiliary forces to keep the Partisans out and to prevent the Croat government from asserting its authority in areas under Italian military occupation but not formally annexed to Italy.[9]

The Partisans and the Emergence of the Yugoslav Communist Party

The Partisans were a broad coalition of Serbs and non-Serbs united by ideological anti-fascism. They were attractive to the Slovenes, whose existence was threatened by the New Order, and also to the Serbs from Croatia and Bosnia-Hercegovina who found themselves threatened with annihilation by the fanatics who served the purposes of the Pavelić régime. The most important source of support was Croatia where Croats alienated by the senseless violence of the Ustaša joined the Partisans in increasing numbers from 1942 onwards. The Bosnian Muslims were attracted to the movement by the promise of autonomy for Bosnia and Hercegovina, as well as protection from the strongly anti-Muslim Četniks; the Macedonians were appealed to by the promise of a Macedonian republic in post-war federation. While the Partisan movement in its broadest sense, drew its support on neither an ethnic nor class basis, it tended to attract the young and unattached, or those who were older but in some way dispossessed. Its membership was not wholly, or even predominantly communist. Its appeal lay in the fact that the leadership under Tito's direction held out the promise of an alternative post-war Yugoslavia as a solution to the ineffective and divisive style of governance which had characterised the pre-war period.

As the German panzer divisions surged across the plains of Russia in late June and early July 1941, the Comintern instructed the European communist parties that they should not 'stand idly by while the precious blood of the heroic people of Soviet Russia is being shed', but rather should mobilise their strength to prevent their countries being 'turned into a base to supply the fascist hordes ...'.[10] Tito claimed retrospectively that he had been putting plans in hand for organisation of a resistance movement for some time prior to this directive. This may be so. Much of the communist core of the Partisan movement had gained invaluable experience of guerrilla warfare with the International Brigades in the Spanish Civil War and was well prepared to pursue a resistance strategy which also sought to bring about a social revolution. Moreover, the Comintern had established a network of radio communications by which it could keep in touch with not just the Yugoslavs but also other communist parties in this region of Europe. By the autumn of 1941, the Comintern was already utilising these resources to direct the KPJ leadership in the organisation of its struggle against the occupation.

The Partisans' strategic vision was diametrically opposite to that of the Četniks. Under orders from the Soviet Union, which was obliged to fight for its very existence, the Partisans were intent on carrying the fight to the enemy, making the occupation as uncomfortable and expensive for the Axis forces and their collaborators as possible. The impact of their actions on the local population was not considered. Indeed the Partisans took the view that reprisals would serve their cause by generating further conflict and thus would act as a recruiting agency for the resistance. The outlook of Tito's movement was revolutionary from the outset, informed by the political objectives for the overthrow of capitalism inherent in Marxist–Leninist philosophy, and conditioned by the generation of clandestine activity, imprisonment and exile to which the KPJ leaders had been subject since their prohibition in 1921.

The Partisan leadership began to place the building blocks for a socialist state as early as the autumn of 1941. In September, they occupied the town of Užice in western Serbia, a strategically important location because of its small arms industry. Here they established a pattern of ordering their host society which they repeated for the remainder of the war, setting up a People's Committee and a People's Court, as replacements for the old administrative and judicial system. The inhabitants found themselves citizens of the 'Užice republic' and were in fact sampling, in simple form, the system of government, which Tito set up in 1945. This pattern of 'occupation' was designed to accustom the population to this new form of organisation, gaining as they did so a measure of popular legitimacy on which they could call once the invaders had been defeated.[11]

War and Civil War

This contest for political power precluded any prospect of the two resistance groups achieving effective co-operation. Nevertheless, the leaderships did pursue desultory contacts during the autumn of 1941 when they aired the possibility of uniting their respective forces. The first such meeting took place on 19 September but with no result; they met again at Brajici on 26 October, when they agreed that the Partisans would supply rifles and ammunition in return for a share in any supplies dropped by the Allies. Tito subsequently claimed that he offered to stand down in favour of Mihailović, an offer that the latter declined, but there is no independent witness to confirm Tito's account. The Germans turned on the guerrillas in November driving them out of Serbia. At the height of the offensive, on 28 November, Tito made a telephone call to the Četnik headquarters at Ravna Gora but was again refused. Mihailović was deeply anti-communist and his suspicions of the political agenda of the Partisan movement, which he recognised would be anti-thetical to the interests of Greater Serbia, were well founded.

At the end of 1941, the Germans crushed the insurrection in Serbia, driving the guerrilla bands into hiding. Mihailović escaped capture, but chose to remain in Serbia where he was assured of widespread support from all levels of the largely homogenous population. The communists, however, embarked on what subsequently became romanticised in Partisan mythology as the 'long march' into Serbian inhabited western Bosnia (part of wartime Croatia), establishing their headquarters at Foča. Here they founded the Proletarian Brigades which linked resist-ance with the wider revolutionary aims.

During the winter, their presence in Foča was tolerated, so long as they did not attempt to cross the Sava River, but in March 1942, they found themselves under renewed attack. Breaking through enemy lines, the Partisans crossed Bosnia, acquiring many new recruits in the process. In September they captured the old Bosnian capital of Bihać and remained there across the winter. It was there that Tito began to develop a national identity for his movement, first by reorganising his army as the 'National Army of Liberation and the Partisan Detachments of Yugoslavia', (NLA) and second by holding the first session of their Anti-Fascist Council for National Liberation (AVNOJ) on 26–27 November 1942. This body, which was inherently political, claimed for itself the role of rallying point for all resistance forces. As such Tito was pursuing two aims: that his movement was national, in the sense of being 'Yugoslav' rather than anti-Serb, and that this represented an alternative political form to that embodied in the Royal Government-in-exile. Further, he was demonstrating that it had a political base which was broader and more widely attractive than a narrowly communist movement. The appointment of Ivan Ribar, formerly Speaker of the Vidovdan

Constituent Assembly, as President regardless of his non-adherence to communism was designed to emphasise this point. Representatives were invited from Slovenia, where the Partisan army had recently withstood a determined effort by the Italians, in concert with Yugoslav fascist forces, to destroy them, and from Macedonia where Bulgarian occupation and adherence to the Tripartite Pact had turned many towards Yugoslav rather than Bulgarian resistance. The Assembly passed resolutions calling for national liberation, the equality of the Yugoslav peoples, respect for private property and private enterprise in industry and agriculture and the promise of free elections after the war. It recognised the national rights of Serbs, Croats, Slovenes and Macedonians.[12]

The British victory at El Alamein in November 1942 combined with the successful Anglo-American landings in North Africa at the end of that month, turned the tide of the war in the West. The retreat of the German and Italian armies in North Africa brought the Balkans into sharper focus as a strategic prize. Hitler believed firmly in the possibility of an Allied landing there and in order to improve the Axis grip on the region, Hitler ordered the pacification of the Yugoslav lands and the destruction of the resistance. During the winter and spring of 1943, against a background of defeat at Russian hands at Stalingrad in January, two major operations were mounted in what was the most determined counter-insurgency operation pursued in the Yugoslav lands during the war and arguably contributed more than any other action to the process of translating this conflict into a civil war.[13] The first, Operation *Weiss*, was conducted in February using combined military forces including Četniks and the Domobranci, and aimed at destruction of the Partisans in Croatia; then, a second Operation *Schwarz*, launched on 15 May, was directed primarily at the Četnik 'Yugoslav Army of the Fatherland'.[14] Both campaigns were prosecuted in such a way as to avoid either giving advantage to the Četniks over the Partisans, or to encourage any reconciliation between Tito and Mihailović.[15] In this way, by driving the rival resistance forces up against one another, the Germans intended that they contribute to each other's destruction.

Such a strategy was unnecessary. By the spring of 1943, the Partisans had come to regard the Četniks as their main enemy. Moreover, they shared German concerns about the possibility of an Allied landing in the Balkans with the Mihailović forces there to meet them. Such an eventuality would be inimical to their revolutionary ambitions. Unknown to the Germans, the Partisans broke out of their pocket north of the Neretva and entered the area north-west of Montenegro into southeast Hercegovina. It was here that the brunt of Operation *Schwarz* took place, falling on the Partisans as much as the Četniks. A month of the most desperate fighting ensued and ended without the German forces delivering a decisive blow to either resistance movement. However, the Partisans were the benefactors, deriving cohesion and confidence as an effective fighting force. From this point onwards, Tito's forces were in the ascendant.

THE BALKANS AND THE GRAND ALLIANCE, 1942–45

During 1943, Yugoslav resistance acquired a new importance to the grand strategy of the major Allies. This was a function in the West of the planning for the invasion of north-west Europe in which irregular forces operating in the Balkan peninsula could play a part to dissipate German military strength. In the East, as the Red Army established its ascendancy over the German forces after Stalingrad, consideration was being given in Moscow to the post-war aspirations for establishment of secure frontiers on Russia's western border. The political disruption caused by the war throughout this region provided the ideal conditions of chaos and potential anarchy in which the still clandestine communist parties could mobilise to acquire power. The Russians were interested not simply in promoting the activities of communist led irregulars in order to create chaos behind the German lines and shorten the war, but were also keen to control them so as to lay the groundwork for the political settlement of eastern Europe in a manner which suited the objectives of the Soviet Union.

Just as the Balkans had formed a buffer between Russian and British imperial interests during the nineteenth century, so it was to be the geographical meeting point of the vital strategic interests of both states in the post-war settlement. The British, whose interest in the Balkans was derived from imperial interests in the Indian Ocean, and requirement for access through the Mediterranean to the Suez Canal, was interested in the longer term in promoting friendly governments in Greece and Italy. They saw post-war stability in Yugoslavia as a *sine qua non* of this ambition. While British consideration of a possible Allied landing in the Balkans was never more than an idea, the Yugoslav resistance, like that in Greece, remained important to the planning of the western allies precisely because its highly active guerrilla fighters could be utilised to pin important German divisions in that theatre, keeping them away from the vital north-west European coast.

News of Yugoslav resistance activity reached Britain in August 1941. Desperate for allies, little time was wasted in sending a mission to investigate. Operating under the auspices of the Special Operations Executive, a special forces mission was put ashore from a British submarine on 19 September. It consisted of a South African mining engineer, Colonel 'Bill' Hudson, who had worked in Yugoslavia before the war, and two Yugoslav officers, Majors Ostojić and Lalatović. Hudson's experiences in the autumn, when he went first to Partisan headquarters at Užice and then on to Mihailović at Ravna Gora, provided portents of the difficulties the Allies were to have for the remainder of the war in utilising these forces to further the Allied war effort. Instead of being greeted as an emissary from an ally, Hudson was regarded by both camps with suspicion and disdain. Tito, in particular, was anxious not to encourage British influence, fearing that they would seek to restore the pre-war status quo. Mihailović wanted to be the sole representative of Yugoslav resistance, with an exclusive link to the Royal government in London and did not want the British, or other foreign powers meddling in this arrangement.

The Russians, meanwhile, maintained an enigmatic posture towards Yugoslav resistance during the early stages of the war. Undoubtedly this was due in part to their preoccupation with the rapidity of the Wehrmacht's advance into Soviet territory, but the ambivalence persisted in their dealings with the Partisans throughout the war. At root of this was Stalin's apparent concern lest Soviet connections with the communist elements among the Partisans instilled in his Allies a destructive distrust of Soviet intentions. Nevertheless, the connections were there and despite Soviet protestations to the contrary, the British were cognisant from the outset that there was a well-established clandestine link between Moscow and the Partisan leadership. The discovery in November 1941 that Radio Free Yugoslavia was broadcast from Kuibyshev, Stalin's wartime capital, was merely confirmation of a widely held suspicion. The official Soviet line, promulgated by the Comintern, was that Partisan movements should emphasise broad anti-fascist and patriotic values rather than revolutionary communist ones, not least because the motherland of communism was itself in great need of British and American support in order to resist the German onslaught. In March 1942 Georgi Dimitrov sent a telegram to Tito pointing out that the priority was to defeat the fascists and that the Soviet Union was allied with Britain and the United States in this cause.[16] The implication was that the Soviet Union would disapprove of any activity which threatened to disturb relations within the Grand Alliance. At the local level, however, the Comintern did issue directives which encouraged Tito to build his movement: on 1 June 1942, Dimitrov instructed Tito that 'this campaign should be waged so as to divide rather than unite all the Četniks to oppose the partisans' struggle. In this regard, your tactical line should be to win over some of the Četniks, neutralize others, and mercilessly destroy the most malicious of them'.[17]

Četniks or Partisans?

Further British missions were infiltrated during 1942 with varying degrees of success. Hudson, who had been abandoned to his fate by the Četniks during the German assault at the end of 1941, rejoined Mihailović in March 1942 and reported spasmodically on the military activities and political ambitions of his connections. His reports built up a picture of the Četnik leadership as ambivalent about the monarchy and government-in-exile, but fiercely pro-Serb. Furthermore, Hudson detected a bias towards Serb-Bulgar understanding, a conception, which Hudson observed, was 'entirely irreconcilable with the idea of a Balkan Federation in which Croatia and Slovenia would have their places'; more worrying from the British point of view, was the fact that this conception, 'would best suit the Russian long-term ambitions in the Balkans'.[18] Undoubtedly the thrust of Hudson's reporting instilled in British minds the notion that Yugoslavia could easily become a second Spain in which the western allies, through their support of the Četniks, could find themselves on the opposing side to their ally, the Soviet Union, in a civil war over which faction should govern post-war Yugoslavia. This in turn impinged on the strategic thrust of British policy towards the Balkans which was certainly conditioned by an axiom that Soviet Russian influence should not be permitted to penetrate the Mediterranean.

This, then, was the paradox at the heart of British policy as it developed during 1943. Communications with the Partisans were officially begun when the mission led by the then Captain Bill Deakin was dropped in late May 1943, arriving at the very moment the Partisans were in the thick of their struggle to survive Operation *Schwarz*. Joining the Partisans during the Battle of Sujetska, the British mission witnessed at first hand the spirit and fighting potential of the Partisan forces. A high profile mission led by Brigadier Fitzroy Maclean followed in September and substantially confirmed Deakin's conclusions that militarily this was the force which could best aid the Allied war effort.[19]

Controversial though this decision has subsequently proven, the logic from a military point of view is difficult to gainsay. The simple truth is that the Partisans, by virtue of their choice of proactive guerrilla warfare, were causing more disruption behind the Axis lines than the Četniks. For this reason the Middle East Defence Committee based in Cairo decided in September 1943 that military aid, in scarce supply, should be directed solely to the Partisans. It is regrettable that this decision was not paralleled at the political level and that the debate continued in British and American circles until the end of January 1944.[20]

The political dimension was more problematic. Mihailović was minister of war in the King's Cabinet in London and the decision to cease the provision of aid was also a rejection of the royalist connections, and more controversially, the Serbian claims to be the rightful leader of the South Slavs. To this has been added the betrayal felt by the British officers who served with Mihailović during 1943 and 1944. Some have subsequently argued that their reports were overlooked or disregarded. It was only a short step from that to the linking of British decision making with the existence of British 'communists' operating within SOE Cairo and also in the field in Yugoslavia to create the notion of a conspiracy within the British establishment which sought to further the communist and Soviet cause. Certainly, the communists would have done what they could to further the Partisans' cause, and undoubtedly a blind eye was turned by agents in the field and evaluators behind the lines to the more unsavoury aspects of the Partisan movement. Such is war. But the conspiracy theory fails to allow for the fact that Moscow was the brake rather than the accelerator on Partisan ambitions.[21]

At the first summit meeting of the Grand Alliance, held at Teheran at the beginning of December, Churchill, Roosevelt and Stalin agreed to give Tito all possible assistance. At much the same time, the Partisan leadership was complicating the political picture by institutionalising its administrative structures. At the second AVNOJ Congress, held in Jajce in November 1943, Tito moved to establish himself as the head of a national government of Yugoslavia. The Anti-Fascist Council was renamed a Presidium, composed of 67 members representing the nationalities of Yugoslavia along with some of the pre-war political groups, assuming legislative and administrative functions. Its Executive

Council, the Council of National Liberation, became effectively a provisional government with Tito, promoted Marshal, as its premier. Yugoslavia would be reconstituted on a federal basis and, controversially, would include some of the territory held by Italy before the war. The question of the King's return and the monarchy in general were to be subject to the people's will after the war.[22]

The Russians, insecure about their relationship with the western front while there was still no second front in north-west Europe, were furious with Tito for advancing his programme so forcefully. But Stalin need not have worried. While both western powers noted these developments with some concern, and were certainly of the opinion that Tito was not acting independently of Moscow, their attention was focussed on preparations for the reinvasion of north-west Europe: they did not want to make an issue over Yugoslav politics and in any case guerrilla activity in the Balkans, whatever its nature, was welcome in so far as it could keep the German forces tied down there. Military considerations prevailed.

However, this did leave the problem of the King and his government-in-exile which during 1943 had become progressively irrelevant to the political struggle going on under the occupation authorities. Following Teheran, the major Allies informed the government-in-exile that 'Yugoslavia, as a state entity, will be restored in full territorial integrity and independence, the question of western frontier and her claims against Italy being settled after the war, bearing in mind the proposal put forward by President Wilson in 1919'.[23] The British, hosts to the King and his politicians, took the lead in attempting to forge a link by engineering an agreement between the government-in-exile and Tito's provisional government.

Allied Attempts to Unite the Royal Government with the National Liberation Committee, 1944–45

In order to facilitate the negotiation, Churchill and Eden persuaded King Peter to appoint a prime minister who had a reputation for compromise as well as links with Yugoslavs outside the traditional Serbian royalist circles. The Croat, Ivan Šubašić was eventually appointed on 1 June. His royal links were well established, having been adviser to King Alexander, but he was also a close associate of Maček and had been Ban of Croatia under the *sporazum*. Sincere, patient and courageous, but devoid of political acumen, Šubašić was appointed in the absence of

anyone better, and during the first two weeks of June 1944 he negotiated
an agreement with Tito which prepared the way for a united provisional government through 'closer co-operation between the Royal
Government and the Partisan's National Liberation Committee'. It
reaffirmed the objective of achieving national unity after the war, and
included a statement to the effect that the question of the monarchy
would be put to the people in a referendum. Tito gave a verbal assurance
that he did not intend to introduce a communist system. While these
arrangements, which amounted to a coalition, placed a degree of constraint on the Partisan leadership, it was the Partisans who were present
in the country, and fighting for its liberation, while Šubašić, King Peter
and the monarchy remained safely behind allied lines. Possession being
nine tenths of the law, the game for post-war control of Yugoslavia was
weighted heavily in the Partisans' favour.[24]

Over the summer, Tito evaded the issue of forming a government of
National Unity, insisting that the issue was of little importance at a time
when the Partisans were engaged in exceptionally hard battles with the
Germans. However, the principle was endorsed by Stalin during discussions with Churchill when the latter visited Moscow on 10–12 October.
At this meeting, Churchill appeared to gain Stalin's acquiescence in an
understanding for an Anglo-Soviet division of the Balkans into spheres of
influence, with Soviet influence predominant in Rumania and Bulgaria,
that of Britain in Greece, with a sharing of influence in Hungary and
Yugoslavia on a fifty-fifty basis. There was no record kept of this discussion and its appearance in Churchill's wartime memoirs has stimulated
great historical controversy. The Yugoslavs certainly were not informed of
this 'understanding', and only found out about it by chance.[25]

The Tito–Šubašić agreement was initialled on 1 November. This was
a modification of the previous agreement which had envisaged the creation of a single state representation, and agreed that the Yugoslav state
would continue in its old form until elections could be held. Within this
ambit, the AVNOJ became the supreme legislative body and a United
Government was formed composed of twelve members from the
National Liberation Committee and six from the Royal Yugoslav
Government. There was no mention of constitutional monarchy, except
by implication through the existence of a three-man regency which
would represent the King prior to a popular referendum on his return.
Yugoslavia would continue to be a monarchy, on paper at least, although
the King would remain abroad and be represented by three regents.
In practice the regents had no authority over the government since

members of the latter were to take their oath to the people. King Peter captured the essence of the agreement when he complained to Churchill that it was a means of getting rid of him 'more or less painlessly'.[26] Several months of uncertainty followed as King Peter attempted to hold out against the agreement, but under pressure from the British with Russian support, he was prevailed upon to cede his power to the Regency Council following which the United Provisional Government came into being on 7 March 1945. Šubašić was appointed foreign minister, and the Serbian Democrat Milan Grol became deputy premier. They were in a minority from the outset as only one third of the seats went to non-communist groups.[27]

Liberation

The coup d'état in Rumania on 23 August broke that country's association with the Axis and opened the way for the Red Army to move against both Bulgaria and Hungary. Given the proximity of Stalin's forces, Tito flew to Moscow on 21 September to conclude an agreement for joint Soviet–Yugoslav military action on Yugoslav territory. Although a Russian military mission had been attached to Tito's headquarters since February, the Partisans had received no effective military aid or supplies from the Soviet Union. Indeed, Tito had been reminded repeatedly since 1941 that the object of the present struggle was the defeat of the fascist forces and not socialist revolution, and furthermore, that 'the Soviet Union has treaty relations with the Yugoslav King and Government and that taking an open stand against these would create difficulties'. It remains unclear whether deprivation of Soviet aid had a political motivation arising from suspicion of Tito's intentions, or whether it was simply a consequence of obvious logistical difficulties associated with the geography of the eastern front.[28]

Soviet troops entered Serbia on 28 September; the Partisans entered Belgrade on 20 October, having been granted the right to take this symbolic honour in an agreement worked out at Soviet military headquarters in Craiova between Tito and the Red Army commander, Marshal Tolbukhin. The Partisans were left immediately to administer their own territory, while the Red Army pursued the retreating Germans north. For the first time, Tito's forces were able to receive Soviet arms and supplies on a grand scale, and they turned these to the task of liberating the remaining occupied areas. This arrangement conferred considerable authority on Tito and lent legitimacy to Partisan assertions that they should organise the peace because they had led the liberation. They wasted little time before imposing their dominance. The Četniks were doomed. Realising that nothing could be done to prevent the establishment of a communist-dominated régime, Mihailović's forces migrated from Serbia en masse, taking refuge in the Sandžak and Bosnia, and leaving Serbia to the Partisans virtually without a fight. In Kosovo, the Albanians revolted against their reattachment to Yugoslavia, and were summarily repressed by a force of some 30,000.[29] The last six months of the war cost the Partisans 30,000 dead and 70,000 wounded as the Germans launched counter-offensives to cover their retreat. Zagreb finally fell on 8 May, VE Day, and the final German units in Yugoslavia surrendered a week later.

CONCLUSION

The legacy of the occupation and partition of Yugoslavia was that it generated a history of violent conflict between the Yugoslav peoples, which had not existed previously.[30] The genocidal philosophy of the Nazi occupiers, which placed the Slavic peoples in much the same lowly status as the Jews, resulted in untold violence between occupiers and occupied. The replication of racialism by the Ustaša, of which the Serb rather than the Jew was the primary demon, and the consequent attempt to eradicate the Serb from Croatia with the same vigour as the Nazis turned on the Jew, created a legacy which would remain an enduring source of weakness unless the post-war régime was strong enough for the questions it raised to be openly addressed.

The success of Tito's wartime strategy to bring about revolutionary change in the power-holding group, can be explained by reference to three factors. First, the Partisan leadership had hoisted the flag of Yugoslav national unity at a time when the vast majority of the people of Yugoslavia had grown tired of the ceaseless Serb–Croat antagonism which had so divided the first Yugoslav state and contributed to their collective demise in 1941. What they could offer was strong and stable governance, a rationalisation of the nationalities problem and the promise of a more even distribution of the society's wealth. Second, Tito was prepared to guarantee and respect Croatian nationality, and indeed to offer a programme in which all identities would be mutually protected. Third, the Partisan leadership had been skilful in obtaining international support in their struggle, by offering to the Allies that which they most needed – active resistance which could keep the occupiers occupied and away from the major fronts. Moreover, they were offering an alternative programme for resolution of the Yugoslav problem and were sufficiently in control of the levers of state power to be able to impose this solution in the face of significant opposition. In short, the KPJ managed to invent itself as the first 'national' party which could stand above the ethnic rivalries and insecurities and assert its authority with the legitimacy bestowed by genuine and significant popular support.

5 Stalinism and Heresy

Post-war Yugoslavia existed within a framework which taught the necessity of the obedience of people to history – that is, to history as a process of social and economic development. Yugoslavia in its second incarnation was created ostensibly to serve such ends. However, it was created by and organised around, a small group of personalities, of which Tito was supreme. A statesman by temperament and outlook, he required a state over which to govern. Yugoslavia, reincarnated, provided just such an entity, and the people, willingly or otherwise, were obliged to follow.

If the Second World War provided the opportunity for the KPJ to achieve the Leninist 'revolution from below', then the period immediately following was when the revolutionary party completed its work by bringing about the 'revolution from above' to transform the state's economic and social base. Initially, the Yugoslav communists, like those elsewhere in eastern Europe, were permitted a certain latitude in how they carried this process out. This was to be a short-lived interval, however, and by the summer of 1947, the Yugoslav leadership found itself pressured from the Soviet Union to adopt greater conformity with Soviet dictates as Stalin responded to Cold War insecurities by imposing greater uniformity among his most immediate allies. The conflict which arose out of Tito's pursuit of Yugoslav 'national' interests and the communist internationalist agenda directed from Moscow, not only drove Yugoslavia from the Soviet bloc, but forced its leadership to redefine communist doctrine in line with the requirements of 'Yugoslavism'. The second Yugoslavia was both Tito's creation, and also a consequence of the Cold War and the clash of ideologies which defined international politics in Europe for over forty years.

CONSOLIDATION OF THE PEOPLE'S FRONT

During the summer and autumn of 1945, the Partisan leadership consolidated its grip on power. The tactics they adopted were those of the Popular Front, expressed in creation of a coalition of left and centre left parties, but one in which the communists were dominant over all others. The background of the war and the need to address the question of collaboration provided the perfect justification for maintaining a high degree of centralisation and security in its aftermath. The AVNOJ held its third and final meeting, when it was expanded to include sixty-eight members of the last pre-war parliament who were not 'compromised by collaboration with the enemy'. Activists for the right and centre politicians were harassed and their publications suppressed. Within the government, the three Cabinet members drawn from the London Government found their freedom to function progressively circumscribed. Grol resigned in August, in protest at the conditions; Šutej and Šubašić followed in late September. The latter still commanded sufficient popular respect to merit house arrest.

Elections were held on 11 November 1945 and there was never any doubt about the result. All the pre-war parties not included in the People's Front were excluded, while intimidation by the secret police ensured that only the very brave or very foolish availed themselves of their right to register a dissenting vote on the ballot paper. In the event, eighty-eight per cent of the eligible electorate of 7.4 million voted; of these, ninety per cent supported the government. The first act of the Constitutional Assembly when it convened on 29 November 1945, was to abolish the monarchy and proclaim Yugoslavia a Federal People's Republic.[1]

Sovietisation

The process of 'Sovietisation', of transformation of the state from a coalition of left and left centre parties into a one party state, which took place throughout eastern Europe in the period 1945–48, was accomplished more swiftly in Yugoslavia than in most of the others. If examined within Hugh Seton-Watson's three-stage model of communist takeover in the region, it can be seen that the first stage, the 'genuine coalition' never pertained, while the second, the 'bogus coalition' existed only briefly and then only to achieve international recognition and legitimacy.[2] By the adoption of the new constitution on 31 January 1946, the KPJ had achieved the complete monopoly over the institutions of the state and could turn to the task of building socialism. Henceforth the socialist parties were forced to 'fuse' with communist parties.

No more political opposition was tolerated in parliament, press or public meeting.[3]

The primary aim of the new constitution was to reduce Serbian power relative to the other republics, while at the same time offering Serbs an incentive for co-operating within the new framework. The former aim was achieved through a re-drawing of the provincial boundaries to create six republics of equal status, thereby subdividing the territory that had been greater Serbia between six administrative units. Thus, Macedonia and Montenegro became republics in their own right and Bosnia-Hercegovina was given republican status delineated by boundaries dating from the Austro-Hungarian occupation. All republican boundaries were drawn along historic, ethnic and national lines and corresponded closely with those of 1918. The second aim was achieved by addressing Serbian nationalist sentiment by leaving Serbia as the largest republic, containing two autonomous entities. The Vojvodina, an autonomous region (*pokrajina*), was populated not only by Serbs and Croats but also Hungarians and other non-Slav groups; Kosovo-Metohija (abbreviated as Kosmet) or 'Old Serbia' became an autonomous province (*oblast*) to recognise its Albanian majority. Within Bosnia, the Muslims were recognised as a distinct ethnic entity for the first time. The creation of the republics of Slovenia and Croatia was less controversial; Slovenia acquired the Julian region from Italy and the small Slovene-speaking region of Prekomurje, annexed to Hungary in 1941. The Croatian republic consisted of Croatia–Slavonia and Dalmatia with the addition of Istria and Zara from Italy, and it acquired Medjumurje, also annexed to Hungary in 1941.[4]

The institutional structure followed the Soviet model of 1936. The legislature consisted of a Federal Assembly composed of a Federal Council (*Savezno Veče*), elected by universal suffrage, and a Council of Nationalities (*Veče Naroda*) comprising equal numbers of representatives chosen by the Assemblies of the six republics and the two autonomous units. Policy was determined by the Presidential Council (*Prezidijum*) which was elected from the Assembly. In 1946, Tito and Ribar retained their assumed roles of prime minister and president respectively. President of the National Assembly was Dragoljub Jovanović, the former leader of the Serbian Peasant Party. Jovanović was deeply critical of the régime from the outset, in particular its economic policies, and despite intimidation continued with this criticism until his arrest in May 1947. At his trial he was accused of being a tool of the British

Secret Intelligence Service.[5] The federal administration was composed of six ministries dealing with defence, foreign policy, the merchant navy, transport, postal services and foreign trade. Then there was a series of 'mixed' federal–republican ministries dealing with finance, the interior, the judiciary, industry, mining, agriculture, forestry, labour and construction, transport. Little was left for the republican governments to administer independently although theoretically they were permitted some cultural autonomy which was reflected in their right to use national languages.

The reality was a centralised and hierarchical political system in which autonomy of the republics and communes was severely circumscribed by the centralised nature of the administrative hierarchy and the parallel organs of the Communist Party which exercised a totalitarian monopoly over the levers of power. Orders flowed down from the Politburo to the lower strata of the Party, whose members exercised day-to-day supervision over the organs of the government. Party and state functions were interlinked, a fact symbolised at the summit by Tito's position at the head of government, army and party.

Alongside Tito, who was supreme, four men dominated Yugoslav politics. Among the most important was the Serbian peasant, Alexander Ranković, who remained at the head of the state security apparatus of which he himself was the architect. His conspiratorial nature had enabled him to remain in the background during the partisan struggle while operating the Party machine under Tito's supervision. During the war, his chief function was to monitor the leadership and see that unreliable characters were replaced with more reliable personnel, while masterminding the KPJ's penetration of quisling forces and the Gestapo.[6] This knowledge was invaluable in securing the communist revolution. Edvard Kardelj, the Slovenian intellectual whose meticulous approach and penchant for abstractions enabled him to assume the mantle of Party theoretician, was appointed foreign minister. Milovan Djilas, the young Montenegrin intellectual, was placed in charge of propaganda. Initially the key area of economic planning was the portfolio of Andrija Hebrang, but his resistance to the Stalinist approach to industrialisation led to his replacement in 1946 with Boris Kidrić, another Slovenian who with Kardelj had organised the Slovenian rising of 1941. Kidrić spent the year of 1944–45 in the Soviet Union where he had studied Soviet economic planning and he returned to Yugoslavia primed to carry out the economic transformation of the economy in the manner and at the pace which Tito expected.

Legitimacy

The Yugoslav communist régime derived its immediate legitimacy from
the fact of being an indigenous movement which had fought bravely
against the occupation during the war and by late 1944 had acquired
de facto power which was consolidated into ownership of a monopoly of
power at the end of 1945. This was complemented by three further
sources of legitimacy. First, the Partisan leadership had acquired international legitimacy during this same period, through paper compromises
with the demands of the western allies in the shape of the Tito–Šubašić
Agreement by which official recognition of the government-in-exile
was transferred effectively to the United Provisional Government of
Tito. The second was derived from the Partisan war myth which all but
deified the veterans of that conflict, the *stari borci*, who had done the
fighting. This romanticised history of wartime resistance gave rise to the
myth of the Yugoslav nations who had united against a common enemy
in order to recreate the unified Yugoslav state. The notion that the
Partisan army had not discriminated on national grounds provided the
starting point for this idea which was encapsulated in the slogan of
'Brotherhood and Unity' (*bratstvo i jedinstvo*) which encompassed this
notion of pan-Yugoslav solidarity and co-operation. This latter also had
class undertones which brings us to the final source of legitimacy which
was that which the Yugoslav Communist Party derived as the vanguard
of the proletarian revolution, the instrument which would hasten and
implement the socialist revolution predicted by Karl Marx. Pursuit of
this teleological goal provided the justification for achievement of rapid
economic development in order to hasten this outcome, which adapted
Marxist political theory for the conditions of industrially underdeveloped countries.[7]

The sources of the state's legitimacy also commit it to follow particular actions. In this case, the supremacy of the Yugoslav Communist
Party, that is the confirmation of the one party state, required that opposition be firmly repressed and even stamped out. The judicial system was
employed to support this process by repressing all opposition. The secret
police, which Ranković had founded in May 1944, was called initially
the Department for the Protection of the People (*Odsek za zaštitu naroda –*
OZNa), and later came to be known the State Security Service (*Uprava
državne bezbednosti –* UDBA). Tito defined its mission as 'to strike terror
into the bones of those who do not like this kind of Yugoslavia'.[8] The
statistics for UDBA arrests in the immediate aftermath of war are very

imprecise, but executions probably ran to five figures in 1946–47, while those incarcerated in concentration camps may have risen to at least to six. The chief charge was collaboration, an elastic concept which, owing to the fact that the Partisans themselves had found it expedient at various stages to hold parleys with the German occupiers, was a charge which was later seized upon by those who subsequently sought to discredit the post-war régime.[9]

Enemies of the State

During the initial post-war years, show trials were staged to make examples of controversial figures with the purpose of discouraging atavistic national sentiments, or contact with overseas connections. Among the most notable was that of Mihailović who was finally captured with the remnants of his supporters in March 1946, tried for collaboration with the Germans, and executed on charges of treason and collaboration. Extermination of the Četniks as a military but more importantly political force was an early objective and other prominent Četniks, as well as the Serbian quislings such as Nedić and his supporters met a similar fate. Certain former ministers and officers in the services of the King were tried *in absentia*. Many collaborators escaped and hid among the refugee camps in Austria and Italy where their destabilising influence inclined the occupation authorities to seek bona fide war criminals and return them for trial by Yugoslavia's courts. Ante Pavelić was pursued by both the British and American authorities with some vigour, but succeeded in escaping through the auspices of the Vatican to Spain and later to Latin America.[10]

The Anglo-American occupation authorities grew wary of responding to Yugoslavia's demands for repatriation of its citizens from refugee camps.[11] Immediately after the war, some 9000 Croat refugees had been forcibly returned by the British from their zone around Klagenfurt, only to be butchered on arrival by Tito's zealots. This exercise was not repeated, and over the summer and autumn of 1945, British diplomats accumulated evidence of the régime's efforts to incarcerate its enemies or even to massacre them wholesale as part of its initial 'social revolution'.

The issues surrounding religious practices were left deliberately vague. Accommodation rather than confrontation was the strategy of the communists, at least in the first summer of the post-war period.

The Orthodox Church had no canonical links with the West, so could be perceived as independent of foreign interference. It had also emerged from the war with tremendous prestige. The Catholic Church, on the other hand, was weakened through its association with the Pavelić régime. In June 1945, Tito attempted to persuade the Croatian Archbishop, Aloysius Stepinac, to accept the detachment of the Croatian Catholic Church from Rome in return for freedom to worship. Stepinac refused and was duly tried on the grounds of collaboration alongside Pavelić's police chief and the Franciscan Provincial in Zagreb. Stepinac was sentenced to sixteen years hard labour, commuted in December 1951 to house arrest, which he served out in his home village of Krasić, dying there in 1960. Both his trial, and the nature of his sentence, reflected the government's recognition of his stature in society and the danger of making a martyr of such a figure. The one consequence they wished to avoid nevertheless came to pass: Croatian Catholic demands for religious rights fused in the post-war years for the first time with wider ethnically defined grievances and thus formed the movement which was to have a deeply corrosive effect on the Yugoslav state one generation later.

Accepting that religion was too important in Yugoslav society to be eradicated swiftly, the régime settled on a policy of subversion, sponsoring in 1947 an association of priests to be established in each republic. This encompassed the Muslims who were persuaded to abandon all pretence of political autonomy in return for state financial support. The tough line towards organised religion generally continued until the early 1950s, but was not successful. The 1953 census, the last to invite the people to register a religious affiliation returned over 86 per cent as declared believers.[12]

EXTERNAL RELATIONS, 1945–48

Revolutionary changes at home were complemented by a high profile policy abroad which was aggressive, chauvinistic and at times interventionist. It brought Yugoslavia into conflict with all the major allies, and contributed significantly to the uneasiness in Yugoslav relations with the Soviet Union. Initially, Tito's government were fervent supporters of the Soviet line, especially in the development of the Cold War with the west, but over a period of three years, they came to realise that Yugoslavia's interests were not necessarily commensurate with those of the Soviet Union. By the spring of 1948, Tito and his closest colleagues had become convinced that not only would Stalin sacrifice Yugoslavia's interests in pursuit of its own, but that he was actively engaged in a policy to deny Yugoslavia's independent statehood.

Territorial Disputes

The Yugoslavs received their first lesson in post-war great power politics in connection with their territorial claims against Italy and Austria. The Partisan leadership had signalled its intention to reopen these questions at the Jajce conference in November 1943. Of the two issues, it was both the extent of Yugoslav claims against Italy and the manner in which they pursued them which resulted in Yugoslavia's isolation at the Paris Peace Conference which opened in July 1946.

It was the sovereignty of Trieste which gave rise to the bitterest, and briefly the most dangerously inflammatory dispute between Yugoslavia and the West. Yugoslav claims against Italy were rooted in their demands for just reparation, and on the fact that four-fifths of the hinterland of Venezia Giulia was ethnically Slovene, even though Trieste city was eighty-five per cent Italian. Having agreed a line of occupation in February 1945, the Partisans then broke the agreement, beating the New Zealand corps in a race to occupy the city of Trieste by one day, and then refusing to withdraw to the demarcation line. After a crisis lasting throughout May, culminating in a joint Anglo-American ultimatum to the Yugoslav government to honour their commitments, the Yugoslav government backed down, probably under private pressure from the Russians who did not want an open conflict with the West at this stage.[13] They remained in occupation of the remainder of the territory they claimed from Italy, and were granted almost all of this at the Paris Peace Treaty of January 1947, except for some districts in eastern Friuli and what became the Free Territory of Trieste where the Yugoslav Army continued to occupy but could not annex an area known as 'Zone B' in the north-west corner of Istria. This intractable dispute soured Yugoslav relations with the British, Americans and Italians, and contributed to the western powers' perceptions that this was a military confrontation designed by the Soviet Union and its east European allies to test Western resolve at the war's end. In fact, Stalin was displeased with Tito's wilful challenging of the Grand Alliance's military agreements, and the lack of Soviet support for Yugoslav claims against Italy was among the first episodes which alerted the Yugoslav leadership to the notion that Stalin could be equivocal about narrowly Yugoslav interests.

The Yugoslavs had a similarly disappointing experience in pressing their claims to southern Carinthia, which they had attempted to further by pursuing quisling forces fleeing in front of the Partisan advance into Villach and Klagenfurt, to which they promptly tried to lay claim on ethnic grounds. On Western insistence, they were evicted from Villach and Klagenfurt, which they occupied, and then found themselves blocked in southern Carinthia by the Red Army which promptly ordered the Yugoslav units out of territory designated for Soviet occupation. At the Peace Conference the Russians initially supported the Yugoslav government in their claims for territorial adjustment. This line was later abandoned once the Russians realised that by so doing their own aims of acquiring substantial German assets in Austria would be accepted by the Western powers as a *quid pro quo*.[14]

The Onset of the Cold War

Throughout this period relations between Yugoslavia and the West steadily worsened, in step with the steadily rising Soviet–Western tension. Western diplomats found their ability to discharge their duties in Belgrade heavily circumscribed; reading rooms were closed and all means of exerting a Western presence progressively cut off. The United States' ambassador was not resident in Belgrade for over eighteen months, in protest at the coercion used during the electoral process in 1945. In 1946, a series of incidents involving overflights of Yugoslav airspace by unarmed Western military transport aircraft culminated in August in a major diplomatic incident when two American transport aircraft were shot down by the Yugoslav air force.

In 1945, Yugoslavia entangled itself in the Greek civil war which had first flared up in 1944 in the wake of the German retreat, as communist inspired guerrilla forces fought with royalists against restoration of the pre-war régime. The preservation of a friendly government in Greece was a *sine qua non* of Western strategy and the difficulties experienced by the British forces in destroying communist insurgency were the cause of deep concern in London and Washington as they pondered the then unknowable extent of Soviet involvement and intentions in the region. The renewal of civil war in 1946 led directly to America's effective declaration of Cold War against communism when Truman announced to a closed session of Congress on 12 March 1947 that the United States would do all possible to shore up the pro-Western régimes in Greece and Turkey which bordered the southern flank of the communist bloc. In fact, the Soviet Union acted more as a brake than an accelerator on the activities of the Balkan communist parties. As in the Italo–Yugoslav frontier dispute, Stalin was probably curious to test Western resolve but not to the extent of open conflict. And he understood the significance of Greece to British security interests in the Mediterranean.[15]

Despite the Soviet urgings to caution, the Yugoslav government was not to be easily dissuaded from their interests in the Greek civil war. Revolutionary solidarity with the EAM (National Liberation Front – *Ethnikon apeleftherotikon metopon*) and KKE (Greek Communist Party – *Kommunistikon komma ellados*) combined with lingering ambitions to barter assistance to the guerrillas in return for acquisition of Greek Macedonia should the KKE take power in Athens, were the motivational factors for continued involvement. In 1944, Tito sent his representative in Macedonia, Svetozar Vukmanović-Tempo, to Greece in an effort to bolster the communists. The first uprising, which took place in November 1944, failed, but a year later, a second was planned at a meeting held in Petrich, this time involving both Yugoslav and Bulgarian representatives. The seriousness with which Tito took these plans is reflected in his deployment of Peko Dapčević, one of his most experienced generals, to head a mission briefed to keep the guerrillas supplied with all manner of aid which could be passed easily across the shared Macedonian frontier. Stalin even gave this initiative a cautious blessing in the spring of 1947. This doubtless encouraged the formalisation of these arrangements which occurred at a meeting with the Bulgarians and Albanians, held at Bled in August, when they agreed to 'organise the rear defences of the Greek Democratic Army with artillery, aviation and infantry'.[16] This seemed to be one step nearer when, at the end of 1947, the Greek insurgents announced that a 'provisional government' headed by General Markos Vafiades had been formed in the free mountains of Greece.[17] For the scheme to advance, however, Moscow's approval was required, but by the end of 1947, Stalin's mood appeared to have changed and the Soviet Union seemed determined to restrain its Balkan allies.[18]

The Soviet–Yugoslav Dispute 1948

Historians still debate the exact sequence of events which drove Stalin to consolidate the Soviet Union's grip on its East European satellites. Some argue that this process was intended from the outset and that while the timing of the final phase might have been brought forward by the decision of the Western powers to consolidate the western sphere, it was nonetheless something which the nature of the Soviet régime required it to do. There is also an argument that consolidation of eastern Europe was not an inevitable outcome, and that it was precisely the decision by United States and Britain to implement Marshall Aid in their sphere which provoked the Russians to seek as near total control over the People's Democracies as they could achieve. In any event, and as one element in the imposition of such control, the Soviet Union sponsored establishment of the Communist Information Bureau (Cominform) which held its first conference in Skarleska Poreba, just inside the southern Polish border, in September 1947. This body was to be the co-ordinating body for national communist parties and included not just those from the Soviet Union and eastern Europe, but also those of France and Italy. The headquarters, the communiqué declared, would be in Belgrade.

Tito and his colleagues were deeply flattered by this since it seemed on the surface to confirm their own opinion that Yugoslavia was the Soviet Union's most important ally. However, Stalin's view was probably exactly the opposite. Far from being a trusted sidekick in the increasingly tense struggle between Soviet communism and Western democracy, Yugoslavia, under Tito's leadership, was viewed in Moscow with increasing suspicion as adventurist and ambitious beyond its allotted role in the socialist camp. Tito's provocative stance over the border disputes with Italy and Austria, and his persistent meddling in Greece were notable manifestations of the difficulties the Russians were experiencing in controlling the indigenous communist leaderships in the Balkans. Another aspect of the problem emerged in the context of the reopening by Tito of the possibility of creation of a Balkan Federation. The Yugoslavs raised the idea at the Yalta Conference in February 1945, but met with a muted response from the Russians and a flat rejection from the British who were concerned about the impact of a Bulgarian–Yugoslav federation upon Greek Macedonia. Following the signature of the Bulgarian Peace Treaty in February 1947, however, Stalin appeared to moderate his stance and indicated that he would welcome an advance in this project. Then, following the Skarleska Poreba conference, Tito embarked on a tour of the communist states on Yugoslavia's borders, beginning in November with Bulgaria, then Hungary and Rumania. The impact was seen first in the adaptations to the popular front governments of Bulgaria and Romania which brought them closer to the Yugoslav model, and second in a series of mutually advantageous treaties which created a customs union comprising Albania, Bulgaria, Romania and Yugoslavia. Dimitrov made it clear that the members were even considering including Greece.[19] At the same time, Tito attempted to advance his designs on Albania which since the war had been subjected to a tutelage by Yugoslavia even more overbearing than that of Stalin over Belgrade. At the end of 1947, Tito sent two divisions into Albania on the pretext of defending Albania from Greece, without consulting either Stalin or the Albanian leader, Enver Hoxha first.[20]

The reaction from Moscow was immediate. Stalin abruptly summoned the Yugoslavs and Bulgarians to Moscow and instructed them on 10 February not to take foreign policy initiatives without his agreement. He then attempted to put a cage around the Balkan communists by demanding that they form the Balkan federation at once, but as a mechanism of Soviet control rather than as a vehicle for asserting greater independence. The Bulgarians were immediately quiescent, but Tito had no intention of having his freedom curtailed in this manner. The proposal was rejected by the KPJ's Central Committee on 1 March 1948.[21]

The Cominform – or Stalin – chose the most symbolic of days in the Yugoslav calendar, St Vitus' Day (28 June 1948) for the publication of the Cominform Resolution which brought the dispute to a head, accusing the Yugoslavs of heresy, of slandering the Soviet Union and of constructing a bureaucratic system which left the Party bereft of inner party democracy. Calling upon the 'loyal' elements in Yugoslav communism to bring the leaders to reason or overthrow them, the Resolution indicted Tito, Kardelj, Djilas and Ranković in particular, for 'errors' in domestic policy and for taking an independent line in foreign policy and treating the Soviet Union on the same footing as other foreign countries. On the domestic front, the Yugoslav leadership was told it had failed to follow the ideological teaching with regard to the class struggle in the countryside and to prepare the way for nationalisation of the land or to liquidate the small peasant farmer class, while their hasty and ill-considered legislation had jeopardised the Five Year Plan. Moreover, they had elevated the importance of guerrilla warfare beyond and had failed to maintain the rigid communist control of the popular front.

This Resolution was in fact the climax of a lengthy correspondence between the Soviet and Yugoslav communist party leaderships which had been conducted since the spring.[22] At the root of the problem was the refusal of the Yugoslav communist party to accept the domination of Moscow. Clearly, the dispute had its origins in the war, in the assertiveness of the Partisans as they consolidated their revolution, and perhaps more importantly in the legitimacy they derived from the population in having led the resistance. The Red Army had played a much smaller role in Yugoslavia's liberation than it had elsewhere in the Soviet bloc and the absence of its presence during the state formation had permitted a popularly supported régime to evolve which was proving to be resistant to Moscow's instruction.

The initial reaction was understandably defensive, with an even more rigorous application of Stalinist principles designed to remove the grounds for Cominform criticism. Draconian steps were also taken to ensure that no divisions were allowed to surface to undermine the unity of the state. Several thousand Yugoslavs suspected of pro-Soviet loyalties were arrested. In fact the Partisan struggle had been so effective in binding the régime and people together that the vast majority in government and out of it remained loyal. Just two functionaries were dismissed, the influential Andrija Hebrang, Minister of Light Industry, and Srejan Zujović, Minister of Finance. Hebrang was shot on the Yugoslav border, presumably attempting to escape.[23] By the autumn, however, the régime went onto the offensive. A series of articles appeared in *Borba* which though unsigned, appeared to have been written by Tito himself. The significance of these lay in the fact that they marked a shift away from the toadying of the past three and a half years to a more critical attitude, seeking to underline the orthodoxy of the Yugoslav interpretation of Marxism, while adopting a condescending attitude towards Stalin himself. Henceforth, 'grandpa' was to be referred to simply as *one* of the great leaders of Marxism–Leninism.[24]

DOMESTIC POLITICS, 1949–53

After 1948, this process of justifying Yugoslavia's stance gathered impetus. Yugoslav communist writers, of whom Djilas and Kardelj were at the forefront, began to denounce the Soviet régime as heretical, as having committed the same ideological errors as those for which Leon Trotsky had been pillaried: its faults were the consequence of bureaucratisation and a lack of obeisance to Lenin's doctrine of the withering away of the state. Through nationalisation of industry, the Soviet régime had generated not socialism but state capitalism. The Yugoslavs argued that from this two courses of action were possible: reactionary dictatorship or socialism and the withering of the state. In the Yugoslav reinterpretation, the difference between the Soviet Union and Tito's Yugoslavia resided here. Unlike the Soviet leadership, the Yugoslav leadership was aware of the dangers inherent in the necessity for the state to play a key role during the transition to socialism.[25] The result was a Titoist version of Marxism which in Western political science was later conceptualised as 'national communism'. This concept had no currency within the communist world.

The siege of Yugoslavia by the communist world was at once a constraint and also, in some sense, a liberating force, precisely because it forced the Yugoslav communist leadership to innovate.[26] In 1949, the abstract debate within the Party which sought to redefine Yugoslav socialism against its Soviet counterpart, received a practical application in the sphere of political and economic organisation. In May 1949, the principal organs of local government, the People's Councils, were given control of their budgets and were permitted to hold public meetings to mobilise support for the régime, both locally and at state level. The following year, on 27 June, a new law on the Management of State Economic Associations by Workers Collectives was passed by the Federal Chamber, marking the point at which Yugoslav socialism definitively changed course. The régime concluded that it should reject the policy of collectivisation of agriculture and micromanagement of industry in favour of workers councils and industrial enterprises managed by the workers themselves. This amounted to a partial destalinisation, although the level of tension generated by the hostility of surrounding states gave Tito adequate reason to use Stalinist practices in the form of the security service to sustain control.[27]

In November 1952 the Party held its Sixth Congress in Zagreb. This was to prove a turning point, its objective being to advance the thesis that there could be many ways to communism which should be pursued in accordance with the specific circumstances of each individual country. The Party was told that it existed no longer to administer government but rather to inspire socialism and political action within the new framework of industrialisation and worker's self-management. Moreover, there was to be a reduction in the use of coercive methods with emphasis being placed on persuasion as the strategy for sustaining popular loyalty to the Yugoslav revolution. Milovan Djilas was entrusted with the task of explaining the theoretical justifications for these changes in the context of announcing that the Party's name had been officially changed from the Yugoslav Communist Party to the League of Communists of Yugoslavia (*Savez komunista jugolsavje* – LCY).

In practical terms this change in direction was implemented through an institutional reorganisation. In order to separate the responsibility for micro-management over all aspects of national life from political initiative, a new body was created to act as a People's Front organisation. Called the Socialist Alliance of Working People of Yugoslavia (*Socialistički savez radnog naroda jugoslavije* – SAWPY) it was in effect an umbrella organisation overarching Yugoslavia's social organisations such as trade unions and youth movements which were affiliated to the LCY, and included membership of the LCY itself. Perhaps its most important function, as it developed, was that of recommending candidates for more senior appointments in federal and republican organisations. In practice, since SAWPY was staffed at the highest levels by members of the LCY, it was the operator of the *nomenklatura* system characteristic of communist régimes in which appointments to party posts were made from lists of recommended personnel and principal instrument through which the Party was able to sustain its control over society.

The 1953 Constitution

The revised constitution, adopted on 13 January 1953, codified the changes of the previous three years. Tito was named President of the Federal Republic, a position he would hold until his death in 1980. At the federal level, the Assembly was reconfigured so that the Federal Chamber of undifferentiated Party or Party-approved representatives now absorbed the previous Council of Nationalities, adding seventy representatives from the republic and provincial (Kosovo and the Vojvodina) assemblies to the 212 chosen for every 60,000 voters.

The new Assembly, called the Chamber of Producers, drew over twice as many delegates from industry as from agriculture (135 and 67) in order to emphasise the superior status of the workers councils which accorded with Marxist teaching, as well as to promote the notion of Yugoslav socialist consciousness. Sovereignty was defined as residing with the people, the latter being defined as the unified Yugoslav working class, whose single unified consciousness, (*jugoslovenstvo*[28]), would replace the various nationalisms discredited during the Second World War. The intellectual lineage of this formulation could be traced back to the nineteenth century 'Yugoslav idea' articulated by the Illyrian movement and the notion of the 'three-named people'. Importantly, for reinforcing this collective identity, the republics lost their rights of secession and sovereignty, granted in 1946. The connection between the self-managed institutions with central government was made through the newly created Federal Executive Council which replaced the Council of Ministers. This body, which had no administrative functions, was intended to assist in the reduction of the state structure.[29]

FOREIGN POLICY, 1949–53

The first step was to exploit Yugoslavia's strategic and propaganda value to the Western struggle in the Cold War in order to obtain economic aid and armaments. The Yugoslav case was greatly strengthened when in June 1950, the vulnerability of small, isolated states to aggrandisement by clients of the superpowers was demonstrated when North Korea invaded the South with Soviet backing. Within three months, Kardelj travelled to Washington, to encourage the West to invest in Yugoslav independence through more formal and extensive trade agreements with the Western powers. He asked initially for more extensive loans and grants to cover the food shortages and finance development projects. The Secretary of State, Dean Acheson, warned Kardelj that the Truman Administration was already having difficulty persuading Congress to vote for military aid and that the deeply anti-communist atmosphere of the McCarthy era would make it very difficult for the United States to undertake a major financial aid programme in Yugoslavia. Nevertheless, recognising the value in Cold War terms of sustaining Yugoslavia as a viable and independent if communist state, Acheson advised Kardelj that the United States would help Yugoslavia, albeit on an ad hoc basis. Some $150 million had been channelled to Yugoslavia by August 1951 and the Korean War had created a climate in which military aid too was approved, amounting to some $60 million worth by the end of 1951. Similar appeals were also made in London. Thus began the Western policy of 'keeping Tito afloat', a phrase coined by both American and British diplomats in the period which led the West to underwrite Yugoslav economic development until the end of the 1980s. Just as Belgrade was opportunistically seeking to gain Western support in return for its neutrality in the east–west conflict, so the West, under no illusion about the political nature of this régime, cultivated Yugoslav dependency, hoping to sustain its independence as a thorn in Soviet flesh as well as for strategic advantages in the event of renewed hostilities in Europe. Ultimately this was to have a deleterious impact on the ability of the state to function, but no thought was given to this at the time.[30]

Simultaneously, Tito embarked on a policy of cultivating relations with the non-aligned states. The Korean War was the first occasion when Yugoslavia co-operated with the newly emerging world to co-ordinate a response at the United Nations. In 1950 and 1951, Yugoslavia was a member of the United Nations Security Council in which it presented a united front with India and Egypt in responding to the outbreak and development of the war. This was a logical extension of the friendly relations which Tito sustained with Aung San in Burma where a similar attempt was being made to follow an independent socialist policy under pressure from a large eastern neighbour. Burma was similarly beset by cultural diversity and was seeking to resolve the difficulties by a federal political system.

The break with the Cominform left Yugoslavia isolated militarily. Numerous border incidents occurred, perhaps as many as 4000 in the period 1949–50, but the country itself, with exception of minor civil unrest in Bosnia, was quiet.[31] Assassination was a constant worry for the senior leadership, as was the threat of invasion. In September 1949, both Britain and the United States let it be known that they would regard an attack on Yugoslavia as an action requiring a Western response (the terms of the response were left deliberately vague). In November of that year, they supported Yugoslavia's election to the United Nations Security Council in preference to Czechoslovakia. But while Stalin lived, Yugoslavia could not rule out the possibility of military attack. There is evidence from the Soviet side that war plans were drawn up and that the plan was completed in the summer of 1950 with roles allotted to all of Yugoslavia's east European neighbours. The Korean War arguably saved Yugoslavia from Soviet invasion because the Western response to Stalin's war by proxy in the Far East convinced the Russians that the West had the resolve to resort to force in order to prevent the forcible extension of Soviet influence. Ad hoc aid carried Yugoslavia through its immediate troubles, which largely ended with Stalin's death in March 1953.[32]

THE ECONOMY, 1945–53

The war left the new Yugoslav régime with a major task of reconstruction. Much of the damage was repaired rapidly with aid from the United Nations Relief and Rehabilitation Administration (UNRRA) which was so generous that by the end of 1946, national income had recovered to the level of 1938. Regarding the future, the régime took draconian steps to bring about socialist ownership of agriculture and industry through land reform and nationalisation. These were enshrined in the first Five Year Plan, prepared by Hebrang, the then chairman of the Economic Planning Council. Despite his warnings of caution, Tito rushed to implement the Plan in 1947, by which time he had replaced Hebrang with the more malleable Boris Kidrić.

The task of converting the peasantry into communist collectivity was an immediate problem for the Tito régime. Many of the Partisan fighters, and even some of Tito's inner circle, were drawn from the peasantry and could be expected to be resistant to the notions of giving up the land for which they had fought. Indeed, AVNOJ passed a resolution during the war which promised to undertake radical agrarian reform in order to extend peasant ownership of the land. The resulting Agrarian Reform Law, passed in August 1945, restricted landholdings to a range of 25–45 hectares, thereby facilitating a reallocation of 80 per cent of the country's land to landless peasants and war veterans. The war had so disrupted agricultural production that the provisional government instituted a policy of forced deliveries during 1945 which met with immediate resistance.

The first step towards collectivisation was taken by the enactment of a Basic Law on Co-operatives in July 1946 which imposed on the peasantry the constraints of fixed prices, compulsory deliveries, high taxes, credit restrictions and prohibitions on hired labour unless they joined a co-operative. At first the government did not coerce the peasants to enter the socialist sector, fearing that such policies would alienate the mass of the population, but following the events of 1948, caution was abandoned. The dispute with the Soviet Union spurred the process, owing to the criticism that the KPJ was soft on the peasantry, that it was 'a party of *kulaks*'. The target of the first Five Year Plan (1947–51) was to raise output by 52 per cent above 1939 levels, not least to feed the rapidly expanding army which Tito was assembling in case of need. The collectivisation of agriculture was speeded up so that collective farms, which numbered 1318 at the start of 1949 were 7000 strong by the year's end. Requisitions were increased to unrealistic levels, forcing those who could not meet the targets to buy produce on the black market and then hand it over to meet their quota. Failure could also result in a spell at a concentration camp. Some resorted to the tactic of hoarding their produce and slaughtering their livestock rather than handing their produce over. Consequently, the collectivisation policy led to a drop in production, reinforced by the severe droughts of 1950 and 1952, which forced the régime to resort to Stalinist solutions.

The small urban middle class together with the richer peasantry had been deprived of any savings they had accumulated during the war by the device of the April 1945 currency reform.[33] The wartime policy of expropriating the property of collaborators meant that over 50 per cent of industry was already in state hands by the end of the war. Industrial recovery was initially rapid and in the five years in which the Plan ran one-quarter of Yugoslav national income was reinvested by the state, with the major proportion going to mining, manufacturing and the improvement of communications. However, the economic Plan was deeply flawed not least because of its impossible targets. In keeping with customary Stalinist practice, resources were assessed unrealistically and there was a concentration on heavy industry to the exclusion of all else. In any case, modelling an economy such as Yugoslavia's on that of the Soviet Union was conceptually flawed owing to the differences between the two states as economic entities. Yugoslavia, a small country with an immature administrative structure, was in no sense comparable to a mineral rich state which covered one-sixth of the earth's surface. Further, the economic development of Yugoslavia was dogged by shortcomings in the administrative system which arose as a result of over-hasty creation of a huge bureaucracy, itself an impediment to effective decision-making and leadership. This dogged the economic development of Yugoslavia until its dissolution in 1991.

The Five Year Plan for Yugoslavia's economic development had been drawn up on the assumption that all necessary assistance in the forms of loans, credits, technical assistance and raw materials would be supplied by the Soviet Union. The degree of dependence on the communist world is evident in the fact that nearly 60 per cent of Yugoslavia's trade was with the Soviet bloc, and prior to the rift with Moscow, further expansion of these trade links was planned. The first consequence of the rift was that not only the Soviet Union but its satellites also cut their connections. The Rumanians ceased rail and postal communication initially and Stalin's determination to destroy the Yugoslav régime was brought home to Tito in February 1949 when the socialist countries did not invite Yugoslavia to attend the meeting in Moscow which established the Council for Mutual Economic Assistance (Comecon). When the Yugoslav Government protested its exclusion, the Soviet Union replied that membership would be possible only 'if the Yugoslav Government denounces its hostile policy towards the USSR and the countries of the People's Democracy and if it returns to the former policy of friendship'.[34]

The trade blockade drove the Yugoslav leadership to seek Western economic aid. As early as November 1948 Yugoslavia's diplomats had begun covertly sounding the principal Western powers about the possibility of short-and long-term trade agreements, including considerable credit provision. The Western powers were initially deeply suspicious of these approaches, but their attitude had softened by the summer of 1949 when Tito demonstrated his commitment to ending Yugoslavia's role as *agent provocateur* in Greece, while privately letting it be known that Yugoslavia might now be interested in joining the European Recovery Programme.[35] A succession of bad harvests deepened the economic crisis. Thus began the relationship of financial dependency the West cultivated in Yugoslavia for the duration of the Cold War which enabled its leadership to delay radical reform of the economy until it was too late.

CONCLUSION

Yugoslavia, in its post-war incarnation, can be said to have been Tito's creation, but it was Stalinist in both conception and method. Highly reliant on the instruments of coercion at the outset, the dispute with the Soviet Union ensured that the Yugoslavs reshaped the role of the Party in a Stalinist mould. Tito himself was among the most insistent that the concentration camps should be retained, and only moderated this view after Stalin's death in 1953. In 1945 Tito had declared that Yugoslavia should not be dependent on anyone ever again: the Cominform dispute gave him both motive and justification for making this so by all means at his disposal.[36]

Paradoxically, the very qualities that enabled Tito to seize power and unite Yugoslavia in 1945–46 were those which led rapidly to his quarrel with Stalin in 1948, and subsequently to successful stabilisation of Yugoslavia as a neutral state in Cold War Europe. Stalin's strategy to dislodge Tito was counter-productive. By facing Tito with a choice of losing control of the state or bartering with the West, his instinct for survival drove him to embrace the latter, but in so doing awarded to the West an advantage in strategic terms of a foothold in the communist camp. For Yugoslavia Western aid both sustained the state and provided it with sufficient independence to foster a unique experiment in state-building. But it also created conditions in which Yugoslavia built up dependency on aid which militated against necessary economic reform, permitting chronic economic mismanagement to be disguised until after Tito's death. The dispute in 1948 was no less than the defining moment for post-war Yugoslavia. More than any other event it defined and shaped the state which became the second Yugoslavia, giving it both strength and endurance, but also the flaws which ultimately led to its undoing.

6 Tito's Yugoslavia Consolidated

Stalin's death on 5 March 1953 marked the end of the tension and uncertainty which had characterised the previous five years. Henceforth Yugoslavia's experiment with communism proceeded within a more stable division of Europe. While its international position remained in some sense ambiguous since it had interests in developing and sustaining working relationships with both East and West in the Cold War, its domestic organisation was innovative, dynamic and highly experimental. Above all, Tito's Yugoslavia was, by the regime's own admittance, peculiar to the specific circumstances of Cold War, retarded economic development and multi-ethnicity with which the LCY leadership had to grapple.

The régime assiduously cultivated the perception, widely held among western practitioners and scholars at least until the early 1970s, that there was a direct line of continuity between the post-Cominform state which emerged in the 1950s and the embryonic political system introduced during 'the great liberation struggle' of the Second World War. This fitted the thrust of post-1948 doctrine which maintained that Stalin and not the Yugoslav leadership, was the true deviant from Marxist–Leninist teaching and that this, rather than wilfulness on the part of Tito and his colleagues, was the real cause of the dispute in 1948. As with all myths which gain widespread credibility, it contained more than an element of truth. Nevertheless, the Yugoslav political system which developed after 1948 was the product of a need arising from unanticipated circumstances inherent in the tensions arising from the divisions which ran through Yugoslav society. Titoism, as Yugoslavia's legitimating ideology came to be known in western scholarship, was the consequence and not the cause of the conflict with Stalin and represented the leadership's response to the challenge Stalin imposed on their continued leadership of the Yugoslav communist movement.[1]

The post-Cominform Yugoslav state was built on three pillars. It obtained ideological legitimacy through the pursuit of communist utopia and by reference to Marxist–Leninist dogma as well as to specifically Yugoslav communist constructions concerning the harmony of the

Yugoslav peoples and the equality of all in the wartime liberation struggle. Worker's self-management and the People's Front provided the
structure through which the teleological goal of communist utopia was
to be achieved. Internationally, the régime sought to meet the basic
requirement to sustain its own security and prosperity by a pragmatic
balancing of its relations with both camps in the Cold War, while extending its influence and raising its profile through a policy of co-operation
with the non-aligned states of the post-imperial world.

POLITICS AND SOCIETY, 1953–61

'Yugoslavism'

Mobilisation of the population in support of the revolution was at the
heart of the Tito régime's policy towards cultural issues from the outset.
The need to sustain popular enthusiasm through what could only be a
difficult period of state-building was behind the equivocal policy
adopted towards the multiple religious authorities which still carried
considerable allegiance with the peoples of Yugoslavia. We have already
seen how this inherently atheistic régime used a combination of repression and compromise in seeking to undermine the ability of the religious
leaders to act as a focal point for their communities, while at the
same time avoiding the appearance of systematic persecution of the
ecclesiastical office holders which might result in generating a coherent
opposition to communism. This was not untypical of the practice of the
European communist regimes throughout this period.

The process of attempting to cultivate a common Yugoslav identity
did not really begin until the mid-1950s. The 1948 census revealed that
the numbers identifying themselves as 'Yugoslav' as opposed to an ethnic identity was as low as 5.1 per cent. While this mattered less prior to
the dispute with the Cominform because the Yugoslav régime was
appealing to internationalist values of the communist movement, in particular worker's solidarity across ethnic and national boundaries, once
the Tito régime was required to develop a theory of the specifically
Yugoslav road to communism, it naturally required that this Yugoslav
identity be given some substance. Accordingly, the régime launched a
campaign to promote the idea of 'integral Yugoslavism' (*Jugosloventsvo*) as
a common culture. The foundations for this were provided by the

Partisan philosophy of 'brotherhood and unity' which conveniently bridged the notion of the particularist identities derived from ethnic and national loyalties with a supranational Yugoslav identity into which the separate national cultures would eventually merge.

The LCY formally adopted this objective as part of the LCY programme at the seventh Party Congress in 1958. However, the problems which this would generate were already evident. Following adoption of the 1953 constitution, the régime had attempted succeeded in obtaining agreement on the standardisation of Serbo–Croat as a common literary language, a development formalised in the Novi Sad Agreement of 1954. With this accomplished the federal government could move towards development of a common educational curriculum which would have a Yugoslav emphasis particularly in the teaching of language, literature and history. Here lay the heart of the problem. Standardisation was a popular idea among representatives from Bosnia-Hercegovina, Macedonia and Montenegro, but it met with unrelenting opposition from the Croats and Slovenes who were convinced that Yugoslavism directed from the federal government in Belgrade (the capital of Serbia) would lead ultimately to effective Serbianisation. Despite the successful creation of all-Yugoslav institutions across the major professions, the field of education, the régime was never successful in establishing either Yugoslav educational norms or even a federal ministry to govern the process. Education, the most powerful element in state-building in multi-ethnic communities, was never fully co-opted to the service of the Yugoslav idea.[2]

Dissent and Repression

No sooner than the 1953 constitution had been formally adopted than dissent began to emerge from within the LCY. The manner in which Tito responded said much about the nature of the régime, its limitations and its agenda. During the summer of 1953, Tito summoned the LCY Central Committee to the communist élite's resort island of Brioni. Here, his favourite retreat, Tito presided over a series of meetings intended to analyse the performance of the party since the seminal sixth Congress. What emerged was a further twist in the internal ideological debate which by January 1954 resulted in the expulsion of two of Tito's closest wartime collaborators from the Party and defined the limits of the régime's toleration of criticism both within and without.

The personality at the centre of this debate was Milovan Djilas. Although he had been a leading figure in the development of the theory behind Yugoslavia's separate road, he was soon disillusioned with what was being created. Among his objections was the growing bureaucratisation of the LCY and the tendency of the Party élite to accrue special privileges. Heedless of the consequences, either personal or political, Djilas developed his thesis in a series of articles published in the party organ, *Borba*, over the autumn of 1953 which questioned the very foundations of the régime. He had three main themes. First, he argued that self-management could only function if the LCY loosened its grip on all areas of the state. The state had to permit the emergence of an opposition, that is, a return in effect to a multiparty democracy and the end of the communist party's monopoly of power. Djilas argued that the break with Stalin had not been accompanied by a break with Stalinism, a fact which was manifest in the irregular judicial procedures which still permitted a security service which could practice arbitrary arrest and detention on merely the suspicion of harbouring pro-Soviet tendencies. Third, Djilas was in general deeply critical of the communist leadership, especially its practice of acquiring privileges – special shops, good housing, vacation retreats – which were all at odds with the socialist ideals they preached and in some instances were outright abuses of power. When he delivered a caustic attack on the social behaviour and luxurious living of his colleagues and their wives, the outrage among the Party élite was complete.[3]

Tito, by now reportedly 'very angry', placed a ban on any further publications and summoned the Central Committee to his retreat on Brioni on 16–17 January 1954. Djilas had always enjoyed great popularity, particularly amongst the intellectuals, the youth and the professional classes. These writings had substantially increased his following and generated commensurate alarm among the more orthodox of his Party colleagues who saw in his work a threat to the very existence of the organisation on which they all depended for their livelihood. Whatever the leadership may have thought of his theoretical arguments, the personal attack on their behaviour was sufficient for them to heap vitriole on him in return, accusing him of every misdemeanour ranging from reactionary deviationism to the more colourful allusion of political pornography. Condemned and isolated from all bar Dedijer, who had hesitantly defended him, Djilas recanted, resigned from the Presidency of the Assembly and some months later, from membership of the Party itself.

Dedijer was similarly ostracised, although in the comparatively liberal climate of the early 1950s, both remained at liberty. However, neither were able to sustain a silence and by the end of 1954, had sprung into the limelight again, this time through interviews published in the *New York Times*. In January 1955 they were tried *in camera* for 'hostile propaganda' and received suspended prison sentences, eighteen months for Djilas and six for Dedijer.[4]

The Djilas affair demonstrated the limits of the Tito's tolerance for reform. During the early 1950s the Yugoslav leadership attempted to ease the pressure on Yugoslav society, attempting to persuade the Yugoslav peoples to accept the communist party's leadership of society, rather than bullying it through the security service coercion. This is the period too, in which Tito as founding father of the Yugoslav state was elevated, or perhaps elevated himself, into the role of cult figure. Accruing for himself the trappings of power, expressed in a growing number of hunting lodges and summer retreats, in the practice of bestowing lavish hospitality on foreign dignitaries, and in the active cultivation of the image and persona of an international statesman, Tito had by the mid-1950s become the very personification of the post-war Yugoslav republic. Perceived by both leadership and people as being above the political struggle, he functioned as the system's supreme arbiter, the one person with authority to force through change or constrain the overzealous would-be liberalisers. At one and the same time, he was both the driving force behind the state's development, and the factor which stultified the growth of a political structure that could function in his absence.

Reform within Yugoslavia's Soviet bloc neighbours had an impact on this process. Under the post-Stalin leadership, the Soviet communist party took a step away from the arbitrary Stalinist practices which had become institutionalised in an oppressive security apparatus. The impact of this partial de-Stalinisation proved unsettling throughout the region, and resulted in a swift rise of pressure for even greater reform not unlike those in evidence in Yugoslavia during the Djilas affair. For Yugoslav domestic politics, the consequence of these disturbances was a resort once more to harsh justice, epitomised in the sentencing of Djilas in November 1956 to three years hard labour, this time without any suspension. Concessions made during the early 1950s in order to gain popular support in the face of external threat and internal economic difficulties, as well as to gain the support of the West, now began to seem dangerous. The tenth anniversary of the founding of the security police was celebrated in May 1954 with emphasis and over the following two years, nearly 2.2 million were imprisoned without trial.[5]

The Djilas affair was still dominating Party debate at the seventh party congress held in Ljubljana in April 1958. Before going into prison, Djilas had sent abroad the manuscript of his book, *The New Class*, which was the first systematic denunciation of the Stalinist régimes and of their apparatus by one who had reached the top. On publication, his sentence was increased to ten years.[6] Bitter at his erstwhile comrade's betrayal of all that had been created, Tito denounced him in brutal terms at the Party congress as 'the traitor and renegade, who spat at the finest achievements of the revolution'. The congress was called to adopt the new party programme which reaffirmed the leading role of the LCY in society and in directing the task of pursuing the socialist revolution. Western influences were condemned, and a reminder issued that individual freedom was permitted only so long as it served that goal. Domestically, Tito reaffirmed the communist party's monopoly of power. Internationally, however, his vision was less orthodox, since it suited Yugoslav ideological needs to promote an ideal of international socialism as polycentric or multifarious where communist parties were as equals with no one party exercising tutelage over the others.

Beneath this façade of control and direction over the Yugoslav experiment the institutions of the state were not developing as envisaged in the constitutional arrangements. Far from achieving the promised withering away of the state, which had provided the theoretical logic of worker's self-management, the new institutions created a duplication of administrative effort. The Federal Executive Council (FEC) was supposed to initiate and enforce policy decisions only, with the task of administering them being allocated to the ministries. In practice, however the distinction became very blurred, in keeping with the functioning of communist systems throughout the region, because the heads of the most important ministries also became ex-officio members of the FEC or were appointed from within its ranks. This bureaucratisation was inefficient and cumbersome, but was accompanied by a more insidious development still. The most damaging feature was the disregard of both the FEC and the ministries for sustaining an ethnic balance in appointing their staffs. While Serbian predominance in the FEC was only briefly evident at the end of the 1950s, the pattern of a disproportionately small Croatian fraction at the top and a heavily Serb and Montenegrin staff was established as early as 1953 and persisted with corrosive effect on the collective identity.[7]

FOREIGN RELATIONS, 1953–61

Following Stalin's death several themes can be discerned in Yugoslav foreign policy. At the centre was a balancing act which sought to keep Yugoslavia on friendly terms with the West. During this period western economic aid, primarily from American sources, provided a safety net for the fragile Yugoslav economy and kept Tito afloat during the most critical period of Yugoslavia's international isolation. This measure of independence gave Tito the strength to handle the Soviet Union's post-Stalin overtures of rapprochement with a judicious coolness which facilitated a resumption of relations without any danger of re-absorption of Yugoslavia by the Soviet sphere. Alongside this, Tito sought to establish himself in the role of international statesman, a function as much of the needs of his own personality as of Yugoslavia's requirement to assert itself abroad. To this end the emergence of growing numbers of newly independent states as a result of post-war European decolonisation provided Tito with a great opportunity.

Until 1956, the western powers conducted a joint policy in Yugoslavia based on an Anglo-French-American tripartite aid programme which had operated there from 1951 onwards with the objective of associating Yugoslavia more effectively with the Western defence system. British and French economic aid came to an end in 1955 by which time the residual problems from the peace settlements of Yugoslavia's neighbours had been resolved. Relations with Italy were normalised after the signature of the London Agreement on 5 October 1954 which formalised the *de facto* partition of Venezia Giulia.[8] Signature of the Austrian Peace Treaty the following year facilitated a similar improvement in Belgrade's relations to Vienna, not least because Austria's neutrality placed it in the non-aligned camp.

To the south, Yugoslavia sought to reassert itself as leader of a Balkan Alliance and Western bulwark in the region by signing a security pact with Greece and Turkey in 1953 which brought increased trade, cultural exchanges and military discussions, and established Yugoslavia in the role of Western bulwark in the Balkans. Inclusion of Greece and Turkey in NATO in 1951 encouraged the West to promote the occidentation of Yugoslav foreign policy and even to consider its integration in the western defence arrangements, which would link NATO's southern flank with its forces in western Europe. This notion never achieved anything approaching reality, however. At the heart of Tito's foreign policy was the notion of sustaining a balance in Yugoslavia's relations with both

East and West, achieving ideological sustenance from a relationship with the communist movement as a whole, while benefiting from Western economic aid and (if need be) military support. When the Balkan Alliance was superceded in 1956 by a bilateral agreement between the Greeks and the Turks, Tito was already deeply engaged in promoting Yugoslavia's interests elsewhere.

Soviet–Yugoslav Rapprochement

The most important factor in Yugoslavia's foreign policy in this period was the drive on the part of the post-Stalin Soviet leadership to 'normalise' relations with Belgrade. In the summer of 1953, Khrushchev, then only tentatively in control of the Soviet Communist Party, hesitantly suggested that the two states exchange ambassadors. The Yugoslavs responded cautiously, anxious not to weaken their bargaining position by revealing how welcome would be a resolution of the schism and an end to the political and economic pressure which had been applied since 1948. Since the rift, Yugoslavia's defence expenditure had trebled, while the dependency on loans from the West was already giving cause for concern. Moreover, one of the ramifications of the Djilas affair and the disturbances which had accompanied it, was the vulnerability of the Yugoslav experiment with communism so long as the estrangement from the Soviet bloc persisted. Indeed, the repression of Djilas was linked with the Soviet overtures since conservative elements within the Soviet leadership, loyal to Stalin's memory, were ready to seize on evidence of dissent in the Yugoslav ranks as reason to veto any reopening of relations with Belgrade.

The formal rapprochement began when Khrushchev visited Yugoslavia at the end of May 1955. No sooner than he had arrived in Belgrade airport, complete with an entourage which included the prime minister, Nikolai Bulganin as well as the foreign trade minister, Anastasii Mikoyan, than Khrushchev as party secretary, made a speech heaping all blame for the breakdown in Yugoslav–Soviet relations on his erstwhile opponents (by which he meant Stalin) whom he vilified in language which hitherto had been employed by the Cominform to describe Tito himself. Khrushchev stopped short of condemning the original Cominform communiqué expelling Yugoslavia for ideological heresy, and concentrated instead on exonerating the Yugoslav leaders for the charges of fascism and espionage which had been heaped on them during the 1949–53 period.[9]

Tito reciprocated, but in a circumspect manner, being careful to defend his own position by reminding the Russians of Stalin's failure to support him in Greece and of the perfidy of the so-called Anglo-Soviet Percentages Agreement of October 1944.[10] An ambiguous declaration, signed at the end of the talks on 2 June, affirmed mutual respect and non-interference in each others affairs, and the resumption of normal relations at the diplomatic level, but specifically avoided any mention of inter-party relations. This followed, however, twelve months later, during Tito's reciprocal visit to Moscow. In April 1956, Khrushchev had dissolved the Cominform and this act, on top of the debunking of Stalin which occurred at the CPSU's twentieth Party Congress in February, made the re-establishment of relations between the two communist parties a possibility. The prodigal son had returned and was duly feasted and glorified as no other visitor to the Soviet Union since the war.[11]

The depth of this normalisation process was abruptly tested by the crises within the Soviet bloc arising from the reform movements in Poland and Hungary. To some extent the Soviet–Yugoslav rapprochement was to blame for the disturbances of 1956. Stalin's last round of purges which had been justified by the need to stamp out 'Titoist deviationism', and for many of the satellites, anti-Titosim was a major factor in régime legitimation. To be told that this was all a mistake was deeply unsettling. Khrushchev visited Tito in Brioni in September and then the two holidayed together in Yalta and on both occasions the Soviet leader tried to impress upon Tito the dangers inherent in the forces released by the twentieth Party Congress which threatened to overwhelm the Party leadership throughout the bloc. Initially Tito supported the moderate reform measures in both countries, but his attitude altered when it appeared that Hungary would proceed to a multiparty system and even leave the Warsaw Pact. On 12 November, after Soviet military intervention, Tito gave an equivocal speech at Pula in which he blamed the original causes of the Hungarian revolt on Stalinist policies but strongly defended the Soviet decision to crush the movement.

The result was another cooling of Soviet–Yugoslav relations, as the Russians suspended the agreement on loans. But the advantages of keeping the lines of communication open outweighed even ideological considerations and the difficulties were smoothed over at a special meeting in Bucharest.[12] Khrushchev was to be enraged by Tito once again a few months later when the latter attended the 1957 conference of world communist parties in Moscow but refused to sign the conference resolutions. Tito remained unprepared to modify Yugoslavia's road to socialism in order to meet criticisms from foreign communists. He explained to Khrushchev that since it was Yugoslavia's policy to avoid alignment with either bloc, it was impossible to sign the resolutions which affirmed the loyalty of all to the communist world. Relations with the bloc deteriorated again as a result of the LCY's new party programme adopted at the seventh party congress at Ljubljana.

During this period, the rise of China as a major power also became a factor in Yugoslav relations with the Soviet bloc. In 1958 the Chinese Communist Party declared Yugoslavia to be not just heretical but the primary cause of the trouble within the communist world. Already, however, there were signs of China's own rift with Moscow which came to the fore as a factor in international politics in the early 1960s. The Sino-Soviet rift, combined with the Albanian government's decision to align with Beijing rather than Moscow, ultimately worked to Tito's advantage since it created the very condition of polycentrism which Tito lauded at Ljubljana and which was necessary to the survival of the Yugoslav road to socialism as defined by Yugoslav ideologues.[13]

Non-alignment

The third strand of Tito's foreign policy was the relationship with the uncommitted states of the 'third world' then emerging from the imperial yoke. The notion of non-alignment as a modus operandi for Yugoslavia in Cold War Europe had become current as part of the ideological baggage developed in the wake of the Cominform dispute. Fortuitously, Yugoslavia's isolation had driven Tito to seek allies at the United Nations, his only recourse, at a time when decolonisation was creating newly independent states in Africa and Asia which required both ideas and material support in the process of economic and social development. Self-assertion in international affairs through definition of their particular interests as separate from those of the Cold War protagonists was the foreign policy expression of these post-imperial third world nationalisms. Membership of the Security Council during 1950 and 1951, and election to the UN's Economic and Social Council in 1952 gave Tito the impetus to pursue such diplomatic contacts in the context of disbursement of development aid to the newly emerging world.

The real awakening in Tito's mind of the potential for Yugoslavia to play a high profile role in international politics, occurred as a result of the Conference of Afro-Asian nations, held at Bandung in April 1955.

Although Yugoslavia was not invited to Bandung, Tito recognised an opportunity to elevate Yugoslavia's standing – and coincidentally his own – through promotion of the community of interest between the Yugoslav peoples and the growing number of newly independent states seeking non-alignment or neutrality in Cold War conflict. Both India and Burma greeted Tito with pomp and circumstance during the spring of 1955 and Tito returned the complement by endorsing the *Panch Sila*, the Five Principles of Peaceful Coexistence, which Nehru and Chou En-lai pronounced in New Delhi in June 1954. These contacts began to extend in this period to include Egypt and Indonesia and a co-ordinated policy between the leading non-aligned states resulted from Tito's meeting with Nehru and Nasser in 1956. From these exchanges, the idea of a summit conference of the Non-aligned movement emerged which took place in Belgrade in September 1961. Yugoslavia was the only European member amongst the fifty-one nations represented, but Tito's prestige ensured that he emerged swathed in the mantel of 'Father of the Non-Aligned Movement'.[14]

THE ECONOMY, 1953–62

The principal economic objective in this period was rapid industrialisation. During the early 1950s, planning was conducted on an annual basis because the uncertainties created by Yugoslavia's ambiguous international status made any other approach impractical. Despite the move towards worker self-management, the state retained control of the exchange rate and monetary system, foreign trade, and investment banking, thereby retaining the power to direct the economy. By 1953, the practices of self-management were sufficiently well established for a second Five Year Plan to be prepared. Here the Yugoslavs were once again the innovators in so far as they adopted a different process to that used under the Soviet type economic systems. The 1953 plan was produced after a lengthy process of consultation in which enterprises, communes, districts and republics all proposed targets in the light of their assessment of their particular needs and possibilities. These were then co-ordinated by the Federal Planning Institute in line with national economic strategy. The plan was then debated in the Assembly and the necessary legislation passed, while overall initiative was left to enterprises in co-operation with communal and republican agencies.

Initially, this management structure appeared to be successful. Yugoslavia had a higher sustained rate of growth during the 1950s in terms of industrial output than most other countries, recording annual growth of 12.56 per cent with average economic growth at 8.5 per cent. The result was completion of the second plan a year early. These figures are deceptive, however. The rapid growth rate was measured from a very low starting point and concealed significant weaknesses. In fact, from the outset, the structure of self-management did not serve economic and industrial enterprises equally, and for those which did not respond well, effective management was hindered by the local party apparatus which remained in a dominant position.[15]

The economy which developed from the reforms of the early 1950s was riven by internal contradictions. As we have seen the devolution of authority was only partial with real power to direct being retained at federal level. Moreover at local level the pre-eminence given to the Party apparatus, was also a significant hindrance to effective workers' control. Often the managers were political appointees who had been given jobs because of their wartime service. Frequently, they were poorly educated, and by the early 1960s, they were presiding over a youthful workforce who were better educated and consequently frustrated by the conservatism of their bosses. Added to this were problems which arose as a result of the insistence on wage equalisation which had the effect of disincentivising skilled workers while reinforcing the grip of the managers on real power. Unlike their Soviet counterparts, the management of the large industrial enterprises which sprang up in this period, had the right to dismiss workers. In the early 1960s they responded to problems by doing just that, resulting in unemployment in the social sector of 7.3 per cent by 1962, which contributed to a deepening sense of social dissatisfaction and an increasingly vocal demand for further reform.

Regarding foreign trade, the seeds of Yugoslavia's economic crisis were being sown through the populations' growing dependence on consumer goods well above the standards experienced by their east European neighbours. The West fed these appetites, seeking to detach the Yugoslavs once and for all from the Soviet bloc. This suited the régime, at least in the short term, because it pacified the populace. But as early as the mid-1950s, a huge balance of trade deficit was being built up as imports greatly outstripped exports, effectively a repetition of the pattern of the interwar years. One of the primary factors was the burgeoning trade with the Federal Republic of Germany, and even more so with Italy following the settlement of the Trieste dispute in 1954, which encouraged this consumerism which gave the Yugoslavs a collective sense of progress and well-being. This was fine until the imbalances in the economy required a squeeze on spending, at which point the readiness of the Yugoslavs to reach for nationalist resentments, made genuine and far-reaching reform a hazardous business.

The crisis emerged in the early 1960s. Despite the success of the 1957 Plan which was completed a year ahead of schedule, the Yugoslav government had been obliged to turn once again to the United States in 1960 for economic assistance, receiving $275 million in short-term credits by the end of the year. In 1961 a new Five Year Plan was implemented which marked the beginning of a series of reforms intended to bring market pressures to bear on industrial enterprises without altering the socialist management structure. The government also devalued the dinar and cut tariffs but the effect was to exert inflationary pressures. Between 1959–62 the cost of living jumped by 30 per cent. The next move at federal level was to slow the market mechanism, retreating from liberal foreign trade. Consequently, production fell for 1961–62, and the Five Year Plan had to be abandoned.[16]

Poor economic performance could be measured in regional terms. By the early 1960s the same patterns that had characterised the interwar period, in which the north was industrialised and relatively prosperous and the south predominantly rural and poor, had been recreated, with the gap between them widening progressively. In 1950 Slovenia's per capita income was three times that of Kosovo, the poorest region; by 1960 the differential was five times. The LCY programme had set out to counter these inequalities by developing the backward regions through a redistribution of wealth via a General Investment Fund. Accordingly, 'political factories' were built to assuage perceptions of disadvantage and discrimination, but these enterprises were frequently founded on a weak economic base and were rarely profitable. This poor grasp of strategic planning and overemphasis on short-term solutions to much deeper social problems had the opposite effect to that intended. Far from softening inter-republican and inter-ethnic jealousies, the poor economic returns which resulted merely encouraged those who were doing the giving to believe that their generosity was being abused, while those on the receiving end concluded that that they were not being sufficiently subsidised. It was only a matter of time before these perceptions fused with the republican and local political organisations to generate hostility defined on ethno-national lines.[17]

CONCLUSION

'Titoism' reached its apogee in the early 1960s, just at the point when the contradictions built into the economy by workers self-management were beginning to emerge in the guise of inflation, unemployment and social malaise. Outwardly, Yugoslavia had weathered a series of domestic and international difficulties and had taken its place among an increasingly polycentric community of communist states. Eastward looking politically, but westward looking economically, Yugoslavia seemed to outside observers to be poised to capitalise on its rising international status among the non-aligned.

The reality, however, was a system which was already creating the framework in which nationalist interests could find renewed expression while simultaneously laying the foundations for catastrophic economic failure which would in itself call the régime's legitimacy to govern into question. Tito, as a convinced Marxist and successful revolutionary, understood the connection between economic prosperity and popular discontent, but the combination of the need to balance the republics so as to assuage latent nationalism with the requirement to operate within a rigid ideological framework prevented the leadership from permitting Yugoslavia to evolve beyond the contradictions which its self-managed socialism had created. While the major western powers were prepared to aid Yugoslavia, simultaneously turning a blind eye to its economic mismanagement, there was little incentive to search for the roots of the problem and in view of the potential for social instability, every reason to avoid such an exploration.

7 Market Socialism and the Resurgence of Nationalism

Following his personal triumph at the Belgrade Conference of the non-aligned states in September 1961, Tito spent the early months of 1962 on an extensive tour of Africa, particularly the Mediterranean states on which Yugoslav foreign policy would focus increasingly as the decade progressed. On his return to Yugoslavia he was presented with an economic crisis that could no longer be ignored.

Tito was already seventy-one years of age and was naturally increasingly resistant to the arguments of those who wanted to innovate. In 1961, the brief liberalisation of the economy had proven alarming and he had called an abrupt halt, probably recognising that if he permitted these reforms to run their course, the economy would be swept into the Western economic system, destroying the foundations of the LCY's rationale for existence. This then, was the heart of the dilemma facing Yugoslavia for the remainder of Tito's life. The logic of liberalisation of the economy required that the Party abdicate from its monopoly of political power and abandon therefore the pursuit of the goals which its doctrine taught were an inevitable outcome of the forces of progress. For reasons of theoretical consistency, and perhaps even more for the preservation of vested interest and personal prestige, protection of the Party took precedence over the requirement for economic reform.

Underneath the debate, which ensued between would-be liberalisers and old-fashioned communist centralisers, several further problems were present. The first concerned the issue of leadership regeneration. The identification of the régime in the person of Tito had been a vital element in establishing the communist revolution in Yugoslavia and provided a guarantee of the unity of Party and state. But as time went by this factor became an insurmountable barrier to effective reform. By the 1960s, a new generation of party apparatchiks had emerged for whom the path to the top was blocked by the presence of a seemingly immovable, and immortal leadership. Increasingly debate within the party became focussed around groups and individuals competing for political favour from the leadership while developing their own agendas. This in turn was linked with the second problem, the re-emergence of sectarian divisions which the communist state had covered up but not resolved. These tensions began to surface once again, becoming conjoined with the issues surrounding both economic reform and leadership renewal.

MARKET SOCIALISM

In May 1962, Tito explained during a visit to Split that the LCY must now take the lead in integrating the economy into a single unit, and through this process to take the development of a uniform socialist Yugoslav culture one stage further. Since the late 1950s, the question of economic reform had been debated frequently within the party and by 1962 had sharpened pre-existing lines of division.[1]

Broadly, two schools of thought existed. One group, commonly referred to as 'conservative communists', thought that the progressive weakening of the LCY's influence was a bad thing in the long run and that what was required was much greater direction from above. The objective of reform, in their view, was to achieve the Leninist goal of rapid capital accumulation which could only be accompanied by planning at the centre and a drastic reduction in emphasis on market forces and profit-making. What concerned the 'conservatives' most was not so much the economic consequences of greater liberalisation, but the impact this would have in political terms on the cohesion and authority of the Party.[2] In their view, the current direction of reform was taking the economy down a road which would ultimately endanger the existence of the Party itself, and therefore their own source of power. The principal advocates of this approach were drawn from Serbia and Montenegro and initially, at least, enjoyed support from Macedonia and elements within Bosnia-Hercegovina.[3]

The alternative viewpoint was based on the assumption that self-management and the parallel decentralisation of political power was the correct approach to Yugoslavia's economic problems. This group resented what they saw as the persistence of so much central administrative control as the principal barrier to self-management's effectiveness. In particular, they objected to the resultant negation of all incentives which, they argued, could lead only to stagnation and chaos. These would-be liberalisers argued for more devolution of power to enterprises and a further reduction in federal and local taxation.[4] The principal advocates of this view were drawn, perhaps not surprisingly, from the prosperous northern republics of Croatia and Slovenia which enjoyed more contact with the prosperous states of central and western Europe. Less predictably they were supported in this, as the debate developed, by Bosnia-Hercegovina, Macedonia and the autonomous provinces of Kosmet and Vojvodina. The explanation for this alignment resides in political rather than economic considerations and more especially the fear of Serbianisation, especially in Macedonia, on which the Croats in particular played to effect.[5]

The debate began, secretly at first, within the Yugoslav association of economists and resulted in preparation of two studies of the Yugoslav economy, after which the issues were discussed more publicly. Eventually, at the end of 1964, Tito and Kardelj were won over to the reformers' point of view. By distinguishing between a reduction in state interference – or *de-étatization* – as distinct from further decentralisation and de-politicisation – a greater dissipation of central executive authority, the reformers won the argument because *de-étatization* fitted in with the Marxist concept of the withering away of the state. This had been a constant theme in Tito's speeches since the early 1950s, not least because it was at the heart of the theoretical feud with the Soviet leadership. Once Tito was convinced that this course could be justified in ideological terms, the matter was decided.

The 1963 Constitution

A fresh Constitution was adopted in 1963 which was designed to support reform of the economy. For the first time, the powers of the federal government were reduced, and even the LCY's central hierarchy lost some measure of authority to the advantage of the republics and regions. The right of republican secession was restored, although this could only be invoked if all republics agreed; a new constitutional court could hear appeals made by the republics against federal laws that infringed on their rights. This set in train a trend which favoured the rise of regional party élites which because the republics were established in 1946 on ethnic and historic lines, created a framework in which national particularisms could become entrenched within the republican party apparatus. The winners, in republican terms, from this round of constitutional tinkering, were the Muslims who were recognised for the first time as a separate nation, at least in so far as the new constitution spoke of Bosnia as a republic inhabited by 'Serbs, Moslems and Croats allied in the past by a common life'. Excluded from this were the Muslims of the Sanjak, the former Ottoman region divided between Serbia and Montenegro.[6]

At the eighth Congress of the LCY held in Belgrade in December 1964, this process was carried a stage further. Henceforth, all republics and regions were directed to convene their own party conferences immediately before the all-party meeting in order to prepare their respective positions on the policy issues of the day. From this moment onwards, Yugoslavia was embarked on a course towards confederalisation of the League. Tito could still assert his authority over any combination of republican leaders and therefore he remained the supreme arbiter of the Yugoslav state, and at least until 1967 republican or ethnic politics remained difficult owing to Yugoslavia's legislative framework. Nevertheless these changes were seminal since they set in motion a shift in emphasis away from the institutions and values which had provided Yugoslavia with unity since the Second World War. The result was a diminution of the importance of 'Yugoslavism' as a defining identity, and thereby tacitly acknowledged the failure of the post-war experiment to build a state which was greater than the sum of its parts. Increasingly, the development of the new 'socialist' self-management with its orientation towards the Western style of market economy and its organisational structure which was increasingly centred on republican and local interests, took on an identity which was defined broadly along ethnic lines. [7]

The year 1965 began with the news that the economic upsurge of 1963–64 seemed to be slipping out of control. The rate of inflation for 1964 jumped by 10 per cent, the largest yet in a single year, and the import surplus nearly doubled. Liberalisation of the banking system was a necessary prerequisite to economic reform. In July 1965 the Federal Assembly introduced a package which provided the legislative framework in which 'market socialism' was to operate. Price controls were abolished over a wide range of goods. Export subsidies were withdrawn and import duties halved. Enterprises were allowed to deal directly with trading partners abroad, but their export earnings determined their allocation of foreign currency. Liberalisation of foreign trade was accompanied by the devaluation of the dinar by 70 per cent and the introduction of a new 'heavy' dinar with a face value of one-hundredth of the old dinar. Since the reforms represented a move towards a market economy, there was no difficulty in obtaining credits from the International Monetary Fund and western banks, particularly those of Britain, France, Italy and the United States, to cushion the shock. Immediately there was a steep rise in the prices of food, clothing, rents and fuel. Although this was partly offset by reductions in personal taxes and social security contributions, the workers councils voted for higher wages in order to fund the rising cost of living.

Meanwhile, Yugoslavia was effectively opened up to the West. Tourism, which had always been a good earner for the economy, became once again a major industry. At the same time the travel restrictions which had been placed on Yugoslav citizens since the war, were lifted in 1963, promoting migration of labour on a grand scale. By the end of the decade, one-sixth of the adult workforce, was employed outside the country. But while the influx of hard currency had a beneficial effect on the economy, its impact on society was more complicated. Both the tourists who holidayed in the country, and Yugoslav workers returning from abroad, brought with them new ideas and raised expectations, and were no longer so willing to accept unquestioningly the tutelage of the Party.[8]

The links which Yugoslavia generated with the West as a consequence of its greater openness, were strengthened further in 1967 by enactment of legislation which enabled private foreign investors to enter into partnership with Yugoslav enterprises. Foreign firms were allowed to invest up to 49 per cent of the capital in joint enterprises and to repatriate their profits. The West Germans, in particular, took early advantage of this opportunity. Meanwhile, licensing and marketing agreements entered into by Yugoslav firms, further encouraged this dependence on foreign partners.

Trade with the Soviet bloc, which recovered rapidly in the late 1950s, remained on a relatively small scale and was conducted on a clearing basis with a year by year balancing of exports and imports. When in 1964 Yugoslavia was granted associate status of Comecon, its trade with that group amounted to less than one quarter of the total, whilst that with OECD countries amounted to almost 60 per cent. During this period the Yugoslav government believed that its ties with the non-aligned world would lead to an increase in trade links with the newly emerging world. In 1965 trade with the non-aligned countries amounted to 15 per cent and Yugoslav construction firms were involved in a series of projects in Africa and Asia. In 1967, the lowering of tariffs between India, Egypt and Yugoslavia was intended to form the basis of a closer economic association among the three countries, but the facts of political and economic geography ensured that it ultimately had little significance.[9]

The Limits of Toleration

The debate about economic reform was accompanied by a similar discussion about society and culture. Broadly, 1960s leadership, so fêted in Western Europe, pervaded the East also and was tolerated by the régime for a while. In March 1962, an amnesty was announced for political crimes committed before 1952, which was extended also to some 150,000 émigrés, an event which attracted great publicity in the West and served to reinforce the impression from outside that Yugoslavia was indeed becoming a more confident and open society. Underneath this façade, however, the Yugoslav state remained secretive, coerced and authoritarian in both outlook and practice.

Throughout the debates of the early 1960s, the most vocal opponent of market reform was Alexander Ranković, Vice President of Yugoslavia since 1963 and widely regarded in this period as Tito's natural successor. Responsible both for the policy of the LCY cadres and for running the UDBA, Ranković had the support of Serb nationalists who instinctively favoured greater centralisation of power over the impersonal market forces which many of the 'liberal' economists favoured. Ranković was a typical party man – an apparatchik – more interested in the retention of power than in revolutionary purpose. He regarded the liberalising tendencies as a threat to the power of the party and probably genuinely feared that polycentrism within the wider communist movement presaged a disintegration of the entire system. He was not alone. Even Tito had significant doubts about weakening party discipline, and in this atmosphere of debate and uncertainty, Ranković used his access to the levers of power to attempt to deter reform through political pressure behind the scenes. Once the reformers had won the internal party battle, Ranković was a target of those who came to perceive him as a negative influence on Tito whose power should be curbed.

It was the autonomous region of Kosovo-Metohija or Kosmet, which provided the scene for Ranković's downfall. Early in 1966, the central government decided to institute a secret investigation into complaints against the activities of UDBA, especially the treatment of Albanians who had long been the focus of police brutality in the region. The most notable post-war incident occurred in 1956 when UDBA had undertaken to search for and confiscate weapons held by the Albanian population. The resistance that ensued led to the death of a number of Albanians before an estimated nine thousand weapons were retrieved.[10] The other aspect to the problem concerned Serbian dominance of most of the key positions in local government and administration, and most importantly had total dominance of the police force and security apparatus, despite the fact that they constituted only 23 per cent of the population. Moreover, Kosmet enjoyed considerably less autonomy than the other autonomous province of Vojvodina. Before 1966, for example, the only education that Albanians were entitled to in their mother tongue was primary schooling. All this reflected badly on a régime which prided itself in racial harmony and social benevolence.[11]

The central government's investigations, which centred on the activities of the Serbian dominated UDBA, were achieved by the army intelligence service which was under the leadership of the Croat, General Ivan Gošnjak. It is not unusual for such investigations to make unexpected discoveries. This occasion was a case in point since what emerged was the true extent of UDBA's covert surveillance of high party officials, including Tito himself. This, if nothing else, decided Tito in the matter and a formal commission of enquiry was set up on 16 June 1966 under the chairmanship of the Macedonia LCY secretary, Krste Crvenkovski. The commission was given just six days to report.[12] Disgraced by the evidence of the unbridled brutality of his officials, Ranković resigned on 1 July at a secret meeting of the Central Committee known as the Fourth Plenum, held once again at Tito's Brioni retreat. He was expelled from the Federal Assembly and membership of the LCY a few weeks later, but remained at liberty. The UDBA and the LCY were duly reorganised and purged of Ranković's supporters amid a plethora of revelations about the brutalities and corruption of the security services which were widely discussed in the press.[13] Crvenkovski was convinced that the military intelligence were up to the same activities and wanted to investigate, but Tito was not prepared to pursue the matter. He remained convinced of the necessity of maintaining a security service, and may well have been turning a blind eye to UDBA's excesses until his hand was forced. While acknowledging that UDBA must be made more accountable, he nonetheless saw that it was reconstructed to perform in much the same role as before as the principal instrument of state coercion against its own citizens.

The summer of 1966 was an important political turning point. The taming of the security service, symbolised in Ranković's fall, opened the way for a generally subservient people to think and speak more liberally at a time when the social climate in Europe as a whole, east as well as West, favoured debate and experimentation and a challenging of the post-war consensus. UDBA's autonomy had been circumscribed in the context of nationalist complaint and this event was supposed to settle the issue of ethnic grievance. Instead, the unmasking of Ranković served as a catalyst for a reconsideration on the part of the republics and provinces of their relationship with the central government. From this point onwards, the struggle between the conservative communists and the reformers took on nationalist undertones that surfaced periodically to threaten the unity of the Yugoslav state and ultimately to overwhelm it.[14]

While the régime demonstrated greater self-confidence in the mid-1960s than it had a decade earlier, the degree to which it would tolerate openly expressed controversy was limited by the degree to which such views threatened the régime's perception of 'Yugoslav' interests at home and abroad, interests which could be defined as broadly as need be once the decision had been taken to curb particular activities. In 1962, Djilas was again at the epicentre of such attention, having written a memoir of his meetings with Stalin which was already safely in the offices of his New York publisher. In March, Djilas was tried *in camera* and re-imprisoned once more, this time for breaking a new law relating to disclosure of official secrets.[15] Meanwhile Mihailo Mihajlov, a scholar of Russian literature at Zagreb University, who was prone to expressing anti-Soviet views at times when Soviet–Yugoslav relations were improving, was driven from his post in 1965, put on trial for spreading 'hostile propaganda' and awarded a suspended sentence. In the same manner as Djilas before him, Mihajlov refused to be intimidated and wrote a series of articles, one of which took the form of an open letter to Tito which dwelt on the theme of the lack of intellectual freedom. This activity was accompanied by the attempt to form an opposition political movement. Another trial and one year's imprisonment followed which was extended in 1967 because he had circulated émigré literature through the post.

The Backlash: Nationalism Resurgent

The dismissal of Ranković provided the excuse for Croat intellectuals to indulge in wider debate of their perception of Serbian hegemony in Belgrade. In March 1967, a group of 130 Croat intellectuals presented a declaration to the Skupština requesting general recognition of a separate Croatian language and demanding that Croatian be used in the schools of the republic. Prior to this they published a declaration rejecting the Novi Sad Agreement of 1954 on the grounds that their acceptance of this modern 'constructed' language had resulted in Croatian

linguistic and literary traditions being relegated to the ranks of regional
dialects. The signatories included many members of the LCY including
one of Tito's own circle, the distinguished writer Miroslav Krleža, who
was subsequently forced to resign from the Croatian Central Committee.
Others were purged or sacked, including the director of Zagreb's
Institute for the History of the Worker's Movement, Dr Franjo Tudjman,
of whom more later.[16]

The Serb intellectual community did not let this go unnoticed. While
conceding some of the points made in the Croat declaration, they
demanded equal status for the Serbian language and use of Cyrillic
script for the Serbs, especially for the 700,000 Serbs living in Croatia.
The disturbance did result in a concession, in so far as facilities for simul-
taneous translation were installed in the Federal Assembly, but more
importantly it served notice that there had been little advance with the
Party's objective of creating a common Yugoslav identity in the ten years
since its formal adoption.

The revival of the language problem was echoed around the
other parts of the country, marking 'the decline if not the fall of the
hopes that some had once held for the creation of "Yugoslav" national
sentiment'.[17] Muslim intellectuals similarly sought to press for recognition of nationality-status within the Federation and in 1968 the Bosnian
League of Communists finally fulfilled the 1963 constitutional provi-
sions by recognising the Muslims as a constituent nation, as opposed to
a minority. Meanwhile the relaxation of police repression in Kosmet
encouraged the Albanians to register their grievances. In 1968, student
demonstrations took place in both Kosovo and the Albanian speaking
areas of Macedonia. These were put down with limited use of force
and the courts gave the ringleaders, mostly young nationalist intellectuals, relatively light sentences. At the same time, the central government attempted to take political steps to meet some of their demands.
Kosovo-Metohija was renamed the Socialist Autonomous Province
of Kosovo and given equal status with Vojvodina. It was allowed
to choose as its flag the black eagle on the red background, which was
the emblem of the Albanian republic. An Albanian university was
founded in Priština to replace the faculties of Belgrade University which
had previously provided higher education in the town, and visiting professors of Albanian language and literature came from Tirana to
develop an awareness of the national culture of the Albanian people.

No sooner than this had been dealt with than student unrest broke out
in Belgrade on 2 June. Most immediately these demonstrations were

rooted in frustration at material conditions and lack of employment but they also drew inspiration from the reform movement in Czechoslovakia and the 'May' events in France. The fierce response it drew from the régime resulted from recognition of the danger that the students' relatively prosaic demands would fuse with wider discontent which rallied around nationalist aspirations, the workers movement and the intellectuals. By the end of the 1960s the reform process had had the effect of displacing the LCY from the centre of power it had enjoyed during the 1940s and 1950s. The relaxed intellectual climate of more recent times had promoted political debate outside the confines of the Party and focussed on a much wider range of topics than economic reform. Various journals had sprung up, reflecting the flourishing political, sociological and philosophical debate within Yugoslavia's universities, and this was reflected in the more controversial tone adopted by the press.

At the centre of these activities was a debating group founded by the Yugoslav Philosophical Association and composed of members of the academic staffs at the universities of Zagreb and Belgrade. The group first came to public notice in 1960 when it challenged the orthodox party dogmatists with their more humanist view of Marxism which was contrasted sharply with the prevailing authoritarianism of the orthodox party ideologists. For eight years, the Association held a series of debates as well as publishing books and journals. From 1963 it organised an annual summer school on the island of Korčula which provided a forum for discussion of current philosophical and sociological trends in Western scholarly discourse. The principal showcase for its ruminations was *Praxis*, an international journal founded in 1964 and published in Zagreb. Owing to its publication in a Western language version as well as Serbo–Croatian, it rapidly became the international forum for innovative Marxian critiques of the modern world.

All this had been viewed by the régime with benevolence until the events of 1968. The event that changed this attitude was the sympathy expressed by the Praxis group for the students' demands. Suddenly, the régime feared that the unthinkable might just occur in the shape of a coherent opposition as a result the combining of students, intellectuals and perhaps even the workers. Perceiving a real threat to the Party's dominance, the instruments of state coercion were swiftly employed to crush it. After a week of violence on all sides, Tito moved adroitly to pacify the students through a skilful television broadcast on 9 June when, speaking as if one of them, he appeared to accept the legitimacy of their grievances by pledging to make himself personally responsible for addressing the problems. Disingenuous this may have been but it achieved the desired results. He then turned on the intellectual community as the easiest candidate for a scapegoat, securing the dismissal of eight professors of Belgrade University associated with *Praxis* and expelling from the LCY all those who were still Party members. Interestingly, the Zagreb element were treated more leniently, which may have been because the Croatian LCY was facing a far more immediate and deep seated problem in tackling nationalist elements within the régime. As for *Praxis*, the funds, which supported their publications, dwindled markedly, and continual harassment by the authorities prevented its adherents from functioning as a source of opposition.[18]

Vigorous in its repression of dissent at home, the Yugoslav Government wasted no time in enhancing its image as a liberal régime amongst the European communists by openly condemning the Soviet invasion of Czechoslovakia in August 1968. Using the old bogey of the security threat to Yugoslavia's independence posed by Soviet aggression, Tito manipulated the occasion in such a way as to assist in the task of quelling domestic unease. Making it clear to the outside world that Yugoslavia would fight if its independence were challenged, additional laws were passed for the defence of the country. These facilitated the revival of Partisan mythology which had founded the Tito régime, and in particular the Yugoslav prowess for guerrilla warfare for which the country was now prepared. Territorial defence units were set up in the republics and all men from the ages of 18 to 65 and women from 19 to 40 were to be prepared to fight in any future war. Arms were distributed to all factories and offices. The spectre of external threat was once more manipulated as a motivation for internal cohesion.[19]

THE CROATIAN SPRING

The *maspok* (*masovni pokret* or mass movement), known in Western terminology as the Croatian Spring marked a turning point for the régime's approach to the nationalities question. Tito's efforts at pacification did not dispel Croatian fears for the future of their national identity nor their disappointment at the results of the economic reforms. During the 1960s, this republic had the highest number of emigrants and one of the lowest birth rates. In 1971, over 5 per cent of the population worked abroad; of these, 50 per cent were below the age of thirty of whom 63 per cent were men. This was a reflection of the lack of career opportunities at home, as well as the attractiveness of the more liberal Western culture for Croatian youth.

The economic pattern of the interwar years was repeating itself as the Croatian communists, as well as the régime's critics came to see the greatest advantage in further democratisation and decentralisation, so as to maximise the power of the republican party organisations at the expense of the federal government. 'Belgrade' remained the metaphor for all that was 'outdated, centralist and authoritarian' while the perceived extent of Serbian influence in the federal government was blamed for the fact that Croatia was not as rich as some of the smaller Western European states. The Croats resented the fact that the headquarters of the large banks and the most prosperous enterprises were located in Belgrade, symbolising the centralisation of Yugoslavia's financial life away from the regions which generated much of the country's wealth. Foreign trade, in particular, was a great source of angst. By far the greatest volume of tourist traffic passed through Dalmatia, while 80 per cent of the Yugoslav foreign trade went through Croatian ports. The Croats objected that so much of this income was dispersed to other parts of the country. They also objected to Serbian domination of both the Yugoslav Army and the police force, even though Croats were predominant in the officer corps of both the navy and air force.[20]

These grievances had significant support with the Croatian communist party. Miko Tripalo, secretary of the Croatian League of Communists, and Savka Dabčević-Kučar, head of the Croatian government and a former economics lecturer at Zagreb University, were leaders of a group of Croatian communists who had matured since the war and now called for yet more decentralisation as well as reform of the banking and currency regulations. As we have seen, this economically motivated dissatisfaction found cultural expression among the intellectuals who were all too ready to revive a sense of cultural particularism among the Croatian peoples. The focal point for such dissent was the Matica Hrvatska, a Croatian cultural organisation which drew on the traditions of the cultural society founded in the 1840s created initially to further the Illyrian movement. Moribund for the early part of the Tito era, the Matica had been revived during the 1960s by a group which included Franjo Tudjman, once an orthodox Yugoslav communist and a Partisan general who was now a nationalist, disillusioned with the Partisan myth. Tudjman declared that the Croats could not be satisfied any longer with a federal state and that Serbo–Croat relations could be managed only within a confederal system.[21] The Matica's periodical,

Kritika, which began to appear in 1968, focussed on discussion of the disadvantageous position of Croat minorities in other republics, particularly Bosnia, and provided a forum for the first attempt in the post-war period by the Croats to stir up the Bosnian Croat issue. By the summer of 1971, the activities of this group, combined with growing dissent from within the Catholic Church as well as the alignment of a number of publications with the reformers, particularly the new *Hrvatski Tjednik* (Croatian Weekly) was concerning Tito deeply. In early July, he summoned the entire Croat leadership to his residence, the Karadjordjevo hunting lodge near Zagreb, and sought to scare them into co-operation by raising once again the old bogeys of fascism and external invasion.[22]

This was to no avail, since the Croatian Party, deeply divided within itself, failed to act and by the end of the year an overtly nationalist political agenda had been drawn up which demanded changes to the Croatian constitution. Regionalism, which had been encouraged progressively by the steady devolution of power, was taking on nationalist characteristics among those who chose to express their grievances about the Yugoslav project in nationalist terms. Fortunately, there was sufficient opposition to the reformers within the Croatian Party for this to be easily suppressed. Tripalo and Dabčević-Kučar were forced to resign along with over four hundred leaders and sympathisers within the party rank and file. The Matica Hrvatska was reorganised and its activities curtailed. On 2 December 1971, Tito appeared on national television and radio to deliver a fierce attack on the nationalists. This time, however, he spread the blame for the unrest across society much more generally. Ideological disputes within the Party, the absence of proper Marxist education coupled with tolerance of pro-Western ideas in the schools and universities, he said, were responsible. And to the extent that these features were the consequence of the liberal ideas which had prevailed since the early 1960s, his argument could not be gainsaid, except in so far as it failed to acknowledge the relationship between this liberalism and the partial marketisation of the Yugoslav economy.

The purges which followed impacted across the Yugoslav federation. The dismissal of Ranković had involved the issue of control of the security forces as well as those of economic policy and Serbian nationalism. The Croatian movement brought up the extent to which a party in one of the republics could follow an independent policy. The cumulative effect of these experiences was to convince Tito that the central organisation should be strengthened and that he would approve intervention by the federal authorities in republican affairs of the republic should the communist system as he defined it, be in danger. Thus, although favouring self-determination and non-interference as standards governing relations among socialist states, he did not intend to apply these principles to the Yugoslav republics.

Action was taken against liberal elements in Slovenia, most notably through the removal of the Slovenian Party leader, Stane Kavčič, at the end of 1971. Henceforth the Slovenian Party was dominated by those such as France Popit who were loyal to the post-war Yugoslav régime and resistant to the ideas of democratisation.[23] In Serbia, the head of the Communist Party, Marko Nikezić, the former Yugoslav foreign minister who had developed a reputation since the late 1960s as a liberaliser, lost his position in October 1972 and other changes in party and state personnel were made. *Praxis* finally succumbed in 1975 when the régime persuaded the printers not to print it. In a restrospective article, Mihailo Marković lamented that 'the mortal sin of the *Praxis* group' lay in taking the ideas of Marx and the Yugoslav League of Communists 'too seriously'.[24]

Leadership Reform and Further Economic Devolution

During the spring of 1971 the régime set in train a further round of constitutional reform which continued down the path towards confederalisation. Twenty-three amendments to the 1963 Constitution provided for still more devolution, not only from the federal to the republican governments but also within the republics to the organs of local government. The now inevitable accompaniment of more economic devolution gave local enterprises control over the local banks in which they had deposited their funds.

Meanwhile, the question of leadership regeneration, or to be exact, the lack of it, had become the central topic of open discussion. Power still lay with the old Partisan command which provided continuity with the wartime foundations of the state, but even their ranks had thinned. Among the younger of the Partisan élite, Djilas and Ranković would have been obvious contenders for the leadership had they not fallen into disfavour. Others, such as Kardelj were not much less old than Tito himself. Tito drew public attention to this impending crisis in a speech in Zagreb on 21 October 1970. The solution he offered was the immediate appointment of a collective presidency at federal level. In April 1971, this proposal was formally adopted with creation of a twenty-two member collective or state presidency composed of three members elected by the republican assemblies and two from each of the autonomous provinces. The LCY had already instituted a collective presidium which paralleled the state presidency the previous year and this formalised the arrangement, conferring on Tito the title of President of the Republic for life, and leaving him with primary responsibility for foreign policy and the maintenance of national unity while permitting the collective body to gradually take on more of the work.

TITO'S CONFEDERATION, 1974-80

Although the régime had reasserted itself through repressive, reactionary policies following the Croatian Spring, the constitutional changes in 1971, which were still in line with the decentralising tendencies of the liberal reformists, were codified by the fourth and final constitution of post-war Yugoslavia promulgated in February 1974. Its purpose was to provide continuity of leadership after Tito's death and it set out to achieve this through creation of institutional arrangements which would prevent any one individual from acquiring the power which Tito had amassed, and any of Yugoslavia's peoples from dominating the federation.

The State Presidency, devised in 1971, was now formalised as the senior decision-making body but reduced in size. From 1974, it consisted of one representative from each republic and province and elected its president in a predetermined order, on a rotating annual basis. The State Presidency would replace the office of President of the Republic on Tito's death. Where Tito was responsible for foreign policy and remained Commander-in-Chief of the military, the State Presidency took control of Yugoslav monetary policy, revenue collection, funding of the under-developed regions and management of the communications and transport networks. Otherwise, the republican and provincial communist parties were constitutionally guaranteed complete control over their respective territories. Their power was reinforced by the fact that the State Presidency was required to reach decisions by consensus, thus giving the republics an effective power of veto at the highest level.[25]

The constitution also codified the arrangements that had emerged from the nationalist disturbances in the late 1960s and early 1970s. Following the events in Kosovo, Tito attempted to apply to the Albanians the same strategy which he had operated successfully to buy the loyalty of the minority of Hungarians living in the Vojvodina. But where the nationalities in Vojvodina traditionally enjoyed good relations and could therefore be persuaded to co-operate through concessions such as having their own schools and media, relations between the Serbs and Albanians in Kosovo had been antagonistic throughout the twentieth century, and, as we have seen, had fared little better under communism than under the monarchy. Even Tito was unable to face down Serbian and Macedonian opposition to Kosovo being granted republican status. Instead, the 1974 constitution formalised the earlier arrangements that were designed to pacify them first through giving both provinces greater autonomy from Belgrade, including the power of veto. Second, Kosovo's allocation from the development fund for the underdeveloped regions was increased to 37 per cent between 1976 and 1980 from the 28 per cent of the first half of the 1960s. Meanwhile, a policy of positive discrimination was successful in increasing the proportion of Albanians in Kosovo's League of Communists in the provincial administration and the security apparatus.[26]

Aside from the person of Tito himself, two institutions alone were providing unity in Yugoslavia's near confederation: the LCY and the armed forces. By the 1970s the former existed more as a debating organisation than an effective centre of power. This was the consequence of the steady devolution of power which had created in the place of one state, eight mini-states which were functioning increasingly along republican lines in both political and economic spheres. Added to which, Tito himself had destroyed much of the innovative talent within the Party ranks during the purges of 1971–72, thereby leaving power in the hands of the more pedestrian of the Party functionaries. Nevertheless, the League of Communists remained the one supranational, all-Yugoslav element in the state architecture.

The army was Tito's creation and, as a bastion of conservative communism, it remained fiercely loyal both to Tito as Commander-in-Chief, and to the Yugoslav ideal. Officers were among the most privileged members of society and were drawn from across the republics albeit with a disproportionately high representation from the Serbian populations. The JNA functioned as the centre of national pride, but under the 1974 constitution its role as the military wing of the LCY was recognised by giving it a seat on the collective Presidency. In this respect its role was to maintain political order within the country and to prevent internal disintegration. Without Yugoslavia, there could be no army. It was a symbol of unity and also a factor in the régime's legitimacy.[27]

Economic Crisis, 1971–80

Despite the retrenchment of 1968 when market socialism was replaced by Kardelj's latest ideological construct of 'consensus economics', the reforms of the 1960s brought the Yugoslav economy to a new state of crisis. By the early 1970s, two problems had become endemic. The first was the growing bureaucratisation of the entire economic system. This was a direct consequence of the fragmentation of Yugoslav industry into thousands of self-managing units, each supported by its own contingent of technocrats and bankers. According to some estimates there were nearly two million self-managing bureaucrats generated by the system in the 1970s, while the banking system had been subdivided to such an extent that almost every enterprise had its own bank. The deleterious effect of these practices on the economy was magnified in turn by the fact that the banks, however, small, were permitted to borrow capital from abroad to make up the shortfall in capital available at home. Indeed, the high inflation rate at home meant that the Yugoslav banks could borrow at negligible interest which led to a huge investment boom. The downside came when the debts began to accumulate (Table 7.1).[28]

One of Yugoslavia's greatest problems was the régime's inability to control inflation, already chronic by 1965. The various reform initiatives implemented since then had made little impact on the problem. At federal level, the difficulty resided in a combination of government expenditure, which was unbounded by any sense of economic management, the parallel failure to control the supply of money and the support of investment programmes which were not economically sound and lacked the backing of adequate resources. Further, the decision-making process had become more cumbersome as a consequence of the steady

Table 7.1 Annual rates of inflation, 1961–80

	1961–70	**1971–75**	**1971–80**
Retail prices	10.6	20.2	18.8
Agricultural produce	14.0	18.8	19.4
Industrial produce	9.2	20.8	18.9
Services	12.9	17.9	17.4
Wholesale prices			
Agricultural produce	5.0	18.0	15.3
Industrial produce	13.8	19.9	19.8

Source: *Yugoslav Survey*, 32, 1 (1991), p. 39.

devolution and was having the effect of discouraging entrepreneurship. Decision-making by consensus required that even more people were involved at each step while the coercive forces required to achieve compliance had been steadily eroded.[29] These factors compounded the consequences of the tendency for enterprises to accumulate large debts. A further decentralisation of power was introduced under the Law on Associated Labour adopted in November 1976. This was, in effect, a constitution to govern the self-managed industries intended to pave the way for complete state withdrawal from economic management leaving market forces to operate within a framework regulated by the decisions of the Basic Organisations of Associated Labour (*Osovne organizacije udruženog rada* – OOUR). Its effect was to decentralise decisions to the lowest levels, leaving the central authorities little in the way of instruments to fine-tune the economy. In short, the economy was so dislocated and bureaucratised that effective decision-making and implementation of central planning had become impossible. To these deficiencies the vulnerability of the economy to world pressures, most notably the rapid rise in the price of oil in 1973, only added.

The incentives for dodging reality were considerable. By the end of 1976 the World Bank had loaned some $1500 million to which it added two further loans of $56 million each in the spring of 1977, the first to support a programme of modernisation in Serbia and Kosovo, and the second for highway construction in several republics. In June 1977 a further loan of $75 million was granted for a nation-wide agricultural programme in which special consideration was to be given to the less developed republics. During 1979 World Bank and European Investment Bank loans of $40 million and $600 million respectively were given for highway construction.[30]

Yugoslavia could only extract itself from this predicament if it accepted the consequences of harsh monetary management and by increasing exports to the West, in order to pay for the imports needed to sustain its industrial growth. This did not happen. Fear of renewed nationalist tension, combined with a sense of importance derived from the West's Cold War enthusiasm for sustaining Yugoslavia's independence, militated against such drastic action. Yugoslavia was, as Dušan Bilandžić wryly observed, a country where profits were nationalised and losses socialised.[31]

In 1979 a concerted effort was made to do something about the debt. Both the IMF and World Bank held their annual meetings in Belgrade in October 1979 when the bankers negotiated the rescheduling

of the debts so as to ease the burden of repayments. Yugoslav indebted-
ness to the Western banks was between $11–$13 billion dollars,
while debt servicing was some $1.8 billion in 1979 and expected to rise
to $2.9 billion in 1981. And these figures did not include the aid being
received from a consortia of Western banks, from foreign governments
and organisations such as the EEC and even Comecon.[32]

Aid for the Underdeveloped Regions

The fifth Five Year Plan, which was finally implemented in November
1971, envisaged promoting greater unity of the state through voluntary
inter-republican economic co-operation so as to remove the economic
basis for the republican rivalry of recent years. In 1965 the Federal
Assembly passed a bill creating the Federal Fund for the Accelerated
Development of the Underdeveloped Republics and Kosovo
(FADURK) funded from a tax of just under 2 per cent on the social
product to be paid by the federal units. Bosnia, Macedonia, Montenegro
and Kosovo were declared the beneficiaries, requiring Serbia, Croatia,
Slovenia and the Vojvodina to be *ergo* the subsidisers. The payments were
interest-free loans rather than grants, and awarded on generous terms.
By the early 1970s, the underdeveloped units were showing growth rates
of some 9 per cent above the national average, but this was well below
the 25 per cent envisaged when the scheme was set up. Increasingly, the

Table 7.2   National income per capita, 1947–78 (Yugoslavia = 100)

	1947	1962	1976	1978
Croatia	107.2	121.3	124.3	129.2
Slovenia	175.3	198.5	201.7	195.3
Vojvodina	108.8	103.4	116.6	123.6
Bosnia-Hercegovina	82.9	72.7	64.2	66.2
Kosovo	52.6	34.0	32.2	26.8
Macedonia	62.0	57.1	68.1	66.2
Montenegro	70.8	66.3	70.3	67.7
Serbia (less the autonomous provinces)	95.6	96.0	98.3	96.6

Source: Based on figures derived from *Statisticki godisnjak SFRJ* (Belgrade,
1955, 1967, 1978, 1980); and reproduced in Singleton, *A History of the
Yugoslav Peoples*, p. 270.

Croats and Slovenes as substantial contributors, grew resentful that their surpluses were being taken and they were not placated by the concessions made in 1972 and 1973 which partly met their demands for the raising of the retention quotas for foreign currency. Similarly, the Serbs, less wealthy than their northern neighbours, resented having to pay subsidies at all, on account of their own relatively underdeveloped economy. Overall, this well-intentioned and imaginative scheme, contributed an extra dimension to growing rivalries between Yugoslavia's constitutent republics.[33] Table 7.2 demonstrates this statistically, reflecting the fact that despite attempts at redistributing income and policies designed to boost the economic performance of the weaker republics by 1978, the five poorer republics, all below the national average in 1947, had, with the exception of Serbia, declined progressively in relative terms.

FOREIGN POLICY, 1961–80

During 1960 and 1961, Cold War tensions between the superpowers increased, manifest in increasingly bellicose statements from both sides, the Soviet resumption of nuclear testing in the atmosphere and renewal of is virtual ultimatum to the West over Berlin. During this period the emergence of so many developing states as a result of the ending of European colonialism appeared to be shifting the power balance in the United Nations away from the West for the first time since the Organisation was set up and this appeared to provide new opportunities for the uncommitted in Cold War struggle to assert their influence diplomatically. Tito sought to capitalise on this process, emerging as the champion of the non-aligned with an innovative system of economic management and social organisation which offered a potential model for third world development. This brought Yugoslavia simultaneously into competition with both East and West which were similarly interested to compete for political influence in the newly emerging world.

Tito's foreign policy in this period has been described as 'the diplomacy of prestige'.[34] It was justified, in the face of mounting domestic economic difficulties by claims that Yugoslavia was thereby contributing to the 'propagation of socialism'. This was a double-edged sword, however, and for a while it appeared that Tito had forgotten Yugoslavia's dependence on equilibrium in its relations with the Soviet Union on the one hand and the West on the other. In 1961, the Non-Aligned Movement's first conference had passed a series of resolutions which seemed to indicate that its bias was pro-Soviet, contributing thereby to Western anxieties about the security in the Mediterranean. A brief interval in 1962 in which the Soviet Union and Yugoslavia appeared to be attempting yet another rapprochement gave credence to this interpretation. As in the 1950s, this episode proved short-lived.

Similarly, the efforts of Tito to promote Yugoslavia's relations with the Arab Middle East backfired when the Egyptians lost the Six-Day War in 1967, forcing Tito to retrench. During this same period, Yugoslavia had disrupted its relationship with France by its support of the Algerian sep-aratist movement, and the traditional close relations between Paris and Belgrade were not resumed until De Gaulle left office. Another element in this which worried the West, in general, was the attempt to promote non-aligned socialism in the Mediterranean lands, denouncing the pres-ence of military forces of powers which did not have Mediterranean coastlines, and encouraging the progressive political organisations in those which did.[35]

The style in which Tito conducted his diplomacy was expensive and open to criticism both at home and abroad. Particularly after 1965, members of the Yugoslav establishment were increasingly inclined to articulate the view that Yugoslavia was living beyond its financial means. Despite Tito's penchant for public hyperbole and diplomatic largesse, Yugoslavia was not a major player internationally, but a small European state with an ailing economy and a dependency on foreign aid which was too great for the giving of aid to third parties to be justifiable. But it suited the style of the régime in Tito's later years. Tito, who enjoyed the trappings of power, whose personal vanity made him susceptible to the temptations to dress in martial clothes and parade his international guests through a substantial collection of official residences, hunting lodges, and island retreats, required an international status which would attract visitors of the appropriate level. Moreover, it gave him connec-tions and information which he could barter as the currency of leverage when Yugoslavia's profligacy resulted in economic crisis. For the most part, however, non-alignment was simply a drain on resources which supplied little of tangible value in return. The needs of the régime in external affairs were ultimately supplied through its management of its stance between East and West.

The Prague Spring, 1968

Developments within Czechoslovakia following Antonin Novotny's replacement by Alexander Dubček were widely applauded by the Tito régime and the Yugoslav media alike. The Czechs, in much the same way as the Yugoslavs, had embarked on a programme of economic liberalisation only to discover that this would not work without some move towards democratisation also. During a visit to Moscow in April, Tito attempted to influence the Soviet view of Dubček's reforms and persuade Brezhnev, who was deeply concerned at the direction events were taking, to take a benign view. 'Any attempt to use force', he argued, 'would have infinitely serious consequences for the Soviet Union itself and for the international workers movement in general'.[36] At much the same time, Tito was cultivating relations with neighbouring Rumania which since the early 1960s had been taking an increasingly independent line, particularly in its foreign policy. The triangular relationship of these 'reform communists' which emerged in the spring of 1968, was curiously reminiscent of the Little Entente of the interwar years which had similarly been formed as an insurance against the re-imposition of control by a hegemonic power.

Tito and Ceauçescu visited Prague during the second week of August to demonstrate their support for the Dubček régime. The Soviet invasion of Czechoslovakia on 21 August 1968 caught the Yugoslav leadership by surprise. Unlike the equivocations of 1956, Tito spoke out strongly against the Soviet action and proceeded to strengthen Yugoslavia's defences. The legacy of the crisis was that it reawakened in Yugoslav minds a deep distrust of the Soviet Union which abided until the demise of communism.

During the 1970s Yugoslavia enjoyed good relations with its immediate non-communist neighbours. Both Austria and Italy were helpful from the point of view of trade, and Italy in particular was a useful bridge to NATO and the EEC. Officially its stance was one of 'active and positive co-existence' and although Tito continued to identify with the non-aligned, it became increasingly difficult for these states as a group to find common objectives outside the broad issues of the day such as disarmament. A succession of non-aligned conferences (Lusaka, 1970; Algiers, 1973; Colombo, 1976) agreed in general terms upon action programmes for economic co-operation between the members in order to accelerate both trade and aid as well as to exert more diplomatic pressure at the United Nations through the Group of 77. The reality was prosaic. Yugoslavia's trade with the non-aligned of Asia, Africa and Latin America amounted to no more than one-sixth of its total overseas trade.

Non-alignment did have, however, a positive impact on Yugoslavia because it helped to break their psychological isolation from the outside world. The very fact of achieving co-operation with non-Marxist groups brought not only self-confidence which in itself contributed to Yugoslavia's stability in this period, but also set their dogmatic preconceptions about the struggle between communism and capitalism in a much broader context of the inequalities between north and south or the centre and periphery in international affairs. Above all, however, non-alignment suited Yugoslavia for domestic political reasons since it was a foreign policy on which all factions were able to agree.[37]

Within Europe Yugoslavia naturally welcomed détente, in both its narrower European incarnation as well as that between the East and West. The final acceptance of the post-war territorial settlement in Europe was to Yugoslavia's advantage as was the Final Act of the Helsinki Agreement of 1975 which gave the international community greater leverage in discouraging the Soviet Union from further interventionism in the affairs of its immediate communist neighbours. However, détente declined sharply after Helsinki, as did Soviet–Yugoslav relations, a development which occurred in parallel with yet another round of Yugoslav–Chinese rapprochement.

TITO'S LEGACY

On 4 May 1980, President Tito died, a few weeks short of his eighty-eighth birthday. He was buried in the specially prepared mausoleum at Dedinje in the suburbs of Belgrade, with foreign dignatories from all over the world in attendance. Two generations of Yugoslavs had known no other leader and the funeral proceeded amid a collective and countrywide outpouring of grief. The interment of the late President was, perhaps, the last event which stirred a collective emotion within the peoples of Yugoslavia. The overseas representation was partly a function of his longevity, as well as his famous hospitality and diplomatic largesse. It was also a recognition of a certain quality of humanity which had enabled him to fight for an idea and win against determined and sustained opposition. He was admired for his leadership of this disparate country and for holding it together for thirty-five years, ruling with a rod of iron but at the same time with a demeanour and style which compelled people to like him. Tito's passing was an event of international significance.

The way in which Tito was remembered is necessarily very much a subjective issue. To many of the Serbs, particularly those who most readily identified with the strident nationalism of the 1980s and 1990s, Tito was yet another instrument of Serbian repression who had denied them their rightful place as leader of the South Slav peoples. In some sense, their subsequent pursuit of Greater Serbia was a reaction against all that was embodied in Titoism, in other ways it was an acknowledgement of the need for a societal goal, a utopian endstate which would fill the void left once Tito's version of communism was no longer credible.

Those who had prospered within Tito's Yugoslavia took the view that Tito's methods, particularly the contradictions of self-managed socialism had prevented them from prospering rather more. It was the nationalities of the traditionally poorer 'southern republics' which had either a weak sense of collective identity, or else contained multiple identities, who saw the Titoist solution, and the creator of the post-war system, as the best of the solutions available, and whose mourning of the late president was rooted in a fear of what the future might hold.

Tito's legacy was three fold. On the positive side, he left the peoples of Yugoslavia with a memory of sustained statehood. He had prevented the resurfacing of Serbo–Croat tensions which paralysed the interwar period and provided the motivation for much of the violence during the war. Under his management, the Muslim population had achieved recognition and the Macedonians had been granted independence from the Serbs as a republic in their own right. Tito had also given the Yugoslav peoples security – security in the form of protection from foreign intervention, and a measure of economic security in so far as the communist economic system provided certain guaranteed conditions for all. Yugoslavia benefitted hugely from its international status, again a product of Tito's vision and style. But, the Cold War tempted the régime to constantly defer facing the costs of its profligacy, resulting in the development of problems that were structural rather than transitory.

The negative aspects of this system were self-evident in the failure of its economy. By 1980, Yugoslavia was widely regarded as an economic catastrophe, and Western businessmen and governments were increasingly loathe to offer yet more investment and loans to offset the consequences of its idiosyncrasies. The shortcomings had fostered a climate in which the methods of corruption and black marketeering were turned to increasingly so that the ordinary person could sustain a viable economic existence. Moreover, as educational levels improved, and people were permitted to travel more freely, the mythology on which the régime was built came increasingly into question. The passing of the generation which had fought the war was an important factor, and the increased questioning of the orthodox version of the history of this period, in particular the re-discovery of traumatic events that had long been taboo, had much to do with undermining the régime's credibility once the figurehead to whom most were loyal was no longer there to manage Yugoslavia's constant state of crisis. Although the drawbacks of the Titoist system were increasingly obvious during the 1970s, it was only after Tito's death that the country was confronted fully with the price of Tito's 'management' of the South Slav conflict.

8   The End of Illusion

Yugoslavia in its post-war incarnation was an expression of two ideals, those of communism and 'Yugoslavism'. The vesting of political power in a single party which maintained an omnipresent control over all aspects of the society's development was key to its ability to define and shape the historical reference points on which the state was founded and which were intended to supersede secular nationalisms with one collective nationalism common to all. But just as communism succeeded only in generating new forms of age-old miseries, so Yugoslavism proved as illusive to the communists as it had to the parliamentarians and monarchists.

The final decade of Yugoslavia's seventy-year history is dominated by three themes. First, the failure of the political system to arbitrate competing interests and outlooks of the most powerful players; second, the confrontation of Tito's economic legacy of crisis; and third the resurgence of ethno-nationalism. The framework within which these issues were played out was the progressive scaling down of east–west conflict and the parallel process of the de-legitimation of communism as a political system. These latter factors, combined with the eventual abandonment of socialist self-management, effectively removed the pillars on which the post-war Yugoslav state was founded.

'AFTER TITO – TITO'

The period immediately following Tito's death was almost startling for its appearance of continuity with the past. The federal government coined the slogan 'After Tito – Tito' in order to reassure the population that despite Tito's death, his spirit as expressed in the Yugoslav régime lived on. This was an acknowledgement of the importance of 'persona' for the legitimacy of the régime and it was accompanied by wide social disapproval of criticism of Tito himself. For two or three years following his death, Tito's memory was beyond reproach and the régime benefited from rising support expressed in an increase in membership of the LCY from 1.8 million to 2.05 million.[1]

In reality a political void had opened. The federal presidency was passed from one uninspiring and little known politician to another. The system, in its various incarnations, had depended upon the presence of the leader who could command co-operation at all levels of society. Without this, there was no single authority which could arbitrate between the competing interests to rise above political squabbles and factionalism. Within a few years, the deference to the past was replaced by growing awareness and open criticism of the legacies that the past had generated for the present. The more permissive atmosphere permitted novelists such as Vuk Drasković, and the literary critic, and former Serbian Party leader, Dobrica Ćosić to publish their controversial works more independently than hitherto. Similarly, only a few years elapsed before attempts were made to reassess both the history of the partisan movement and the life of Tito himself. In the vanguard of this process were the hagiographical enterprises of Vladimir Dedijer, but once an iconoclastic mindset gained an audience, it was not long before the credibility of the mythology built on Partisan resistance and the harmony of the Yugoslav peoples had been undermined to the detriment of the cohesion of the state. Once the principle of open dissent from the status quo was established, popular disrespect for the régime became palpable.[2]

The 1980s debate about political and economic reform was in many ways a reprise of that of the 1960s, but without the boundaries set by rigid party discipline of the middle years of Tito's rule. There were two distinct poles in this discourse. The recentralists objected to the confederalisation of the LCY. Drawn largely from Serbia and Serbian elements in Bosnia, they argued that devolution had gone too far in the widest sense, and focussed on the degree of autonomy granted to Kosovo and Vojvodina in particular. In their view there was an urgent requirement for retrenchment, with greater co-ordination among the republics by the centre particularly in the key spheres of education, transport and pricing policy, with a commensurate tightening of Party discipline. Sometimes, the recentralisers posed as guardians of Tito's legacy, although this changed in the mid-1980s when a new figure of stature rose above the crowd to lead them. The confederalists, on the other hand, wanted the existing level of decentralisation institutionalised by making central committee members responsible to the republican parties which elected them rather than to the Party's central committee, as hitherto. They also wanted to scale down the power of the LCY presidium and especially to secure abandonment of the Leninist principle of democratic centralism which had guided the central party's conduct and constituted one of the only remaining checks of liberalisation of politics. These concerns, together with those relating to the rise of ethno-nationalism among the Albanian population, the progressive deterioration of the economy, and the widespread lack of confidence in the Party's competence to govern effectively, were the debating points for the Twelfth Party Congress which was held in Belgrade 26–29 June 1982.[3]

Kosovo, 1981

The first political crisis of the post-Tito era occurred a year earlier, in Kosovo, less than one year after Tito's death. It is important for two reasons: first as a harbinger of what was to come and second, as a challenge to the authority of the state presidency and therefore to the federal government. The events centred on student riots which occurred in the first week of March 1981, initially for the reason of registering protest at the conditions prevailing at Priština University. However, these primarily materialistic demands quickly fused with overtly nationalist issues. At their most extreme the protesters' agenda included an extension of Kosovo's boundaries to encompass the Albanian speaking areas of Macedonia. For the most part, however, the Kosovar Albanians identified with the more modest objective of republican status within the confederation. The Serbs remained equally determined to reverse the decisions of the 1974 Constitution, and alighted on Albanian agitation and demonstration as proof that such a move was necessary for security reasons.

Initially the official response was muted, but when the demonstrations spread and workers became involved, violence ensued. Thirteen people were killed in clashes with police on 11 March, and open street battles took place in most of Kosovo's municipalities following violent demonstrations at the University on 1 April. A news blackout was imposed to halt the wide publicity the violence was receiving, and martial law was declared in the province. The federal government shied away from identifying the disturbances as nationalist and dismissed it in communist language as counter-revolutionary activity, organised by outsiders conspiring to achieve the unification of Kosovo with Albania.[4]

The real causes were several-fold. Certainly an Albanian separatist movement existed in both Kosovo and Albania and had become an acknowledged fact at federal level by the end of the 1960s. However, the provincial leadership of Kosovo had managed to conceal the extent of its following, seeking to avoid giving the Serbs any reason for retracting the concessions granted since 1968. The irony in the situation was that the nationalist agenda had been fuelled by the very reforms which had been implemented in order to dissipate such tensions. Despite the investment of almost half the funds allocated to underdeveloped regions to Kosovo during the latter part of the 1970s, the socio-economic conditions of the population remained grievous. In 1977, Kardelj had warned that something had to be done to ameliorate this problem if peace were to be maintained.[5] The problem lay in the way the incoming funds were used. What was required was the expansion of manufacturing industry which would relieve unemployment; instead funds were directed into prestigious capital-intensive projects such as power generation which sprang up as a means of appeasing the educated Kosovar Albanians, but brought little relief to the poverty experienced by the vast majority of the 600,000 population. By 1980, the per capita income in Kosovo had dropped to just 28 per cent of the Yugoslav average, having been some 48 per cent in 1954.[6]

Similarly, the funds directed to expansion of Priština University were producing some 10,000 graduates a year for whom there was little suitable employment. The university's acknowledged role as nurturer of Albanian culture, and in particular its adoption of Albanian rather than local dialect as the principal literary language, together with its proactive cultivation of close links with its counterpart in Tirana, established it as the institutional epicentre of the promotion of Albanian nationalist culture. By 1980, it had 35,000 students enrolled, all with expectations raised well beyond the standard of living enjoyed by the peasant farming community from whence many of them had emerged. By 1981 substantial numbers were unemployed, frustrated and antagonistic to the minority Serbian community which comprised merely 13 per cent of the population but could generally entertain higher expectations in terms of access to professional employment and living standards. The underprivileged, unemployed urban youth resorted to registering their frustrations by striking out at the Serbian students and desecrating Serbian graves and churches.[7] Under such conditions it was only a matter of time before discontent founded in economic deprivation fused with nationalist sentiment to produce potentially explosive pressure for major reform.

The attempts at pacification which followed the events of March and April failed to halt the deteriorating security situation. The state responded to the challenge by implementing ritual purges of the League of Communists of Kosovo and other official bodies, and suppressing the more worrisome journals. Between 1981 and 1987 the predominantly Serbian police brought criminal charges against some 5200 Kosovar Albanians. Not that the Albanians were passive. For their part they demonstrated their rejection of the legitimacy of the status quo by resorting to the methods of non-violent as well as violent protest and did not confine these activities to the province. Skopje, Ljubljana and Zagreb all felt the physical manifestations of this rejection of what the Albanians perceived as Serbian repression.[8]

ECONOMIC CRISIS, 1981–91

Perhaps the most significant factor in undermining the legitimacy of the Yugoslav state during the 1980s was the economic crisis which spiralled downwards with increasing velocity. The second oil crisis of the early 1980s led to high interest rates which combined with the exceptionally strong dollar to generate a recession across Europe. This magnified significantly Yugoslavia's foreign debt which by 1981 had risen to just under $19 million, nearly a one-third increase on the figures for 1979.[9] Moreover, Tito's death undermined international confidence in Yugoslavia. As inflation took off and standards of living fell accordingly, dropping by almost 10 per cent between 1982 and 1989, the perception of Yugoslavia as an economic catastrophe became firmly established in the minds of international financiers who were increasingly reluctant to offer further loans except on the most punitive terms. Finally, the problems of inefficiency, bureaucratisation, parochialism and cronyism which socialist self-management produced, when combined with the *nomenklatura* system of appointments operated by the Party, made genuine reform almost impossible. Political power was so diffused in the confederation that there was no one element strong enough to direct and enforce the stringent reforms required.[10]

The conflict management strategy employed by Tito was much to blame. By the 1980s all eight of the political entities comprising Yugoslavia were running their economies on a republican rather than national basis. Each insisted on having its own 'modern' industries, however unproductive and wasteful this strategy might be. Strategic industries were a particular case in point. For instance, the giant iron-ore processing plant at Kavadarci in Macedonia. Its construction had begun in the 1960s, and absorbed almost half of one billion dollars in convertible currency loans and an equivalent amount of domestic investment before being scrapped in the 1980s because the available local ore was too deficient in iron to make the plant feasible, a fact known before the project was begun. Another example can be found in the decision to build ports at both Koper and Bar so that Slovenia and Montenegro respectively could draw even with Croatia which already had an excellent port at Rijeka, and moreover a port with sufficient capacity to handle all Yugoslavia's sea trade. The result of such politically motivated profligacy was steadily rising debt, but with no tangible benefit.[11]

These problems were magnified by other decisions, such as the devolution of the banking system which succeeded mainly in facilitating corruption on a vast scale. By the 1980s, the federal authorities interfered with republican financial arrangements at their peril. Instead of a single economy, Yugoslavia had a series of mini-economies and worse, some of these began waging economic warfare against one another.[12]

Long-Term Stabilisation Programme, 1983

Between 1980 and 1989, the Yugoslav government was trapped in a cycle of price freezes, devaluations, restructuring plans, price and wage freezes and bridging loans which created 'stagflation' rather than stabilisation (see Table 8.1). Various attempts were made at arresting the crisis. In July 1983 the federal government launched the so-called Long-Term Stabilisation Programme with the assistance of a large financial aid package prepared by Western governments. This included a drastic reduction in overseas expenditure as the grants to non-aligned clients in the developing world were wound up, while many of Tito's extravagant embassies which his régime had sustained to promote Yugoslavia's international status were closed. At home, the opulent palaces which had provided the backdrop for Tito's statesmanship were

Table 8.1   Annual inflation increases, 1985–89

	1985	1986	1987	1988	1989
Wholesale prices	82	71	99	203	1306
Retail prices	76	88	118	199	1256
Cost of living	74	89	120	195	1252

Source: *Yugoslav Survey*, 32, 1, 1991, p. 39.

converted into hotels. Tourism remained the most valuable part of the economy, while Tito's legacy was being viewed increasingly as a milestone.

The extent of Yugoslavia's economic problems was admitted to Parliament by the then Prime Minister, Branko Mikulić, in 1987. He acknowledged that over half of Yugoslavia's borrowings had been used for consumption or invested in mistaken projects, while the attempt at inter-republic redistribution of wealth in which the economic development of Bosnia-Hercegovina, Montenegro, Macedonia and Kosovo was to be subsidised by the relative wealth of Slovenia, Croatia, Serbia and Vojvodina, had also failed since the gap had widened rather than narrowed. In 1945, the per capita income in Slovenia, the wealthiest republic, was about three times that of Kosovo, the poorest unit. By the 1980s this disparity had doubled.[13] This deterioration was encouraging the growth of corruption and the black market as households were driven to increase their income by any means available. At the same time, elderly workers were inclined to defer retirement owing to the inadequacy of existing pensions, which created a significant increase in unemployment among the young. Social services became overburdened as health care infrastructure declined, reducing the level of public health while education fell further behind the standards of the developed world.[14]

The Marković Reforms, 1989–90

The last attempt at economic reform was made in 1989 when Ante Marković replaced Mikulić as prime minister in March. A successful industrialist from Croatia, of which he had also been president, Marković determined to institute radical reform with the aim of turning Yugoslavia into a market economy, a reaction in part to the liberalisation of the Soviet economy under *perestroika* which had legitimised the discussion of private enterprise throughout the communist world. Marković attempted to outflank both the republics and the party. Where Mikulić's five attempts at instituting reform had failed because they had to be vetted by the presidencies and party leaders, Marković went straight to the legislature. He appointed new ministers on ability rather than party connections and promised that they would be responsible to the federal assembly. He sought to use the assembly's committees to promote his plans, as per the norm in parliamentary systems. For over seven months the lack of political consensus among the republics delayed implementation of the reform package. Croatia and Slovenia broadly supported the policies, they were concerned lest they strengthen the federal centre, and thereby pave the way for a different prime minister to recentralise. The strongest opposition came from Serbia where the squeeze on credit to loss-making enterprises, and the liberalisation of imports was threatening the survival of its bankrupt industries. When the programme was presented to the respective republic assemblies in December 1989, Serbia and Kosovo both rejected it. This notwithstanding, the reform package was accepted on a majority vote and went into effect on 1 January 1990.

Immediately, self-management was abolished and the banking system given independence. At the centre of strategy were drastic measures to tackle inflation. Using a cushion of some $10 billion hard currency reserves, the new 'heavy' dinar was pegged to the deutschmark (at a rate of 7 : 1), and made freely convertible. A balanced budget was introduced, a six-month wage freeze imposed and the worthless promissory notes that Yugoslav firms had been handing to each other were peremptorily cancelled. The result was that foreign exchange reserves rose dramatically with a commensurate decline in the foreign debt. Control of the money supply was restored and inflation, which was running at some 2500 per cent in 1989, was halted almost at once. The international response was encouraging: some 3000 firms initialled agreements during 1990 and the first few months of 1991, bringing investment of $1.2 billion to the Yugoslav economy.[15]

However, this international popularity for Marković was not echoed within the country. Non-Serbs saw him as a centralising communist trying to reimpose Belgrade's hegemony on the rest of the country. Pro-Milošević Serbs criticised him for undermining socialism and ruining Yugoslavia on behalf of foreign bankers. Either way, his control of the economy was tenuous and short-lived. As soon as the six-month freeze on wages expired, workers everywhere demanded increases and got them. The federal bank's inability to keep track of the money supply reached a climax in December 1990 when Milošević subverted the system by diverting some $1.8 billion of federal funds for Serbia's use, passing it out in bonuses, wage increases, subsidies and interest free loans, in effect a vote-buying spree in the month prior to Serbia's elections in December 1990.[16]

THE DELEGITIMATION OF COMMUNISM AND THE RISE OF NATIONALISM, 1986–90

Central to the unravelling of the post-war Yugoslav state was the disintegration of the League of Communists in 1990 which followed upon the wider delegitimation of communism throughout eastern Europe. A series of factors combined to promote this development. As we have seen, Yugoslavia was an economic catastrophe in this period, the régime unable to deliver a stable economic environment, let alone rising prosperity. Increasingly, these hardships appeared to the wider population as senseless, particularly as western Europe was enjoying a boom during the middle of the decade which served to sharpen the Yugoslavs sense of deprivation.

During this period, the security environment altered as a consequence of the reform process embarked upon by the new President of the Soviet Union. Mikhail Gorbachev's policies of *glasnost* and *perestroika*, introduced in 1986 and 1987 respectively, together with the abandonment of the so-called 'Brezhnev Doctrine' of limited sovereignty in eastern Europe in the spring of 1989, altered the security environment in which Yugoslavian exceptionalism within the communist world had been defined. The rapid dismantling of communism in eastern Europe which followed the breaching of the Berlin Wall in November 1989, and most graphically for Yugoslavia, the popular and shockingly violent overthrow of the Ceauçescue régime in Rumania, less than two months later, removed much of the foundations on which the legitimacy of Yugoslavia's League of Communists was founded. The teleological goals on which the post-war Yugoslav state had been focussed – the creation of socialism in preparation for the development of communism – were by the end of 1989 largely discredited as falsehoods. Europe, liberated from the anxiety generated by Soviet–American ideological confrontation and cold war, turned to its own future, while Yugoslavia, once the most prosperous and self-satisfied of the People's Democracies, was in economic and political disarray. Stripped of its Cold War strategic importance and without an effective leadership, Yugoslavia could no longer command the international financial and political attention which had sustained it for over forty years.

During the mid-1980s, power began to pass perceptibly from the old Partisan generation to a new constellation of leaders. In 1986, many of the personalities who were to lead Yugoslavia into dissolution, had risen from obscurity in their respective republican party systems. We shall look at each republic in turn.

Serbia

The Serbs refused to accept that Kosovo had been granted full autonomy. The task of overturning the 1974 Constitution was the centre of gravity in the political debate within Serbia for the remainder of Yugoslavia's existence. Dragoslav Marković, president of Serbia during the final years of Tito's life, presented the Serbian critique of the elevation of Kosovo's status in a confidential 'Blue Book' during the 1970s, but the issue was never publicly discussed. Once the mourning for Tito was over, however, Serbian historians wasted little time in exploiting the comparatively liberal atmosphere of Yugoslav philosophical debate in the early 1980s to publish overtly Serbian works. They were encouraged in this by the seemingly insatiable demand from the general populace which eagerly devoured literature and history which reinstated the case for the revival of Greater Serbia. At the forefront of this process was Dobrica Ćosić, an old Partisan who had joined Tito's resistance movement in 1941 believing that communism was the best vehicle for protecting and furthering Serbian national interests. Since the war he had developed a reputation as a writer of popular historical epics set mostly during wars and littered with references to Serb mythology. The liberalisation of the Kosovar Albanians in 1968 stimulated him to develop a complex theory of Serb national persecution under communism which constituted the foundation for the Greater Serb programme of the mid-1980s.[17]

This debate gathered momentum when the Serbian Academy of Sciences (SANU) joined the fray. Its contribution appeared as a memorandum 'to raise the most important social, political, economic, educational and cultural problems' for Serbia and Yugoslavia. Completed in draft form on 25 September 1986, it presented a radical analysis of Yugoslav politics and in particular Serbia's position within the polity. At the centre of its argument was the claim that Tito and his successors had discriminated against the Serbs by pursuing a policy of 'a weak Serbia, a strong Yugoslavia', and blamed Serbia's poor economic condition on its inability to control its destiny. Further, the decision to raise the autonomous republics to almost republican status in 1974 had, in SANU's opinion, denied the Serbs the right to their own state by dividing its territory into three parts. Serbs were not only being persecuted in Kosovo, it argued, but were also being threatened elsewhere, especially in Croatia, where their numbers had declined significantly relative to the Croatian population.[18]

The Memorandum posed a challenge to the very foundations of the post-war Yugoslav state and was widely condemned within Yugoslav society for that very reason. But the Memorandum was not rejecting Yugoslavia as such: its criticism was levelled at the Titoist vision of the unitary South Slav state. Their point was that Serbs had flourished most effectively under Royalist Yugoslavia which awarded the Serb peoples the leading role which they believed to be consistent with their contribution to building a South Slav state in the nineteenth and early twentieth centuries. Since the Second World War their position in relation to the other nationalities had been progressively eroded, a process which should be halted.[19]

This intellectual statement of Serbian nationalist aspiration found its champion in the Belgrade lawyer and party functionary, Slobodan Milošević who emerged from obscurity in February 1986 with an agenda of modernisation and experience of business management, most recently as President of the Bank of Belgrade. Born at Požarevac in 1941 Milošević was a hardline communist, a fanatic from a disturbed background whose populist approach and powerful oratorical style enabled him to manipulate mass opinion with aplomb. Milošević was commended as Serbian Party leader by his mentor, Ivan Stambolić, who was obliged to resign the post on elevation to the Yugoslav presidency. The two men shared the view that the Serbs had been treated harshly under the Tito régime, but where Stambolić was careful to frame the issue in Yugoslav terms, Milošević perceived the problem exclusively in terms of Serbian interests. While Stambolić was at heart a negotiator who believed that differences of opinion should be tolerated within the Party, Milošević was a Stalinist whose support within the party organisation was, not unlike Stalin's, derived from his ability to 'get things done and not waste a lot of time talking'.[20] Initially, his actions were in keeping with those of conservative communists; he demanded a re-imposition of party discipline and strong leadership to fill the post-Tito vacuum. But within a year of taking office, he began to move adroitly to the nationalist side of the debate, bringing about the very situation that Tito had striven to avoid, the fusion between nationalist 'opinion' and political power.[21]

Initially, Milošević's agenda was not so obvious. When he took office, Stambolić was wrestling with the Kosovo issue, and attempting to negotiate a closer relationship between the region and Serbia. Milošević joined him in condemning Serbian generated unrest as nationalist. The following year however, when Stambolić sent him to Kosovo to meet with the militants, a more insidious agenda emerged. Addressing an excited crowd of some ten thousand Serbs and Montenegrins on

24 April 1987, Milošević spoke not only as a communist, but also with nationalist overtones, using the phrase 'No one is allowed to beat you', the meaning of which was ambiguous, but which was certainly interpreted by those of nationalist inclination to mean that Serbian nationalism would not be repressed as hitherto.[22]

This event was the beginning of Serbia's post-Tito order. The thrust of his policy was to reverse the Tito–Kardelj confederalist solution, which he saw as the root of both Serbia's ills and those of the whole of Yugoslavia. Milošević began a process which he termed 'differentiation' through which the party was purged of all who would not give him total loyalty. One of the most notable casualties was his erstwhile friend and supporter, Stambolić, who was driven from both the Serbian party and the Yugoslav presidency by the end of 1987. The re-imposition of party discipline was a plank in his strategy to prevent collapse of the régime itself, and in this he drew the bulk of his support from conservative elements within the army and the older generation who believed in Yugoslavia as a centralised if authoritarian unified state. Having championed the nationalist demands of the academics, he won their allegiance too by liberalising Belgrade cultural life. The support of the intellectuals, who were wooed into a suspension of judgement, was a key element in the process of legitimising his régime. At the same time, he gained control of the media, particularly the broadcasters, by more overt means, placing his own appointees in key positions.[23]

Milošević kept attention directed to the Kosovo issue which was made easy by the increasingly vociferous protests from the Serb population there that their numbers were dwindling owing to persecution by the lawless, irredentist Albanians. In fact the evidence indicates that there was mutual discrimination between the two populations, but that the very fact of a much higher Albanian birth rate was having the effect of increasing the Albanian population relative to that of the Serbs while the parlous economic circumstances of Kosovo, exacerbated by well-meaning but ill conceived enterprise initiatives were aggravated by high unemployment and the tendency of both populations to migrate to the other republics, thereby diminishing the economic base of the region still further. A strike by Albanian miners at the Trepča zinc and lead mines in February 1989, brought matters to a head when Milošević arrested the strikers on the grounds of counter-revolutionary activity. On 28 June 1989, with human rights organisations developing an increasing interest in events in Kosovo, one million Serbs descended on the province to celebrate the 600th anniversary of the battle of

Kosovo Polje. To mark the occasion the remains of Prince Lazar were exhumed and paraded, an event which served as a chilling reminder of the sanctity of Kosovo Polje to Serbian Orthodoxy on which Serbs based their determination to sustain their rule over the province. The Republican Party leaders were obliged to accompany Milošević to Kosovo for the 'celebration' and witnessed at first hand a speech in which he reminded the onlookers that the Serbs had fought for their rights in the past and would do so again if need arises.[24]

Milošević formally overrode the 1974 constitutional arrangements in March 1989 when he pushed a series of amendments through the Assembly which placed limits on the rights of both Kosovo and Vojvodina to act independently. The lesson of this episode was the powerlessness of the federal government. Milošević was imposing his agenda through manipulation of mass political opinion while simultaneously packing the legislative bodies of both Kosovo and the Serbian government with his own appointees to the extent that he could afford to ignore opposition to his policies mounted from the other centre of power. Just as in Kosovo, Milošević had used populist political methods which played on economic under-privilege and nationalist fears to rally substantial support in Vojvodina and Montenegro, thereby acquiring effective control of 50 per cent of Yugoslavia's eight federal units. The Macedonian Party was also supporting him, ensnared as it was in the same conflict of sectarian interests with both Serbian and Albanian dimensions. Fear of further violence, particularly among the Croats and the leadership of Bosnia-Hercegovina which were required to confront a substantial Serbian diaspora if they resisted Milošević, led to a stand-off in which the other republics were inclined to leave the Serbs to assert themselves in Kosovo in the hope that Yugoslavia itself could thereby be saved.

Slovenia

Historically, Slovenia's cultural individuality had protected it from the resentments of the Serbs and the Croats. For much of the post-war period it had appeared the most contented of the constituent parts of Yugoslavia, modestly prosperous, enjoying full employment and access to trading partners of the Alpen-Adria group of central European states. Slovenia suffered less than some of the other republics in the repression following the Croatian spring and generally took advantage of the distinctiveness of its language to encourage a more liberal policy towards the intelligentsia than was practiced elsewhere. By the early 1980s, Slovenia was already developing the basis for a civil society which would carry it through the transition from communism.

During the spring of 1986 the leadership changed. The old guard conservative communists retired and Milan Kučan was elected to the Party presidency. An adherent of the liberal wing of the Slovenian communist party, he had not resigned during the 1971 purges, believing that he could do more from within the organisation than outside it. Kučan was born in 1941 in Prekumurje. A lawyer by training who had spent many years as the Slovenian representative in a number of the federal party organisations, during which he had acquired a deep understanding of Belgrade politics. While not a radical, he was immediately tolerant of the emergence of demands for greater democratisation.[25]

Among those clamouring for reform by the late 1980s were the environmental pressure groups whose agenda had been written following the 1986 Chernobyl disaster. Then there were the conscientious objectors to military service who saw in Serbian actions in Kosovo a tangible expression of disparity between the outlooks of Yugoslavia's constituent republics. The artistic community was also vigorous in this period, parodying Yugoslavia and elevating everything which was officially taboo. Hitherto such activities had been tolerated as a safety valve for unorthodox ideas, but by the late 1980s, the alternative discourse which dominated the Slovenian Communist Youth movement, was becoming a much more significant force in the republic and could not be disdained by the political leadership any longer.

The event which galvanised the Slovenian democratic opposition, bringing these forces into closer alignment, was the celebrated trial of four editors of the journal *Mladina* (Youth) which was published by the Socialist Youth League. They had transgressed the limits of the Defence Minister's tolerance by criticising him for selling arms to Ethiopia and then accusing the federal government of conspiring with the Swedes to send arms to Libya. They were arrested ostensibly for betraying state secrets after a copy of Kučan's speech to a secret session of the party presidium on 29 March had been found in the desk of Janez Janša, one of the editors. The article prepared on the basis of this document claimed that the army was planning a *putsch* against the most important Slovene political figures in order to curb the growth of Slovenian nationalism. Not only was the trial held *in camera* but it was also conducted in Serbo–Croat. Both factors convinced the already alienated Slovenian population that the trial was not really about state secrets but was an attack on Slovenia.[26]

Protesters responded to this authoritarian action by forming a Committee for the Defence of Human Rights and succeeded in obtaining an investigation of the army. Within months, four political parties had emerged from this group, supposedly under the Socialist Alliance, but in fact new formations which joined with the Slovenian Writers Union to draw up a political programme advocating pluralism, demanding multiparty elections in the spring of 1990, and expressing a desire to live in a sovereign state of the Slovene people. Parallel demands were made for western style democratic socialism and the establishment of parliamentary democracy by breakaway groups of socialists united variously as the Social Democratic Alliance of Slovenia and the Slovenian Democratic Alliance.

The response from the Slovenian communist party was to seek accommodation with these emerging forces. Initially, Kučan attempted to persuade them to remain under the umbrella of the Socialist Alliance but this strategy was soon abandoned in favour of a move on the part of the Party itself towards a more plural polity. Secret but nevertheless contested elections for the Slovenian representative to the Yugoslav state presidency were held in April 1989 which returned Dr Janez Drnovšek. Kučan hoped that by welcoming a more open and liberal culture he could revive the fortunes of the Slovenian Communist Party, but the pressure towards greater democratisation which was in substantial part a reaction to the events in Belgrade and Kosovo, overwhelmed such ambitions.

During the spring of 1989, a rift opened up between Serbia and Slovenia which proved irreconcilable and led directly to Yugoslavia's disintegration. For the previous two years, Kučan had studiously avoided direct conflict with Milošević at federal level, including withholding overt opposition to the imposition of martial law in Kosovo and the use of the army and police to deal with the protesters by force. But the miners strike of March, and particularly the manner in which the strikers were lured into abandoning their hunger strikes only to be arrested, spurred the Slovenian people as a whole to take a stand against the policies being pursued by the Serbian authorities. In September the new political parties followed the Serbian precedent and pushed constitutional changes through the Slovenian assembly, declaring Slovenia a 'sovereign and independent state'. The Assembly asserted Slovenia's right to secede, claimed the authority to veto the use of armed force in its territory and deleted the provision that the League of Communists should play the leading role in society.[27]

Sensing the import of this challenge Milošević responded swiftly, employing the same tactics as elsewhere; endless allegations were directed through the mass media, which Milošević now controlled, while Serbia began an economic boycott of Slovenian goods, thereby beginning, in effect, a trade war within Yugoslavia itself. Finally, Milošević and his agents overreached themselves. In mid-November 1989, the so-called Committee for Meetings set up by the Kosovo Serbs decided to hold a mass rally in Ljubljana on 1 December to explain the Serbian views to the Slovenes. The Slovenian leadership, by now in a strong position domestically, refused permission for this event. The immediate consequence was a deepening of the trade war which had been waged between the two republics for over a year, while Slovenia withheld 15 per cent of its annual contribution to the federal budget and sent its usual contribution to FADURK directly to Kosovo. Thus, by the end of 1989, the federal government's credibility as a centre of political power had received a profound challenge.[28]

Croatia

Since the repression of the Croatian Spring, Croatia had lapsed into sullenness. Unlike the Slovenes the Croats were not insulated geographically from the rest of Yugoslavia and were ever conscious of the potential for centralisation to promote Serbianisation under the guise of sustaining Yugoslavism. Repression had in fact strengthened pro-independence sentiment in Croatia, but it had driven it underground. For much of the 1980s, the republic remained overtly quiescent, leaving the Slovenes, their allies in the centralist–decentralist debate, to make the running in challenging the atavistic policies of Belgrade. Under the prime ministership of Ante Marković, Croatia was the agent of compromise and always mindful of the consequences of outright confrontation. Accordingly, this period was given the epithet, the 'Croatian silence', but their covert identification with Slovenian developments was inherent in their broader alignment with the forces of confederalisation to which they had adhered since the 1960s.

Part of the problem was that Croatia was not unified, either as a republic or as a communist party. Liberal elements, both Croat and Serbs existed alongside nationalist elements and old-fashioned communist dogmatists similarly drawn from both identities. The president of the Croatian party, Stipe Šuvar, elected in May 1986, represented a so-called 'Yugoslav synthesis', pro-Yugoslav and inherently federalist, which only gradually began to define a 'Croatian synthesis' out of the necessity of defending the republic's interests against those of other Yugoslavs. In order to avoid confrontation his idea was to offer the Serbs in Croatia greater autonomy and in return to obtain greater autonomy for the Croatian state within Yugoslavia.[29]

This strategy brought Croatia into collision with the centralising policies of Milošević. Croatia had refused to support the revision of the 1974 constitution and was inclined to take the side of the Kosovar Albanians. Meanwhile the equivocations of the Croatian republican authorities had created a period of ambiguity at a time of political turmoil at the federal level. Full advantage was taken of this by the more stridently and narrowly nationalist elements led by Franjo Tudjman who prepared a new, Croatian nationalist view, to counter that of Serbia. Although Tudjman was of impeccable Partisan origin, having joined the resistance in 1941 at the age of nineteen and served in the Army from which he retired with the rank of Major General in 1961, he had subsequently adopted the outlook of a narrow Croatian nationalist. These views had been refined during several spells behind bars, the first in the early 1970s when he was a victim of Tito's purges, and then again in 1981, also for nationalist activities. In that sense he was little different to the other nationalist leaders which emerged within Yugoslavia in this period, in so far as he was motivated primarily by a desire to advance his own career and chose to achieve this by taking up the cause of protecting the rights of Croatia's nationals against encroachment from other equally aggressive nationalist politicians. However, Tudjman's nationalism was particularly odious because it resonated overtly with the fascism of the interwar period raising once again the spectre of the genocide which Europeans believed had been expunged from the continent by forty years of inter-ethnic co-operation.

CONCLUSION

For the majority of Europeans, the end of 1989 was a moment of triumph and hope. The rapid destruction of an immutable and oppressive system and the ending of the division of Europe, a constant reminder of the catastrophes of the first half of the twentieth century, marked the end of an unlamented era in European history. For Yugoslavia it was the moment at which the South Slav people stood at the edge of the precipice, propelled by the forces of change sweeping eastern Europe and compelled by the logic of their own multiple nationalisms which had taken over as the defining force in Yugoslav politics when the credibility of communism, and particularly Yugoslavia's self-managed variant of it, finally evaporated.

9 Nemesis

Yugoslavia began to disintegrate at a moment of profound disturbance in European politics. Disorientated by the sudden and unanticipated ending of the Cold War, the major European states were unprepared either institutionally or politically to provide firm direction to a demanding and complex state at its periphery. Yugoslavia's dissolution was just a part of the difficult process of transition from communism experienced by all the states of eastern Europe in the early 1990s. However, Yugoslavia was exceptional. Of all the east European states created after the First World War, it was the most ethnically convoluted and intermingled. It carried the bitterest of legacies of multifaceted ethnic violence which the Second World War generated among European peoples. Its experiment with communism was also exceptional, as was its transition not least because it was controlled and directed from outside. Yugoslavia in 1990 was a multi-ethnic sovereign state without a functioning centre of power. While its constituent parts recognised the need for internal reorganisation, none had the power to coerce the remainder into co-operation and the international 'community' did not attempt to supply the necessary power until the process of dissolution was already beyond the point of return.[1] Although reform rather than dissolution remained a possibility up to the secessionist crisis of 1991, the centrifugal forces generated by rising nationalist sentiment in the absence of effective leadership or the will to mediate inter-republican disputes, placed any course other than dissolution ultimately beyond reach.

THE DOMESTIC CONTEXT OF YUGOSLAVIA'S DISSOLUTION

Demography was one element in the context of Yugoslavia's dissolution. The figures in Table 9.1 give an indication of how the constituent populations measured against one another numerically during the final decade. While the principal founders of Yugoslavia – the Serbs, Croats and Slovenes – had each declined marginally as percentages of the

Table 9.1 Yugoslavia's population, by nationality, 1981, 1991

Nationality	1981	Per cent	1991	Per cent	Growth/decline
Serbs	8,140,507	36	8,526,872	36.2	4.68
Croats	4,428,043	19.7	4,636,700	19.7	4.71
Muslims	1,999,890	8.9	2,353,002	10.0	17.65
Albanians*	1,730,878	7.7	2,178,393	9.3	25.85
Slovenes	1,753,571	7.8	1,760,460	7.5	−1.35
Macedonians	1,341,598	6.0	1,372,272	5.8	2.28
Yugoslavs	1,209,024	5.4	710,394	3.0	−41.25
Montenegrins	579,043	2.6	539,262	2.3	6.87
Hungarians	426,867	1.9	378,997	1.6	−11.22
Others and unknown	818,174	3.7	1,070,878	4.6	30.88
Total	22,427,585	100.00	23,528,230	100.00	

* Figures estimated on the basis of the 1981 census where nationality not given. This applies to the Albanian populations which boycotted the census.

Source: 'The National Composition of the Yugoslav Republics', *Yugoslav Survey*, vol. 33, no. 1 (1992), pp. 3–24.

total population since 1918, they retained a similar balance between themselves with the Serbs and Croats the most dominant in 1991 as they had been in 1918.

Throughout Yugoslavia's seventy-three year history, no one element in the population ever achieved anything approaching a numerical majority. Consequently, equilibrium was never properly established because the fundamental dispute over state organisation, which had impeded the first Yugoslavia, remained unresolved in the second. For a time Tito succeeded, through application of Marxism–Leninism, to create a federal government which was greater than the sum of its parts, but co-operation was coerced and easily threatened once liberalisation produced challenges that the régime was too weak to contain.[2]

Following Tito's death Yugoslavia depended for its unity on two institutions – the League of Communists and the Army. Their importance to the cohesion and continuity of the federation was recognised in the framing of the 1974 Constitution which institutionalised the role of both at federal level. However, by 1990, the authority of these organisations had been challenged and undermined by the actions of each of the three most powerful members in the federation.

The Demise of the League of Communists

By the beginning of 1990, the League of Communists which had been the cement of Yugoslavia for over forty years, was itself in the process of disintegration. Disorientated by the rapid collapse of the communist systems in the east European states, the League called an extraordinary Fourteenth Congress which was held in Belgrade on 20–22 January 1990 and devoted to the task of addressing the question of the régime's future legitimacy. The Party leadership placed before the delegates a draft resolution proposing a fresh political and economic compromise. While arguing in favour of Marković's economic reforms, the draft called for creation of a mixed economy rather than a pure market system. On the political front it proposed that the LCY seek political legitimacy in future through free elections, but it refrained from suggesting that these be multiparty elections. The Serbian constitutional changes of 1989 were to be confirmed. The Slovenes were swift to counter this by offering a substitute motion calling openly for creation of a multiparty system, the adoption of secret ballots, and asymmetric federalism with creation of a federal league of communists composed of separate independent parties. They also called for democracy in Kosovo and abolition of democratic centralism.

This was a reiteration of the two fundamentally opposed conceptions which had been at the centre of Serb–Slovene conflict since the mid-1980s. In the absence of any willingness to negotiate a way forward, or even a sense of any common ground, the Slovenes took advantage of the Serb rejection of their draft, to walk out. The Croats, whose delegation also walked out, then compounded the impact of this action. Neither the Bosnians nor the Macedonians were prepared to continue the discussions and the congress was suspended without even electing a new leadership. The next morning *Borba* declared, 'The League of Communist No Longer Exists'.[3] On 22 January, the 'leading role of the League of Communists' was removed from the Constitution.

The Role of the Army

The demise of the LCY had profound implications for the other unitary and centralist institution, the Yugoslav army (JNA). Although the JNA, as befitted its political role in the Yugoslav state, had been directed to give practical expression to the Partisan notion of 'brotherhood and

Table 9.2   Ethnic composition of officers in the
Yugoslav People's Army (JNA)

Nationality	1971	1981	1990
Croats	8.4	12.6	12.5
Slovenes	3.7	2.8	2.3
Serbs	60.4	60.0	54.3
Montenegrins	7.0	6.2	5.2
Yugoslavs	6.1	6.7	9.6
Moslems	1.3	2.4	5.3
Albanians	0.3	0.6	1.5
Macedonians	5.8	6.3	7.3
Hungarians	0.5	0.7	1.0
Others	1.5	1.6	1.4
Total	100.00	100.00	100.00

Source: L. Cohen, *Broken Bonds*, p. 182.

unity', by striving for proportionality in both the officer corps and
the ranks, this policy proved difficult to implement. From the 1960s
onwards, Serbs and Montenegrins consistently formed a far greater proportion of the officer corps than of the Yugoslav population in general
as Table 9.2 demonstrates. This imbalance can be accounted for in part
by the fewer career opportunities available in the poorer republics, and
perhaps the use in the armed forces of Serbo–Croat as the official language, which was particularly unattractive to the Slovene and Albanian
elements in the population. Given the Army's role as the military wing
of the League of Communists, this became a problem increasingly for
its legitimacy as a unifier and symbol of statehood once the League itself
began to disintegrate. Consequently, as the civilian government failed to
resolve the crisis, so the military began to play a more political role and
became overtly critical of the politicians, playing a leading role in stirring up resistance at federal level to Slovenia's constitutional amendments in September 1989.[4]

The JNA's defensive role within Yugoslavia, which was essentially to
protect the state against an internal disintegration, had been substantially reorganised following the Warsaw Pact invasion of Czechoslovakia
in 1968. Since then Yugoslavia's planners had evolved a strategy called
General People's Defence which was based on the concept of the nation
in arms. In addition to the division of the country into five military
districts, each republic had its own territorial defence force (TO).

These forces which were organised and commanded by retired generals of the JNA were paid for and equipped by the republics. Clearly these formations were yet another development that reinforced the growth of the republics as semi-autonomous entities. In recognition of the danger this contained, the JNA moved to dismantle these organisations during 1989. This proceeded in parallel with the generally supportive attitude taken by the Minister of Defence, General Veljko Kadijević, towards the Marković reforms. After all, the armed forces as an all-Yugoslav institution enjoying high status and extensive privileges, had a vested interest in the continued existence of a unified Yugoslav state. However, this outlook combined with its related adherence to communism, brought it into dangerous alignment with Milošević, while at the same time becoming an easy target for the decentralisers among the Slovenes and the Croats as they built their case against a return to greater centralisation.[5] Thus, the JNA, the sole remaining unifying institution left to Yugoslavia, was caught between two fundamentally opposing forces. Since Yugoslavia was essential to the Army's survival, it was for this that it chose to fight, only to be destroyed by Milošević as soon as it had served his purpose.

Post-communist Elections

At the beginning of 1990, Slovenia and Croatia were already prepared for the disappearance of the League of Communists. Each had scheduled elections for the spring in recognition of the requirement to obtain popular legitimacy for new governments which would implement the decision to depart radically from the status quo. Two weeks after the failure of the Fourteenth Congress, Kučan announced the formation of an independent Slovenian Communist Party, based on the principles of social democracy but with no affiliation to the LCY.[6]

Slovenia was the first to hold elections in 1990, with the two rounds being held on 8 and 22 April. DEMOS (a contraction of *DEMokraticke Opozicije Slovenije*), an alliance of six opposition groups together with the unaffiliated united essentially in opposition to communism and in their demand for independence, won 55 per cent of the vote giving it 127 seats of the 240 available in the Assembly. However, it was the Party of Democratic Renewal (the former League of Communists) which was returned as the biggest single party. Accordingly, its candidate, Milan Kučan, was returned as Slovenia's first post-communist president.

Elections were held in Croatia on 22 April and 6–7 May. Unlike the Slovenes, the Croats had prepared belatedly for this occasion. The best organised and largest of the parties which emerged by polling day was the Croatian Democratic Union (*Hrvatska demokratska zajednica* – HDZ), a right wing party campaigning on a platform of conservative social values, economic prosperity and Croatian nationhood. The HDZ leadership, headed by Dr Franjo Tudjman, had exploited the advantage of being the first nationalist party to take the field by securing hard currency support from the Croatian diaspora overseas. In January 1990, the various cultural institutions which had been stirring up Serbian nationalist sentiment in Croatia formed the Serb Democratic Party (SDS) under the leadership of Jovan Rašković, a psychiatrist originally from Knin who lived and worked in Sibenik on the Dalmatian Coast. Initially it was intended to be an extension of Serbia's Democratic Party, a liberal opposition party, but was increasingly taken over by a militant wing loyal to Milošević. When the SDS decided to spread its activities into Bosnia-Hercegovina, Rašković simply contacted his professional colleagues there to get the party off the ground. The result was that another psychiatrist, Radovan Karadžić, became President of the Bosnian SDS and in time war leader of the Bosnian Serbs. The issue which dominated the election was Croatia's relationship with the Yugoslav state, and the result, an overwhelming victory for the HDZ, which won 42 per cent of the vote, represented a delayed expression of pro-independence sentiment among the ethnic Croatian population. This result gave it control over two-thirds of the seats in the Sabor and Tudjman was elected president. The League of Communists of Croatia, which lacked a leadership with Tudjman's charisma, received just 25 per cent of the vote. The left was supported by the majority of the Croatian Serbs who were strongly opposed to plans for converting Yugoslavia into a loose confederation. However, the political left was weakened by the existence of a coalition of parties composed of former communists, the existence of which divided the vote between the coalition and the League.[7]

Having gained a groundswell of support, not least through the liberal use of bribery and corruption, combined as control of the media, Milošević called elections in Serbia suddenly in late 1989 and permitted only his own candidates to run. Despite his genuine popularity in this period, particularly among the rural communities and Serbia's businessmen, Milošević was determined to take every possible measure to ensure that he would continue to rule. During the summer of 1990 he organised a referendum on 1–2 July persuading 97 per cent of the electorate to endorse changes to the Serbian constitution before holding elections. The changes included the abolition of the autonomous provinces and the elimination of the word 'Socialist' from the republic's name. The overwhelming support was testimony to the fact that the majority of Serbs believed that Milošević alone could represent Serbian interests effectively.

When elections were held to the Serbian National Assembly in December a hastily organised opposition to the Serbian Socialist (ex-communist) Party was mounted by the Serbian Renewal Movement (*Srpski pokret obnove* – SPO), under the leadership of Vuk Drašković, a flamboyant figure with intellectual pretensions whose bearded appearance and racist ideas were reminiscent of the Četnik movement. Drašković was in many respects even more extreme than Milošević himself. The second opposition party was formed peremptorily from a composite of ten loosely organised and generally democratically inclined opposition parties. Calling itself the United Serbian Opposition, it lacked focus and in any case Milošević had too firm a grip on the levers of power for such a hastily organised group to make itself heard among the wider Serbian public. His Socialist Party emerged with over 77 per cent of the vote, giving them 194 out of the 250 seats in the Assembly and Milošević was returned as president with a mandate of 65 per cent.[8]

Culturally similar to the Serbs, the loyalty of the Montenegrins had been ensured by Milošević in January 1989. The elections held there in December 1990, gave the League of Communists of Montenegro a mandate of 66 per cent, and its leader, Momir Bulatović, who also became president, was prepared to suppress his personal wishes for a reform of the communist system in favour of giving total support to the centralisers.

During the political crisis of the late 1980s, the Bosnian League of Communists remained the strictest in its continued support of 'brotherhood and unity'. However, the party was enfeebled by internecine rivalries as well as by corruption which manifested itself in the form of clientilism, the extent of which had been revealed by the Agrokomerc scandal of 1987. This had developed from the disclosure that this Bosnian based firm, one of the largest in Yugoslavia, had issued promissory notes equivalent to $500 million without collateral. At the top of the clientele network was the senior Bosnian communist leader, Hamdija Pozderac whose hitherto distinguished career in Bosnian republican politics was cut short, but not before the scandal had exposed the extent to which leading politicians were conniving in financial malpractice through the creation of illegal networks in order to line their own pockets.[9]

In January 1990, the Bosnian party decided to adopt a new constitution and introduce a multiparty system. So as to prevent the latter developing along national lines, the creation of parties under national names was expressly forbidden. This solution quickly proved unworkable, however, and the ban was lifted. But, despite the determination of the city dwellers, the managers and intellectuals to avoid the politics of ethnicity, there was little enthusiasm for democratisation which was seen as leading dangerously, if only inadvertently, towards a confrontation with Bosnia's tripartite ethnic identity. Instead, the majority of Bosnians were content for the continuance of an authoritarian Yugoslav solution which avoided the difficult decisions which might destabilise the complex ethnic intermingling of the population.

The elections were held on 18 November 1990 and produced a vote which divided the seats in the legislature between the three parties representing the main ethnic groups in numbers roughly comparable to their population size. The Party of Democratic Action (*Stranke demokratske akcije* – SDA) which attracted the Muslim vote, received 30.5 per cent of the seats, which was lower than their 44 per cent of the population. Karadžić's Serbian Democratic Party (*Srpska demokratske stranke* – SDS), received 25.2 per cent, and the Croatian Democratic Community (HDZ – Bosnia), led by Stjepan Kljuić, a Croat from central Bosnia, received just 15 per cent. The Communists, with 10 per cent, were a spent force in Bosnian politics and simply disappeared.

A coalition government was formed and the key posts were allocated according to the election results, with the leader of the SDA, Alija Izetbegović, being elected President. Izetbegović had a history of dissident activity stretching back to the Second World War when he had been imprisoned early in the Tito era for participation in the Young Muslims. He was tried and imprisoned for a second time in 1983 as a nationalist dissident and in particular for spreading seditious literature.[10] This gave him credibility among the Muslim population but left him dangerously vulnerable to the attacks of others who wanted to undermine his authority. He presided over a republic which was endangered by a series of complex pressures from within and without and had declared during the election campaign that the Muslims, together with other nations, would defend Bosnia from partition with armed force if need be.

In Macedonia the old party leadership was voted out of office at the Tenth Congress of the Macedonian Party, held in Skopje at the end of November 1989. The new leadership was younger and reform minded and concerned that Milošević's ambitions might extent to a recreation of

Greater Serbia on the pre-First World War model, at the expense of Macedonia's independent identity. Following the abortive LCY Congress in January, alternative political associations were permitted to organise. Free elections to the Parliament (the *Sobranje*), took place on 11 November 1990 in which the IMRO–Democratic Party for Macedonian National Unity emerged with the 38 seats of the 120 available, the largest share of the votes, while the Party of Democratic Transformation, formerly the League of Communists, finished in second place with 31 seats. The government was formed after weeks of negotiation from a multiparty coalition led by the reform-orientated communist, Koro Gligorov, President of Macedonia, which left the nationalists in opposition. Gligorov founded post-communist Macedonia on the principle of a citizen's state rather than one based on Macedonian people, thereby renouncing at the outset Macedonian nationality as an organisational focal point.[11]

By the end of 1990 then, all of the six Yugoslav republics had elected in more or less free elections, new legislatures and presidents. The only important figures in the country who remained unelected were at federal level, namely the federal assembly, the presidency and of course Ante Marković. But these were now essentially anomalous because they presided over a near confederation of national leaderships, which with the exception of Serbia and Montenegro were either partly or predominantly coalitions of non communist parties.

Ethnic tensions continued to rise over the summer of 1990. At the centre of the conflict was a revival of overt Serbo–Croat antagonism, which was easily provoked in the context of a more stridently nationalist tone from the Serbian government in Belgrade and the upsurge of long suppressed Croatian nationalist sentiment. Just as in Slovenia, Montenegro and the autonomous provinces, the Serbs had organised protest rallies and even instituted commemorative services to the victims of the Ustaše concentration camps of the Second World War.

Milošević exploited the media at Croatia's expense to the extent that towards the end of 1988, the Croats were being accused of dumping radioactive waste in Serb villages in order to poison the Serb communities. The outcry this generated was so great that the authorities dug up the alleged sites in order to investigate the matter. The allegations had little foundation. Nevertheless, this episode had a deleterious impact on sections of the Croatian Serb community. While the vast majority of Croatia's Serbs were city dwellers who were well integrated into Croatian society and were suitably offended by this crude nationalist activity, the rural populations of the villages around Knin and the communities which had settled eastern Slavonia on the border with Vojvodina immediately after the Second World War were a different matter. During August, the towns of Knin and Benkovac demonstrated that they as a community were growing increasingly fearful for their security by setting up blockades to prevent the Croatian police functioning effectively. They were encouraged in this atavism by Serbian special forces acting as provocateurs. Then in October, this process was carried a stage further when the villages in the Knin area declared themselves an independent Serb enclave which they called the *krajina*.[12]

All this suited Tudjman's purposes since it gave him occasions to respond to nationalist rhetoric in kind. In the wake of the Serb rebellion in August 1990, Croatia hastily trained some 20,000 gendarmes (*specijalci*), in addition to the existing police, arming them with light weapons bought abroad. But despite the enthusiasm for independence, Croatia's vulnerability to the pressure from its southern neighbour and the Yugoslav army caused Tudjman to hesitate. Throughout 1990 he continued to press for a further loosening of the federal arrangements while retaining the Yugoslav state. The change of policy in favour of full independence was signalled by the Sabor's adoption of a Bill on 21 February 1991 which asserted the primacy of the Croatian laws and the Croatian Constitution.

During March 1991 the republican presidents agreed to hold weekly meetings in what proved a final effort to prevent the ultimate crisis. These meetings proved to be merely the final forum in which the stand-off between the two camps was aired. Croatia and Slovenia reiterated their view that Yugoslavia should become a voluntary association of sovereign republics and were duly countered by Serbia and Montenegro which wanted Yugoslavia to remain a united state in which the federation would exercise control over the key aspects of sovereignty, including security, economic policy and foreign affairs. In the middle of this debate were the presidents of Macedonia and Bosnia-Hercegovina who proposed a third alternative – an 'asymmetric federation' – a proposition which was never properly clarified. In May the federal government finally lost all credibility when the customary rotation of the presidency was not observed. The incoming president was due to be the Croat, Stipe Mesić, who had promised to investigate conditions in Kosovo as soon as he took up office. The Serbs exploited their control of Serbia, Montenegro, Vojvodina and Kosovo to block the changeover. The federal executive was thus discredited and Slovenia and Croatia then depleted the federal assembly by ordering their representatives to walkout in protest at Serbia's tactics in the presidency.[13]

War: Slovenia and Croatia Versus Yugoslavia

The Slovenian Assembly had adopted a secession law on 20 February and on 8 May announced its intention to secede on 26 June. Having a well-integrated population, which was over 90 per cent Slovene, and no common border with Serbia, its decision to seek independence was not domestically controversial. Despite the depletion of its Territorial Defence Force since May 1990, Slovenia was ready to ward off the attempt by the federal forces to prevent its secession. In a 'Ten Day War' which began on 25 June, the JNA believed it could dissuade Slovenia from leaving Yugoslavia by a short, sharp display of military force. In the event, it was outmanoeuvred on the ground by clever defensive tactics on the part of the Slovenian Territorial Defence units. These were backed up by a combination of diplomacy and propaganda which persuaded international opinion that the JNA's use of force was illegitimate and had to be stopped by the threat of sanctions. Accordingly, it was opprobrium from outside Yugoslavia which pressured the cessation of hostilities and led to the recognition of Slovenia's *de facto* independence, even though it agreed to suspend this for three months. The withdrawal of JNA personnel was complete at the end of October and Slovenia received formal recognition by the European Community member states on 15 January 1992.[14]

The Croatian government similarly proceeded towards secession, forming a Croatian National Guard Corps on 11 April as a response to the deployment of tanks by the Yugoslav Army when Serbs were murdered in the Croatian Plitviče National Park. It was used first to occupy a village near Knin on 29 April. Then on 12 May, the autonomous region voted in its own referendum to remain part of Yugoslavia while one week later a referendum in Croatia voted 90 per cent in favour of secession.

The fighting which ensued on 25 June between the Croatian forces and the JNA was much more protracted than that in Slovenia. Like the Slovenes, the Croats agreed on 7 July, following mediation of the European Union Troika, to suspend independence for three months. But at the end of July, Tudjman finally turned his back on negotiation of a Yugoslav solution when he boycotted meetings of the Collective state

Presidency. Zagreb's relations with Serbia were formally broken on 4 August and the conflict with the Serbs entered a new phase on 22 August 1991 when Tudjman sent an ultimatum to the Yugoslav presidency demanding an end to the JNA's arming of the Serb militias. When this demand was not met, the Croatian government ordered general mobilisation in preparation for a 'war of liberation'.

The conflict which dragged on through the autumn wrought large-scale destruction and a death toll of over 10,000 Croat service personnel and civilians. Hundreds of thousands became refugees. Ultimately this carnage contributed positively to Croatia's campaign for recognition which it achieved from the Europeans in January 1992. The ceasefire, which ended what the Croats call the 'Homeland War' was concluded on 2 January and received backing from the United Nations which put an interposition force into the Serb Krajina to keep the peace. Yugoslavia, the once proudly independent socialist unitary state, effectively had ceased to exist.

INTERNATIONAL CONTEXT OF YUGOSLAVIA'S DISSOLUTION

Yugoslavia had been deeply affected by the processes of transition from communism which had been under way since the mid-1980s. The speed with which communism lost its legitimacy caught the Yugoslav leadership, both federal and republican, off balance and contributed to the speed with which they turned to mobilise nationalist sentiments in order to build up their support as the ideology of communism was progressively discredited. Outside Yugoslavia, there was an awareness of the dangers which its dissolution might hold. It was not so much that the warning signs were ignored, but rather that they occurred at a moment in time when so much in international affairs was being revolutionised as a consequence of the steady retreat from Cold War which began in the mid-1980s. The implications of this for the institutions which had developed in the context of the Cold War to manage security and trade were profound. When Yugoslavia went into dissolution, the United States was in the middle of a partial withdrawal from Europe, the European Community (EC) was reorganising itself in order to develop a political dimension particularly in fields of defence and diplomacy and NATO, created as a defensive organisation and the bastion of western defence against the perceived Soviet 'threat' for forty years, had to adapt itself to the post-Cold War environment, or face dismantlement. The revolution in international affairs was completed when the Soviet Union co-operated with the United States, through the United Nations to develop a co-ordinated response to the Iraqi invasion of Kuwait in September 1990.[15]

The impact of these developments on Yugoslavia was several-fold. First, it removed the Cold War corset,[16] the framework of security which had provided a near constant source of collective threat to the peoples of Yugoslavia, discouraging them from indulging in the politics of division lest these lead to an attempt by the Warsaw Pact to stabilise the region through invasion. Second, with the Cold War at an end, Yugoslavia had lost its strategic importance to both sides. It was no longer to be indulged by the West and courted by the East as a matter of course. Third, the international community was fully preoccupied with the momentous developments the changing international environment occasioned and in particular with the challenge to it mounted by Saddam Hussein.

The 'Hour of Europe'

When on 25 June, the JNA invaded Slovenia, the European Community insisted that this was a crisis which it would handle without interference from the United States. In part this was a response conditioned by the collective failure of the EC to co-ordinate a coherent approach to the Gulf crisis, despite its rhetoric about developing a common defence and diplomatic architecture. Immediately, the EC Troika, in this instance the foreign ministers of the Netherlands, Italy and Luxembourg, made a hastily arranged visit to Belgrade at the request of the Slovenian government, where they obtained agreement on a three-point plan drawn up by Ante Marković. It called for a suspension of the implementation of the declarations of independence for three months, a resolution of the presidential crisis which had precipitated the demise of Yugoslavia's federal executive and legislature, and the return of the JNA to its barracks. The initial agreement for a ceasefire broke down immediately and the troika adjourned to Brioni where it negotiated a peace agreement which awarded *de facto* recognition to Slovenia. The agreement required Slovenia to deactivate its territorial defence units and to permit the presence of an observer mission to monitor the ceasefire.

The initial triumphalism within the EC that this apparent success occasioned was quickly dispelled. The Serbs were prepared to concede Slovenian independence, but the vigour of the EC intervention encouraged the JNA to concert with the leadership of Serbia in working actively to prevent the success of Croatian secession. Despite the upsurge of Serbo–Croat violence as the war for possession of the Krajina got under way, the EC attempted to carry the negotiating process a stage further by inviting the warring factions to a conference at The Hague, convened on 7 September under Lord Carrington's chairmanship. This conference set out to consider Yugoslavia as a whole, and throughout the negotiations Carrington treated all parties in the dispute as equally responsible for the crisis. A series of proposals were put before the delegations representing the federal government and the six republics and the two provinces, amounting to a reworking of the various settlements which had been proposed within the presidency between March and May, with the addition of a grant of special status to the national minorities in areas in which they constituted a majority. These concessions amounted to substantial judicial and legislative powers and it remains unclear exactly how the arrangement was supposed to work. It foundered because it required the Slovenes and Croats to give up the gains they had already won. On 8 October both reiterated their declarations of independence.[17]

Sanctions imposed by the EC on 25 June, and by the UN on 25 September, were designed to contain the war and prevent any of the parties acquiring additional armaments as had the Croats during 1990. Such measures probably deepened the crisis, however. For one thing the JNA had succeeded in disarming the republics before the war started and thus the federal authorities in Belgrade held an overwhelming advantage militarily over the rest of Yugoslavia. Moreover, Yugoslavia as a net exporter of weapons was not short of munitions, although the location of the principal armaments factories in Serbia and Bosnia-Hercegovina similarly prejudiced the balance of forces in favour of the Serbs.

While the EC Conference was in progress, a judicial commission under the chairmanship of Robert Badinter was tasked to consider applications for independence. Having failed to persuade the delegations to accept a restructuring of Yugoslavia, the EC foreign ministers shifted towards a partial recognition of independence, declaring on 29 November that Yugoslavia was 'in the process of dissolution'.[18] This shift, which was confirmed at a meeting of EC foreign ministers on 16–17 December, amounted to acknowledgement that the best the

EC could now do was to offer to guarantee the independence of the new states as they emerged. The result was that majority populations were being left to dominate the minorities. The Germans had been the first to switch from a policy of seeking reform of Yugoslavia to recognition of the newly independent state, citing the gratuitous nature of the violence in the Serbo–Croat war as justification for identifying the Serbs as aggressors, but their policy was also conditioned by being in the forefront of states receiving Croatian refugees as well as having successfully changed German borders in order to absorb the former East Germany. Detractors from a policy of recognition, which included Britain, the United States and, to a lesser extent, France, argued that this was motivated by the belief that far from halting the war, as the Germans argued, it would lead to further fighting. Both sides in the argument were right and both were wrong.

Internationalisation of the conflict brought a halt to the war in Croatia, and also opened the way for the warring factions to request an interposition force in the Krajina. The United Nations, which had been active in the mediation process since October, successfully negotiated a ceasefire in early December. However, stability on this front opened the way for a renewal of conflict elsewhere.

BOSNIA'S WAR FOR INDEPENDENCE

The Bosnians did not want independence for themselves, and were resistant to the break up of Yugoslavia to the very end. In January 1992, Izetbegović requested that recognition of Croatian and Slovenian independence be withheld, raising the spectre of ethnic war in Bosnia if this process were to be completed. The disintegration of communism had led Bosnians like other Yugoslavs, to seek security within their own ethnic groups, but unlike the other republics in which there was one segment of the population holding an absolute majority, in Bosnia the population contained three substantial minorities which were intermingled throughout the republic. Consequently, a move to secede as a unit from Yugoslavia would only work if it had the full support of the majority of each of the three ethnic components.

Although war did not break out in Bosnia immediately upon international recognition of Slovenia and Croatia, it is nonetheless difficult to sustain the argument that there was no direct causal link between these latter events and the onset of the Bosnian war just a few months later.

The secession of the two northern republics left the Bosnian government facing an impossible choice. It could either remain within the rump Yugoslavia, where there was now no counterbalancing force to the centralising policies of the Serbs, or alternatively it could opt to leave the federation, in which case its substantial Serbian community, increasingly militant throughout since 1989, would object on the grounds that it saw its best interests as lying within a continuation of the federal relationship with Belgrade.

A series of factors converged to render Bosnia unstable by the beginning of 1992. Socially, there was a clear division between the educated town-dwellers who adopted a sophisticated approach to Bosnia's complex society, and the countryside which remained almost feudal in its outlook and simple in its political allegiances. The stridently nationalist tone of both Serb and Croat political rhetoric during the late 1980s struck a resonant chord in such communities, giving rise to a sense of communal fear in an environment in which stability depended upon trust and co-operation across ethnic divisions. To this was added the development by the SDS of a military wing similar to that of the Serb militias in the Krajina which were armed and organised by Serb special forces. The parallel disarming of the Territorial Defence Units by the JNA left the non-Serb Bosnians in a situation which was militarily asymmetric since only the Serb community was left with means at its disposal to wage outright war. The SDS was able to rally support from the wider population by raising the spectre of Islamic fundamentalism through rigorous exploitation of Izetbegović's dissident past. Twenty years before Izetbegović had published a tract called 'Islamic Declaration' in which he set out the arguments for the superiority of Islam over communism and Christianity. The fact that such polemics were no longer part of the Bosnian president's political thinking was beside the point in such a highly charged atmosphere. A referendum on independence was held on 28 February and 1 March 1992 and the 63 per cent turnout from the Croat and Muslim population was overwhelmingly in favour of independence. The SDS, however, had organised a boycott, having held a referendum of their own the week previously which declared their determination to remain federated to what was left of Yugoslavia. The battle lines were drawn and war began on 6 April, the day independence was formally declared.[19]

Serb war aims were to unite the Serb communities in north-west Bosnia with the majority of Serb communities in the lands adjacent to Serbia and Montenegro. The tactics were similar to those used in the Kraijina, and involved mass terror and war-fighting practices of annihilation of people and property last seen in the region during the summer of 1941, by which the Bosnian Serb army attempted to eradicate all traces of the Muslim and Croat communities.[20] These aims had been achieved by the late summer of 1992, with the exception of the Muslim enclaves of Srebrenica, Žepa and Goražde. Here the Serbian forces settled down to wait, having achieved occupation of roughly two-thirds of Bosnian territory.

Negotiations

The first attempted settlement was organised by David Owen, Lord Carrington's successor as EU negotiator, and the UN's envoy, Cyrus Vance, in the spring of 1993. Vance–Owen Peace Plan was based on the assumption that the settlement must not reward the aggressors. Their plan proposed a cantonisation of Bosnia, in which the republic would be divided into ten provinces, nine based on ethnic lines and one mixed, under a weak federal government in Sarajevo. The stumbling block to its acceptance was that it required the Bosnian Serbs to give up territory for which they had fought, and this they were unprepared to do, even though Milošević was beginning to heed the economic consequences of the sanctions ring which had been imposed on the rump Yugoslavia by the UN on 30 May 1992. The plan had received a less than enthusiastic response from the external powers since it was unenforceable without the commitment of 50,000 ground troops, an undertaking which the international community was unprepared to accept so soon after the end of the Cold War had brought demilitarisation to Europe.

What the failed peace negotiations did bring, however, was a new conflict, this time between the Bosnian Croats and the Muslims, a response to rising tensions in the Croat areas consequent on the arrival of large numbers of Muslim refugees fleeing from the fighting in and around Srebrenica. A second variation of the Owen peace plan was proffered in July 1993, this time on the basis of a federal solution dividing Bosnia into three semi-autonomous republics. The Muslims discovered to their horror that their position had weakened owing to the second round of fighting. Still adamant that they would not accept any solution which amounted to a partition of Bosnia, their stubborn refusal to sign the latest peace plan was encouraged by the equivocal signals being sent by the United States during the summer of 1993 which led the Muslims to conclude that the sanctions ring, which stood between them and rearmament from outside might soon be lifted. Thus they chose to continue to fight in order to establish a more favourable territorial balance.[21]

A third plan, put forward in June 1994, was prepared by the five nation Contact Group which brought Russia into the negotiating team alongside the United States, Britain, France and Germany. This also outlined a confederal solution and envisaged a Croat–Muslim federation in Bosnia offering them 51 per cent of the former republic's territory including most of the major cities while awarding the Serbs control over the remaining 49 per cent. Its basis was the agreement in principle made in September 1993 on the establishment of a Union of Republics, and the agreement brokered by the United States in secret talks between the Croats and Muslims in February 1994 on a Bosnian Federation. The Plan was presented to the various parties on a yes or no basis. Although the Bosnian Serbs still held out against a settlement, Milošević acted this time to cut off their military supplies, thereby changing significantly the balance of forces on the ground and clearly diminishing the ability of the VSO to continue the conflict.[22]

Over the winter of 1994–95, Milošević reopened his contacts with Tudjman. The result was that Croatia was permitted to retake the Krajina unopposed and, in July and August launched an offensive with American and Bosnian Muslim agreement, which took the Croatian army into territory occupied by the Bosnian Serbs. The latter, starved of military supplies and lacking even political support, retreated. They were driven back until their territory corresponded to roughly that which was under offer in the Contact Group agreement.

The Bosnian war was brought to an end in October 1995 for four reasons. First, one of the principal antagonists, Croatia, was ready to make peace because it had achieved most of its territorial objectives. A second antagonist, the Bosnian Serbs, had been beaten on the ground and not by NATO action, but by the attritional consequences of sustained Croatian and Muslim war fighting. Third, the economic situation in Serbia itself was becoming desperate and Milošević saw peace as expedient in order to save his political position. He was prepared, therefore, to enforce a settlement on the Bosnian Serb leadership regardless of their protests. Finally, the warring parties had wearied of the conflict and the ethnic separation of the population had been largely achieved. Added to this, NATO applied the weight of its air power capability to the situation in September and October, hastening the various factions to accept an invitation to the conference table.

The Dayton Agreement, negotiated in November 1995, imposed a solution not dissimilar to that which had been offered in 1993. The new Bosnian state consists of Bosnian–Croat Federation and a Bosnian Serb Republic under a weak central government in which a president, prime minister, parliament and constitutional court, preside over the traditional key competences of foreign policy, monetary policy, and foreign trade. However, almost all other powers have been devolved including those of policing and armed forces. This settlement has required the supervision of a substantial peace enforcement mission. The war had cost the lives of some 200,000 people, and generated a refugee crisis of comparable magnitude. Despite the continuing presence of the international community, only a small percentage of the refugees have chosen to return, a reflection of the deep distrust which the conflict instilled. Moreover, all attempts at developing the federation towards the projected Union of Bosnia-Hercegovina have foundered on the refusal of the Serbs to co-operate.

MACEDONIA'S PEACEFUL TRANSITION

Macedonia carried the same potential for instability and violence as Bosnia owing to the tensions which had arisen during the late 1980s between substantial Albanian minority and the Slavic community. In this case it was the anti-Albanianism of the Serbian communist party which was the instrument of the breakdown of trust between the Macedonian populations.

The Macedonian population voted for independence in a referendum held on 8 September 1991, although the Albanian population declined to vote. The decision to opt for secession was a direct response to fear that Macedonia's ethnically divided population rendered it vulnerable to the same destabilisation as had occurred further north. Independence was duly declared on 21 November 1991 but despite the Badinter Commission's endorsement, was not recognised by the European Community until December 1993. This was due largely to the objections of neighbouring Greece, which was reluctant to accept establishment of a new Macedonian state since, in their view, Macedonia was simply a geographic expression. For this reason Macedonia was obliged to adopt the cumbersome appellation of FYROM (Former Yugoslav Republic of

Macedonia) and even then only received recognition from Greece after an eighteen-month trade embargo in which the Greeks delayed the passage of supplies to Macedonia from the port of Salonika and under pressure from both Russia and the United States.

The central figure in Macedonia's stability has been the President, Kiro Gligorov, a lawyer by training who had impeccable Partisan credentials, having joined the KPJ in 1944. He was a member of the Yugoslav presidency in the 1970s but as supporter of the marketisation of the Yugoslav economy, he disappeared into obscurity during the 1980s and reappeared during the Marković reform period when his enthusiasm for liberalisation of the economy and the introduction of multiparty elections resulted in his return to federal politics. It was there that he established the reputation which subsequently gave him the political weight to impose his vision on post-communist Macedonia.[23] Under Gligorov, Macedonia has been governed through a series of coalitions in which care has been taken to include the Albanian Party for Democratic Prosperity. Even so there have been constant difficulties in the field of education and culture, resulting in spasmodic periods of tension which have been contained by the presence of a United Nations preventive mission and also by the action of NATO-led armed force.

SERBIA: THE ENEMY WITHIN

The new Federal Republic of Yugoslavia, which Serbia and Montenegro proclaimed in 27 April 1992, did not receive international recognition until 1994 and then only as a device to assist with halting the war in Bosnia. The two remaining elements of Yugoslavia had things in common. Apart from ethnic affiliation, since the Montenegrins are largely Serb, both communities had elected communist-dominated governments during the transition. Nevertheless, the relationship between them was persistently complicated by Montenegro's fear that Milošević might be prepared to further Serbia's interests at the expense of its smaller counterpart.

After Dayton, the Kosovo issue continued to dominate and served as a distraction from the precipitous deterioration of the economy. The issue at the root of the contest in Kosovo is the legitimacy of Serbia's claim to sovereignty over the territory of Kosovo. Like Macedonia, Kosovo applied to the Badinter Commission for its case for independence to be considered, but this was largely ignored both within

Yugoslavia and by the major international states which were wary of dealing with the Kosovo leadership on the same level as to the region's other politicians. In part this is a function of geography and Kosovo's perceived lack of economic viability as an independent entity; in part it is the consequence of a widely held assumption that Kosovo is at the heart of Balkan stability and that any attempt to change its status in respect to sovereignty will destabilise the equally delicate ethnic balance further south in Macedonia, as well as in Bosnia and will have ramifications in Albania.[24]

During the wars in Bosnia and in particular in the context of the peace settlement in 1995, the major external powers became trapped in the logic of this dilemma, since resolution of the Bosnian conflict was built on the premise that the government in Belgrade had to be kept positively engaged in sustaining the peace and making the Dayton settlement work. This conveyed to the Serbs the notion that they had a free hand to order Kosovo as they chose.

This approach impacted on the situation in Kosovo in two ways. First, it emboldened Belgrade, encouraging the government there to persist with policies which amounted in effect to the creation of an apartheid regime. That this was possible was due in no small measure to the strategy of non-violent resistance adopted by the Kosovo Albanian leadership, in particular that of the proclaimed pacificist intellectual, Ibrahim Rugova, who was elected in 1992. Rugova's view was that it would be self-destructive for the Kosovo Albanians to take on the Serbs and he accordingly attempted to defend the Albanian population from repression by acquiescing in the creation of parallel political structures.[25] However, this had a deleterious impact on the more radical elements in the Albanian community, especially in the light of the Dayton settlement which conveyed the impression that armed conflict was the most effective means of obtaining redress in an ethnically divided community. The Kosovo Liberation Army (KLA), the principal organisational expression of radical Albanian politics in the rump Yugoslavia began to be a threat to the status quo following the collapse of the Albanian state in 1997 which provided the opportunity for the KLA to arm itself from the unguarded weapons arsenals of the former communist regime. Proclaiming a political programme which at its most extreme was advocating pan-Albanian Union, it thereby opened up the prospect of further regional destabilisation.

Violence on both sides, which occurred from 1997 onwards restricted in turn the options for a resolution. On the one hand, the moderates among the Kosovo Albanian politicians were undermined as figures of authority within their community and consequently it was the extremist agenda which came increasingly to the fore. At the same time, the very fact of violence which the Serbs perceived as terrorist provided a reason by which the Milošević government could justify internal security measures, and this in its turn, provided the KLA with a justification for reprisals. The result was a steady escalation of violence on both sides as the perception of threat increased. At the same time, this raised the stakes of the settlement to the point where only the most extreme solutions were being aired, thereby making the possibility of settlement the conflict through peaceful means increasingly remote.

The major external powers became actively engaged in the conflict during the summer of 1998 as the violence threatened to create a refugee crisis as Kosovo Albanians in droves began to move south and east to escape the persecution from the Serb internal security forces. Diplomacy was conducted through the six nation Contact Group which conducted a form of indirect negotiations through its envoy Christopher Hill who shuttled between the various factions over the summer in an effort to establish some common ground. The Contact Group sought to balance the competing interests of the two parties while avoiding any discussion of Kosovo's status and accordingly it based negotiations on a succession of draft proposals which offered a state infrastructure for Kosovo, within existing international boundaries, in which a large measure of self-governance would be permitted. The agreement was to implement with the support of NATO, an issue of vigorous international dissent, with a review at the end of three years which technically at least would provide a fresh opportunity to examine the question of sovereignty.

Some measure of consensus appeared to have been achieved in mid-October when Richard Holbrooke visited Belgrade and emerged with a document known as the Eleven-point Plan. Milošević had been persuaded to accept an OSCE (Organisation for Security and Co-operation in Europe) monitoring mission in Kosovo in return for an undertaking that sovereignty of the rump Yugoslavia would not be an issue in the settlement. Within a few months, however, the violence on both sides resumed and the Contact Group was obliged to summon the warring factions to the conference at Rambouillet in the middle of February under the threat of NATO air strikes should they fail to comply.

The Rambouillet talks were unproductive, since neither party was prepared to sign the settlement placed before them. The Serbian delegation hid behind its legal claim to sovereignty and the support of the Russians who were unwilling for the Contact Group to back the negotiations through the use of military force. The settlement on offer was less satisfactory to them than the status quo and they saw little incentive in signing up to it. Furthermore, the NATO alliance had not demonstrated internal cohesion over the threat of force and Milošević may have concluded that it would not be able to sustain an attack if one were ordered. Moreover the UN Security Council in its Resolution 1199 of 23 September 1998 which declared a humanitarian emergency threatening peace and security, had stopped short of authorising the use of force. For their part the Kosovo Albanians believed they had more to gain from direct NATO involvement than from a peaceful settlement.

In the event, Milošević chose to call NATO's bluff. The war which lasted from 24 March to 9 June reversed the balance between the protagonists. For the remainder of 1999 and into 2000, the KLA took advantage of the power they had achieved as a result of the war to terrorise the Serbs in return. As in Bosnia, an ethnic separation has been achieved through armed conflict, but the peace continues to require a substantial international presence.

CONCLUSION

The cost of these wars to the inhabitants of the former Yugoslavia can be measured in the standards of living which, with the exception of Slovenia, are either at or below those of 1990. It is reflected less tangibly, but with rather more long-term implications, in the breakdown of inter-communal trust which the wars have generated and which only the passing of several generations will soften. The cost to the international community can be measured in the commitment which it has subsequently been obliged to make to the stabilisation and reconstruction of the successor states. What Europeans failed to do wholesale in 1990, they have been obliged to undertake piecemeal, but under even more difficult circumstances.

Conclusion

Yugoslavia's history spans a distinct historical epoch in European history bounded by the beginning and end of the experiment with communism. It was created a little over a year after the October Revolution of 1917, and dissolved some eight months before the Soviet Union's demise in December 1991. This was an age of ideology, of the pursuit of radical new ideals, a reaction to the certainties of political stability and economic growth that characterised Europe in the nineteenth century. Yugoslavia was in 1918 a product of its times. It was an idea, developed by intellectuals and the seekers of political power, which was translated into reality because events, somewhat unexpectedly, created the opportunity for its attainment, and because no one could suggest an alternative.

During this era of seventy-three years, Yugoslavia was created and later recreated, at the instigation of its own peoples, and twice destroyed under pressure from changes taking place in the European continent as a whole. In addition to communism, its leaders experimented with constitutional monarchy, monarchical dictatorship and with various forms of centralisation and federalism. None succeeded in overcoming the deeply held prejudices, the distorted historical perceptions, the mythologies and above all the communal fear and nihilism which had been instilled as a consequence of centuries of foreign rule and which all the efforts of communist educational practices did nothing to ameliorate.

From the outset, the South Slav state-building project was undermined by the paradoxes which it contained. This was manifest most clearly in the struggle between the Serbian vision of a centralised state and that of the more extreme elements among the Croats who saw a loose federal structure as the only political form in which their culture could flourish. While extremes of opinion generally exist in most functioning modern states, they are generally counterbalanced by those who occupy the middle ground in between and constitute the consensus forming majority. Such a majority was singularly absent from Yugoslavia for much of the interwar period, thereby providing the opportunity in which sustained struggle between Serbs and Croats could establish itself as the defining tension of the South Slav state. In post-war Yugoslavia, this paradox remained, but another concealed it for a time. Under the Tito régime, Yugoslavia was torn between the opposing forces of communist internationalism which emphasised workers solidarity, and nationalism expressed as Yugoslavism which became necessary as a consequence of Yugoslavia's isolation from the Soviet controlled communist movement. Once Yugoslavia was directed down its own road to socialism, the communist dogma was manipulated to serve as the principal tool in management and containment of the national question. The outcome was the progressive devolution of power to nationally defined republics until there was so little remaining at the centre that the federal authorities were no longer able to impose all-encompassing policies. Once communism failed to deliver on its economic contract with the people, it was overrun and consumed by the nationalist pressures it had sought to deny and suppress. Workers self-management, itself a mass of contradictory pressures, merely provided a forum in which this struggle could be played out.

This brings us to the use of coercion. In both its monarchical and communist forms, Yugoslavia's leaders resorted to coercive methods to impose solutions and obtain co-operation. This was a function not simply of the types of régime but of the political immaturity of the Yugoslav peoples. Such methods were effective in the short term at enabling the incumbent régimes to govern; in the long run they militated against the growth of consensus and the habits of negotiation and compromise, serving only to reinforce existing social divisions. This proved particularly damaging following the death of the founding 'father' of post-war Yugoslavia, leaving the state without the one person who could command the attention and obedience of the majority.

External factors played a major part in ensuring Yugoslavia's survival or demise. Just as political leaders manipulated communal fears in the late 1980s to emphasise divisions, so at various stages the leadership exploited such mentalities to focus the population on one readily identifiable common interest – freedom from external attack. Even the Serbs and the Croats had been persuaded to come to a compromise once Hitler and Mussolini had raised the stakes sufficiently. The question of what would have been the outcome in 1990–91 had a new external threat to the South Slav peoples appeared in place of the Soviet Union's menace used by Tito to generate cohesion for so long, is a matter for speculation.

Reform of Yugoslavia was possible, and probably the solution for which the majority of its population wished, but it could not be achieved from within. In 1990, war in Europe was widely regarded as unthinkable, still less a recurrence of wholesale persecution of ethnically defined populations. Precisely because these events were considered outside the normative values of modern European society, there was a resistance on the part of the major European states to taking preventive action. To do so would mean confronting the fact that fifty years of multi-ethnic state-building across the western half of the continent had rendered the persecution of minorities and armed conflict between peoples no less possible than they had been prior to 1945. This approach, a product of naiveté which is the necessary concomitant of political idealism, was at the heart of the international inaction which delayed coercive intervention until Yugoslavia's crisis had proceeded beyond the point when reform was any longer a possibility.

Notes

INTRODUCTION

1. C. Gati, 'From Sarajevo to Sarajevo', *Foreign Affairs*, 71, 4, (1992), pp. 64–78; E. Hobsbawm, *The Age of Extremes. The Short Twentieth Century 1914–1991*, (London: Michael Joseph, 1994), pp. 2–3.

2. Hobsbawm, *The Age of Extremes. A Short History of the Twentieth Century 1914–1991*, (London: Michael Joseph, 1994), pp. 2–3.

3. S.K. Pavlowitch, *The Improbable Survivor: Yugoslavia and its Problems 1918–1988*, (London: Hurst, 1988), p. 1.

4. See I. Banac, *The National Question in Yugoslavia: Origins, History, Politics*, (Ithaca and London: Cornell University Press, 1984) and J. Lampe, *Yugoslavia as History. Twice there was a Country*, (Cambridge: Cambridge University Press, 1996).

5. For example R.D. Kaplan, *Balkan Ghosts. A Journey Through Yugoslavia*, (New York: St Martin's, 1993).

6. For example, S.P. Ramet, *Nationalism and Federalism in Yugoslavia, 1962–1991*, 2nd edn, (Bloomington & Indianapolis: Indiana University Press, 1984).

7. For example, G. Schöpflin, *Nations, Identity, Power. The New Politics of Europe*, (London: Hurst, 2000).

8. For example, Pavlowitch, *The Improbable Survivor*.

1. THE EMERGENCE OF THE SOUTH SLAVS

1. The most comprehensive and authoritative discussion of this topic can be found in Banac, *The National Question in Yugoslavia*.

2. F.R. Bridge and R. Bullen, *The Great Powers and the European States System*, (London: Longman, 1980), p. 5.

3. A. Watson, *The Evolution of International Society. A Comparative Historical Analysis*, (London: Routledge, 1992), pp. 249–50.

4. For a critical analysis of the debate about the sources of nationalist identity and the nature of nationalism see J. Hutchinson and A.D. Smith, *Nationalism*, (Oxford: Oxford University Press, 1994).

5. Banac, *The National Question in Yugoslavia*, p. 71.

6. M. Djilas, *The Contested Country: Yugoslav Unity and Communist Revolution, 1919–1953*, (Cambridge, MA: Harvard University Press, 1991), p. 21.

7. F. Singleton, *A Short History of the Yugoslav Peoples*, (Cambridge: Cambridge University Press, 1985), pp. 24–54.

8. Djilas, *The Contested Country*, p. 23 ff.

9. Ibid., p. 24.

notes

10. J. Lampe, *Yugoslavia as History*, (Cambridge: Cambridge University Press, 1996), p. 58.

11. Djilas, *The Contested Country*, p. 31.

12. Banac, *The National Question in Yugoslavia*, pp. 86–8.

13. Djilas, *The Contested Country*, p. 33.

14. Lampe, *Yugoslavia as History*, pp. 76–7.

15. B. Jelavich, *History of the Balkans. Twentieth Century*, vol. 2, (Cambridge: Cambridge University Press, 1983), p. 55.

16. V. Meier, *Yugoslavia. A History of its Demise*, (London: Routledge, 1999), pp. 51–3.

17. Petrovich, *History of Serbia*, (New York: Harcourt Brace Jovanovich, 1976), pp. 27–81.

18. Lampe, *Yugoslavia as History*, p. 46.

19. Banac, *The National Question in Yugoslavia*, pp. 64–6.

20. N. Malcolm, *Bosnia: A Short History*, (London: Macmillan, 1994), pp. 55–8.

21. For a detailed account of the emergence of the Kingdom of Serbia, see M.E.B. Petrovic, *History of Serbia 1804–1918*, 2 vols, (New York: 1976). M. Crnobrnja, *The Yugoslav Drama*, (London: I B Tauris, 1994), pp. 35–44.

22. B. Petrovic, *History of Serbia*, vol. 1., pp. 230–5; D. MacKenzie, *Ilija Garašanin: Balkan Bismarck*, (Boulder, CO: East European Monographs, 1985), pp. 42–3.

23. Djilas, *The Contested Country*, p. 29.

24. Crnobrnja, *The Yugoslav Drama*, p. 37.

25. M.D. Stojadinovic, *The Great Powers and the Balkans, 1875–1878*, (Cambridge: Cambridge University Press, 1968).

26. A.J.P. Taylor, *The Struggle for Mastery in Europe 1848–1918*, (Oxford: Oxford University Press, 1954), p. 252.

27. Lampe, *Yugoslavia as History*, p. 64.

28. Pavlowitch, *The Improbable Survivor*, p. 116.

29. Jelavich, *History of the Balkans*, p. 28.

30. E. Barker, 'The origins of the Macedonian dispute', in J. Pettifer, ed., *The New Macedonian Question*, (London: Palgrave, 1999), pp. 3–14. See further E. Barker, *Macedonia. Its place in Balkan Power Politics*, (London: RIIA, 1950).

31. C. Dumba, *Memoirs of a Diplomat*, (London: George Allen & Unwin, 1933), p. 116.

32. *Parliamentary Debates* (Hansard), CXXIII, (1903), p. 946. S.G. Markovich, *British Perceptions of Serbia and the Balkans 1903–1906*, (Paris: Dialogue, 2001), p. 65.

33. S.K. Pavlowitch, *History of the Balkans*, 1804–1945, (London: Longman, 1999), p. 174.

34. Lampe, *Yugoslavia as History*, p. 82

35. W.S. Vucinich, *Serbia Between East and West: The Events of 1903–1908*, (Stanford: Stanford University Press, 1954), pp. 180–9.

36. R.W. Seton Watson, 'The Role of Bosnia in International Politics 1874–1914', in L.S. Sutherland, *Studies in History. British Academy Lectures*, (London: Oxford University Press, 1966), pp. 262–93.

37. Singleton, *A Short History of the Yugoslav Peoples*, p. 111.

38. Lampe, *Yugoslavia as History*, p. 91.

39. Quoted by J. Remak in '1914 – The Third Balkan War: Origins Reconsidered', in H.W. Koch, ed., *The Origins of the First World War. Great Power Rivalry and German War Aims*, (London & Basingstoke: Macmillan, 1972), p. 98.

40. Lampe, *Yugoslavia as History*, p. 96.

41. M. Glenny, *The Balkans 1804–1999. Nationalism, War and the Great Powers*, (London: Granta, 2000), p. 299.

42. D. MacKenzie, *Apis: The Congenial Conspirator. The Life of Colonel Dragutin T. Dimitrijevic*, (Boulder, CO: East European Monographs, 1989), p. 64 ff.

43. Lampe, *Yugoslavia as History*, p. 100 ff.

44. Jelavich, *History of the Balkans*, p. 106.

45. G. Stokes, 'The Role of the Yugoslav Committee in the Formation of Yugoslavia', in *Three Eras of Political Change in Eastern Europe*, (Oxford: Oxford University Press, 1997), pp. 93–108. This article appeared originally in *The Creation of Yugoslavia*, D. Djordjevic, ed., (Santa Barbara, CA: Clio Press, 1980), pp. 51–72.

46. Jelavich, *History of the Balkans*, p. 117; Lampe, *Yugoslavia as History*, p. 100.

47. J. Reed, *War in Eastern Europe. Travels through the Balkans in 1915*, (London: Orion Books, 1994), pp. 3–4.

48. Lampe, *Yugoslavia as History*, p. 108.

2. THE COLLISION OF IDEALS

1. A. Sharp, *The Versailles Settlement: Peacemaking in Paris, 1919*, (Basingstoke: Macmillan, 1991), p. 130.

2. A. Sharp, *The Versailles Settlement*, pp. 130–58; S. Marks, *The Illusion of Peace: International Relations in Europe 1918–1933*, (Basingstoke: Macmillan, 1976), pp. 1–24.

3. Sharp, *The Versailles Settlement*, p. 131.

4. I. Lederer, *Yugoslavia at the Peace Conference. A Study in Frontiermaking*, (New Haven, CT: Yale University Press, 1963), pp. 276–308, H. Temperley, *History of the Peace Conference of Paris*, vol. 4, (London: HMSO, 1920–24), pp. 307–37.

5. Lampe, *Yugoslavia as History*, p. 112.

6. D. Mack Smith, *Mussolini*, (London: Paladin, 1981), pp. 43–4.

7. Sharp, *The Versailles Settlement*, pp. 141–2.

8. Banac, *The National Question in Yugoslavia*, pp. 49–58.

9. Lederer, *Yugoslavia at the Paris Peace Conference*, p. 137.

10. Ibid., pp. 228–45.

11. For example, Pavlowitch, *History of the Balkans*, pp. 257–65.

12. S. Jovanović, 'The Jugoslav Constitution', in *Slavonic Review*, vol. 3, 1924–25, p. 169.

13. Ibid., pp. 173–4.

14. Glenny, *The Balkans*, p. 368.

15. Singleton, *A Short History of the Yugoslav Peoples*, p. 147.

16. Pavlowitch, *Yugoslavia*, (New York: Praeger, 1971), pp. 65–74.

17. Djilas, *The Contested Country*, pp. 49–78.

18. M. Glenny, *The Balkans*, p. 404.

19. Pavlowitch, *History of the Balkans*, pp. 261–2.

20. R.W. Seton Watson, 'The Background to the Yugoslav Dictatorship', *Slavonic & East European Review*, vol. 10, 1931–32, pp. 363–76.

21. Lampe, *Yugoslavia as History*, pp. 143–5.

22. Singleton, *A Short History of the Yugoslav Peoples*, p. 115.

23. Lampe, *Yugoslavia as History*, p. 118.

24. E.H. Carr, *International Relations between the Two World Wars 1919–1939*, (Basingstoke: Macmillan, 1947), p. 25.

25. Seton-Watson, 'The Background to the Yugoslav Dictatorship', p. 366; Singleton, *A Short History of the Yugoslav Peoples*, p. 146.

3. DICTATORSHIP AND COMPROMISE

1. Pavlowitch, *A History of the Balkans*, p. 274.

2. Ibid., p. 276.

3. R.W. Seton Watson, 'Yugoslavia and the Croat Problem', *Slavonic and East European Review*, vol. 16, (1937–38), pp. 102–12.

4. This idea is discussed fully in Lampe, *Yugoslavia as History*, pp. 168–70.

5. R.J. Crampton, *Eastern Europe in the Twentieth Century*, 2nd edn, (London: Routledge, 1997), pp. 164–8.

6. Lampe, *Yugoslavia as History*, pp. 174–7.

7. Public Record Office (Kew), FO 431/1 R5735/30/92 Belgrade d. 28, 27 Feb. 1939.

8. Seton Watson, 'Yugoslavia and the Croat Problem', p. 105.

9. Lampe, *Yugoslavia as History*, pp. 179–80; J.B. Hoptner, *Yugoslavia in Crisis 1934–1941*, (New York: Columbia University Press, 1962).

10. G. Swain and N. Swain, *Eastern Europe since 1945*, 2nd edn, (Basingstoke: Macmillan, 1998), pp. 12–15.

11. Biographies of Tito range from the hagiographical, such as P. Auty, *Tito*, (London: Longman, 1970) to the iconoclastic N. Beloff, *Tito's Flawed Legacy. Yugoslavia and the West, 1939–1984*, (New York: Victor Gollancz, 1985). Of the biographies written by Tito's comrades and available in English, V. Dedijer, *Tito Speaks: His Self-portrait and Struggle with Stalin*, (Wiedenfeld & Nicholson, 1953) and M. Djilas, *Tito: The Story from Inside*, (London: Wiedenfeld & Nicholson, 1981) should similarly be read in conjunction with each other for balance. For a short synthesis which takes a critical viewpoint, see S.K. Pavlowitch, *Tito: Yugoslavia's Great Dictator. A Reassessment*, (London: Hurst & Co, 1992).

12. S. Clissold, *Yugoslavia and the Soviet Union 1939–1973. A Documentary Survey*, (London: Oxford University Press for the Royal Institute of International Affairs, 1975), pp. 1–11, 115–21. Swain and Swain, *Eastern Europe since 1945*, pp. 12–15.

13. D.T.A. Stafford, 'SOE and British Involvement in the Belgrade coup d'état of March 1941', *Slavic Review*, vol. 36, no. 3, (September 1977), pp. 399–417; M.C. Wheeler, *Britain and the War for Yugoslavia 1941–1943*, (New York: Columbia University Press, East European Monographs, 1980), especially pp. 34–61.

14. C. Ford, *Donovan of OSS*, (Boston: Little Brown, 1970), p. 103.

15. Quoted in E. Barker, *British Policy in South East Europe in the Second World War*, (London: Macmillan,1972), p. 87.

16. I. Jukić, *The Fall of Yugoslavia*, (New York: Harcourt Brace Jovanovich, 1975), p. 57, cited in B. F. Smith, *The Shadow Warriors: OSS and the Origins of the CIA*, (London: Andre Deutsch, 1983), p. 52.

17. G. Ross, *The Great Powers and the Decline of the European State System 1914–1945*, (London: Longman, 1983), p. 133.

18. Singleton, *History of Yugoslavia*, p. 173.

19. E.H.Carr, *The Twenty Years' Crisis 1919–1939*, (London: Macmillan, 1946 edn,), p. 224.

4.   CIVIL WAR AND COMMUNIST REVOLUTION

1. Jelavich, *History of the Balkans*, pp. 262–3.

2. S. Trifkovich, 'Rivalry Between Germany and Italy in Croatia, 1942–1943', *The Historical Journal*, vol. 36, no. 4, (1993), p. 882; Jelavich, *History of the Balkans*, p. 263.

3. Trifkovich, Rivalry Between Germany and Italy in Croatia', p. 880.

4. S.K. Pavlowitch, 'The King who Never Was: An Instance of Italian Involvement in Croatia, 1941–43', *European Studies Review*, vol. 8, (1978), pp. 465–87.

5. Pavlowitch, 'The King who Never Was', p. 481.

6. The figures for deaths during the conflict are not accurate. See for example, Jelavich, *History of the Balkans*, pp. 264–5 and Lampe, *Yugoslavia as History*, p. 207, note 10. See also J. Tomasevich, 'Yugoslavia during the Second World War', in W.S. Vucinich, ed., *Contemporary Yugoslavia. Twenty Years of Socialist Experiment*, (Berkeley: University of California Press, 1969).

7. S.K. Pavlowitch, 'Neither Heroes nor Traitors: Suggestions for a Reappraisal of the Yugoslav Resistance', *War and Society. A Yearbook of Military History* in B. Bond and I. Roy, eds, (London: Croom Helm, 1976), pp. 227–42.

8. See M.J. Milazzo, *The Chetnik Movement and Yugoslav Resistance*, (Baltimore and London: Johns Hopkins University Press, 1975); J. Tomasevich, *The Chetniks. War and Revolution in Yugoslavia 1941–45*, (Stanford: Stanford University Press, 1975).

9. C. Cviic, *Remaking the Balkans*, (London: Pinter for RIIA, 1991), pp. 19–20.

10. Quoted in D. Wilson, *Tito's Yugoslavia*, (Cambridge: Cambridge University Press, 1979), p. 21.

11. Singleton, *A Short History of the Yugoslav Peoples*, p. 193.

12. W.R. Roberts, *Tito, Mihailovic and the Allies 1943–1945*, (Rutgers University Press, 1973), pp. 76–8; D.Wilson, *Tito's Yugoslavia*, (Cambridge: Cambridge University Press, 1979), p. 25.

13. Trifkovic, 'Rivalry between Germany and Italy in Croatia', p. 895.

14. Operation Weiss came to be known by the Partisans as the Fourth Offensive.

15. P. Hehn (ed.), *The German Struggle Against Yugoslav Guerrillas in World War II: German Counter-Insurgency in Yugoslavia 1941–1943*, (New York & Boulder: East European Monographs, 1975), pp. 3–35. M. Milazzo, *The Chetnik Movement and the Yugoslav Resistance*, (Baltimore and London: 1975), pp. 149–50, quoted in Trifkovic, 'Rivalry Between Germany and Italy in Croatia, p. 898.

16. A. Dallin and F.I. Firsov, *Dimitrov and Stalin 1934–1943. Letters from the Soviet Archives*, (New Haven and London: Yale University Press, 2000), pp. 216–17.

17. Ibid., p. 221.

18. A. Lane, 'Perfidious Albion? Britain and the Struggle for Mastery of Yugoslavia 1941–1944: A Re-examination in the Light of 'New' Evidence', *Diplomacy & Statecraft*, vol. 7, no. 2, (July 1996), pp. 345–77.

19. F.W. Deakin, *The Embattled Mountain* (Oxford: Oxford University Press, 1971). F.H. Maclean, *Eastern Approaches*, (London: Jonathan Cape, 1949).

20. A. Lane, 'Perfidious Albion?', pp. 345–77.

21. For example N. Beloff, *Tito's Flawed Legacy*, (London: Gollancz, 1985); D. Martin, *The Web of Disinformation: Churchill's Yugoslav Blunder*, (New York: Harcourt Brace Jovanovich, 1991).

22. Wilson, *Tito's Yugoslavia*, p. 29.

23. S. Clissold, *Yugoslavia and the Soviet Union*, p. 33, note 114. President Wilson had proposed that the Italo-Yugoslav frontier in Istria should be drawn in accordance with the principle of national self-determination. This 'Wilson Line' was rejected by the Italians.

24. Djilas, *The Contested Country*, p. 146.

25. Much has been written on the so-called 'Percentage Agreement' of October 1944. Among the most useful are P.G. Holdich, 'A Policy of Percentages? British policy in the Balkans after the Moscow Conference of October 1944', *International History Review*, vol. 9, no. 1, (February 1987), pp. 28–47; A. Resis, 'The Churchill-Stalin "Percentages" Agreement on the Balkans, Moscow, October 1944', *American Historical Review*, vol. 83 (2), (April 1978), pp. 368–87.

26. Roberts, *Tito, Mihailovic and the Allies*, pp. 303–4.

27. M.C. Wheeler, 'Pariahs to Partisans to Power: the Communist Party of Yugoslavia', in T. Judt, ed., *Resistance and Revolution in Mediterranean Europe 1939–48*, (New York: Routledge, 1989).

28. Clissold, *Yugoslavia and the Soviet Union*, pp. 23–5.

29. Singleton, *A Short History of the Yugoslav Peoples*, p. 214.

30. This argument is developed particularly clearly by Stevan Pavlowitch in *The Improbable Survivor*, pp. 1–15.

5. STALINISM AND HERESY

1. The conventional wisdom holds that the communists would have emerged the winners even without coercion, but this view is challenged by Aleksander Pavkovic in *The Fragmentation of Yugoslavia: Nationalism and War in the Balkans*, 2nd edn, (Basingstoke: Macmillan, 2000), p. 216, note 14.

2. H. Seton Watson, *The East European Revolution*, 3rd edn, (London: Methuen, 1956), pp. 167–229; Seton Watson's model has been challenged in recent years by the Swains who argue that since the communist revolutions in the Balkans were carried out by indigenous communists, Stalin's desire to Sovietise them was of little importance. Swain and Swain, *Eastern Europe since 1945*, p. 7.

3. H. Seton Watson, *From Lenin to Khrushchev. A History of World Communism*, (New York: Praeger, 1960), pp. 248–70; the standard work on the political

evolution of post-war Yugoslavia is D. Rusinow, *The Yugoslav Experiment 1948–1977*, (London: Hurst, 1977).

4. Singleton, *A Short History of the Yugoslav Peoples*, p. 210.

5. Wilson, *Tito's Yugoslavia*, p. 44.

6. Maclean, *Eastern Approaches*, p. 327.

7. Rusinow, *The Yugoslav Experiment*, pp. 13–14.

8. Ibid., p. 15.

9. An excellent summary of the debate and its contributors appears in Pavlowitch, *The Improbable Survivor*, p. 140 fn. See also Lampe, *Yugoslavia as History*, p. 235.

10. A. Lane, 'Putting Britain Right with Tito: the displaced persons question in Anglo-Yugoslav Relations, 1946–47', *European History Quarterly*, vol. 22, (1992), pp. 217–46.

11. See R. Knight, 'Harold Macmillan and the Cossacks. Was there a Klagenfurt Conspiracy?', *Intelligence and National Security*, vol. 1, (1986).

12. Pavlowitch, *The Improbable Survivor*, pp. 101–3.

13. V. Mastny, *Russia's Road to the Cold War*, (New York: Columbia University Press, 1979), pp. 282, 288.

14. Clissold, *Yugoslavia and the Soviet Union*, pp. 45, 83–4.

15. M. Djilas, *Conversations with Stalin*, (New York: Rupert Hart Davis, 1962).

16. Clissold, *Yugoslavia and the Soviet Union*, p. 48. The text of the agreement appears in F.A. Voigt, *The Greek Sedition*, (Berkeley, 1969), p. 165.

17. M. Djilas, *Rise and Fall*, (London: Macmillan, 1985), pp. 227–8; E. Barker, *Macedonia. Its Place in Balkan Power Politics*, (London: RIIA, 1950), p. 117.

18. E. Barker, 'Yugoslav Policy Towards Greece, 1947–1949', in L. Baerentzen, J.O. Iatrides and O.L. Smith, (eds), *Studies in the History of the Greek Civil War*, (Copenhagen: Museum Tusculaneum Press, 1987), pp. 263–308.

19. Swain and Swain, *Eastern Europe since 1945*, p. 58.

20. Clissold, *Yugoslavia and the Soviet Union*, p. 46.

21. Swain and Swain, *Eastern Europe since 1945*, pp. 56–8.

22. Royal Institute of International Affairs, *The Soviet–Yugoslav Dispute. Text of the Published Correspondence*, (London: RIIA, 1948).

23. M. Djilas, *Tito. The Story From Inside*, (London: Weidenfeld & Nicholson, 1981), p. 125, C. Andrew and V. Mitrokhin, *The Mitrokhin Archive: The KGB in Europe and the West*, (Penguin, 1999) pp. 464–5.

24. 'Grandpa' was the Comintern nickname for Josef Stalin.

25. Seton Watson, *From Lenin to Khrushchev*, pp. 266–7.

26. Lampe, *Yugoslavia as History*, p. 250.

27. R. Crampton, *A Short History of Modern Bulgaria*, (Cambridge: Cambridge University Press, 1987).

28. *Jugoslavenstvo* in Croatian.

29. Wilson, *Tito's Yugoslavia*, pp. 68–74.

30. D. Acheson, *Present at the Creation: My Years in the State Department*, (New York: W W Norton & Co, 1969), p. 333; Djilas, *Rise and Fall*, pp. 273–4.

31. Djilas, *Rise and Fall*, pp. 235–6.

32. B. Kiraly, 'The aborted Soviet Military Plans against Tito's Yugoslavia', in W.S. Vucinich, ed., *At the Brink of War and Peace: the Tito–Stalin Split in a Historic Perspective*, (New York: Brooklyn & Mega Press, 1992), pp. 273–88; G. Partos,

The World that came in from the Cold, (London: RIIA, 1993), pp. 21–2. Andrew and Mitrokhin, *The Mitrokhin Archive: The KGB in Europe and the West*, p. 464.

33. Swain and Swain, *Eastern Europe Since 1945*, p. 23.

34. Clissold, *Yugoslavia and the Soviet Union*, p. 227, no. 146, 'Soviet Reply to Yugoslav Protest', 11 February 1949.

35. A. Lane, *Britain, the Cold War and Yugoslav Unity*, pp. 125–49; L. Lees, *Keeping Tito Afloat: The United States, Yugoslavia and the Cold War*, (Pennsylvania State University Press, 1997).

36. Clissold, *Yugoslavia and the Soviet Union*, p. 165.

6.   TITO'S YUGOSLAVIA CONSOLIDATED

1. Pavlowitch, *Tito: Yugoslavia's Great Dictator*, (London: Hurst, 1992), p. 103.

2. A. Pavkovic, *The Fragmentation of Yugoslavia: Nationalism and War in Yugoslavia*, 2nd edn, (Basingstoke: Macmillan, 2000), pp. 61–3.

3. The principal sources for this section are D. Rusinow, *The Yugoslav Experiment 1948–1974*, (London: Hurst for RIIA, 1977), pp. 70–80, and Pavlowitch, *Yugoslavia*, pp. 252–6.

4. Pavlowitch, *Yugoslavia*, p. 252.

5. Ibid., p. 253.

6. M. Djilas, *The New Class. An Analysis of the Communist System*, (New York: 1957); see also Pavlowitch, *Yugoslavia*, p. 269.

7. Wilson, *Tito's Yugoslavia*, p. 82; Lampe, *Yugoslavia as History*, p. 257.

8. J.C. Campbell, ed., *Successful Negotiation Trieste, 1954*, (New Jersey: Princeton University Press, 1976).

9. Swain and Swain, *Eastern Europe since 1945*, p. 77.

10. A. Ulam, *Expansion and Co-existence. The History of Soviet Foreign Policy, 1917–67*, pp. 562–3.

11. Clissold, *Yugoslavia and the Soviet Union*, p. 66.

12. S. Talbot, ed., *Khrushchev Remembers*, (Boston: Little Brown & Co, 1971), p. 383.

13. Jelavich, *History of the Balkans*, p. 391; Ulam, *Expansion and Co-existence*, p. 563.

14. Singleton, *A Short History of the Yugoslav Peoples*, pp. 238–9.

15. Lampe, *Yugoslavia as History*, p. 272.

16. Ibid.

17. Jelavich, *History of the Balkans*, pp. 391–2.

7.   MARKET SOCIALISM AND THE RESURGENCE OF NATIONALISM

1. Lampe, *Yugoslavia as History*, pp. 277–8.

2. Pavlowitch, *Yugoslavia*, p. 302.

3. Rusinow, *The Yugoslav Experiment*, p. 136.

4. Wilson, *Tito's Yugoslavia*, pp. 140–2.

5. Ramet, *Nationalism and Federalism*, pp. 16–17.

6. Quoted in Glenny, *The Balkans*, p. 586.

7. Lampe, *Yugoslavia as History*, pp. 277–8.

8. Crampton, *Eastern Europe in the Twentieth Century*, p. 309.

9. F. Fetjö, *A History of the People's Democracies*, trans. D. Weissbort, Pelican edn, 1974, pp. 376–7; Lampe, *Yugoslavia as History*, pp. 281–4.

10. Ramet, *Federalism and Nationalism*, p. 188. Accounts of this event vary widely, some sources enumerating the number of deaths as rather higher.

11. Bennett, *Yugoslavia's Bloody Collapse*, p. 71.

12. Fetjö, *A History of the People's Democracies*, pp. 197–9.

13. Rusinow, *The Yugoslav Experiment*, pp. 186–7

14. A. Carter, *Democratic Reform in Yugoslavia. The Changing Role of the Party*, (London: Pinter, 1982).

15. His book was duly published in the United States as *Conversations with Stalin*, op. cit.

16. Glenny, *The Balkans*, p. 585.

17. Jelavich, *A History of the Balkans*, p. 396.

18. Rusinow, *The Yugoslav Experiment*, pp. 217–18.

19. Ibid., pp. 240–41.

20. Ibid., p. 249; Jelavich, *History of the Balkans*, p. 395.

21. D. Wilson, *Tito's Yugoslavia*, p. 201 fn. 8.

22. M. Tanner, *Croatia. A Nation Forged in War*, (Yale: New York and London, 1997), pp. 200–1.

23. V. Meier, *Yugoslavia. A History of its Demise*, trans. S. Ramet (London: Routledge, 1995), pp. 35–6.

24. M. Markovic, 'Marxist Philosophy in Yugoslavia: The Praxis Group', in M. Markovic and R.S. Cohen, *Yugoslavia: The Rise and Fall of Socialist Humanism*, (London: Bertrand Russell Peace Foundation, 1975). An extract is reprinted in G. Stokes, ed., *From Stalinism to Pluralism: A Documentary History of Eastern Europe since 1945*, 2nd edn, (Oxford: Oxford University Press, 1996), pp. 116–21.

25. Rusinow, *The Yugoslav Experiment*, p. 327.

26. C. Bennett, *Yugoslavia's Bloody Collapse. Causes, Course, Consequences*, (London: Hurst, 1995), p. 72.

27. J. Gow, *Legitimacy and the Military. The Yugoslav Crisis*, (London: Pinter, 1992), pp. 26–62; Bennett, *Yugoslavia's Bloody Collapse*, pp. 75–7.

28. Lampe, *Yugoslavia as History*, pp. 308–15.

29. D. Plestina, ' "From Democratic Centralism" to Decentralised Democracy? Trials and Tribulations of Yugoslavia's Development', in J.B. Allcock, J.J. Horton and M. Milivojevic, eds, *Yugoslavia in Transition: Choice and Constraints*, (New York & Oxford: Berg, 1992), pp. 125–68.

30. Singleton, *A Short History of the Yugoslav Peoples*, p. 268.

31. Quoted in C. Cviic, *Remaking the Balkans*, 1st edn, p. 59.

32. Singleton, *A Short History of the Yugoslav Peoples*, pp. 265–9.

33. Ramet, *Nationalism and Federalism*, pp. 150–61.

34. Pavlowitch, *Yugoslavia*, p. 360.

35. Pavlowitch, *The Improbable Survivor*, p. 17.

36. Clissold, *Yugoslavia and the Soviet Union*, p. 80.

37. A. Rubinstein, *Yugoslavia and the Non-Aligned World*, (Princeton, NJ: Princeton University Press, 1979), especially pp. 326–9. For a summary of

Yugoslav foreign policy in the 1970s, albeit with an anglocentric bias, see Wilson, *Tito's Yugoslavia*, pp. 255–9.

8. THE END OF ILLUSION

1. Singleton, *A Short History of the Yugoslav Peoples*, p. 280.

2. For a wide ranging discussion of Yugoslav historiography in this period see I. Banac, 'Yugoslavia', *American Historical Review*, October 1992, pp. 1084–104. Stevan Pavlowitch has dwelt at length on Tito's biographers in a review essay, 'Dedijer as Historian of the Yugoslav Civil War', *Survey*, 28, 3, (1984), pp. 95–110.

3. Ramet, *Nationalism and Federalism*, pp. 214–15.

4. Ibid., p. 197.

5. Ibid., pp. 194–5.

6. M. Baskin, 'Crisis in Kosovo', *Problems of Communism*, 32, (March–April, 1983), p. 65; G. Stokes, 'The Devil's Finger: the Disintegration of Yugoslavia', in *Three Eras of Political Change in Eastern Europe*, (Oxford: Oxford University Press, 1997), pp. 122–3.

7. Singleton, *A Short History of the Yugoslav Peoples*, p. 273.

8. Ramet, *Nationalism and Federalism*, p. 199; Stokes, 'The Devil's Finger', pp. 122–3.

9. Lampe, *Yugoslavia as History*, p. 319. See further H. Lydall, *Yugoslavia in Crisis*, (Oxford: Oxford University Press, 1989).

10. Bennett, *Yugoslavia's Bloody Collapse*, p. 69.

11. Ibid., pp. 74–5; Stokes, 'The Devil's Finger', p. 120.

12. Glenny, *History of the Balkans*, p. 625.

13. Bennett, *Yugoslavia's Bloody Collapse*, p. 70.

14. J. Seroka, 'Variation in the Evolution of the Yugoslav Communist Parties', in J. Seroka and V. Pavlovic, *The Tragedy of Yugoslavia: The Failure of Democratic Transformation*, (London: M E Sharp, 1992), pp. 67–88.

15. Cviic, *Remaking the Balkans*, p. 60.

16. Stokes, 'The Devil's Finger', p. 131.

17. Bennett, *Yugoslavia's Bloody Collapse*, pp. 76–8, R. Thomas, *Serbia Under Milošević: Politics in the 1990s*, (London: Hurst, 1999), pp. 40–1.

18. Memorandum of the Serbian Academy of Sciences (SANU), trans. D. Rusinow, 1986, in G. Stokes, ed., *From Stalinism to Pluralism: A Documentary History of Eastern Europe since 1945*, 2nd edn, (New York & Oxford: Oxford University Press, 1996), pp. 275–80.

19. Cviic, *Remaking the Balkans*, p. 66.

20. A. Djilas, 'A Profile of Slobodan Milošević', in *Foreign Affairs*, vol. 71, no. 4, (Summer 1993).

21. Thomas, *Serbia Under Milošević*, p. 42.

22. This speech, often reported, was extemporised in the heat of the moment and various version of the precise words used exist. Pavlowitch seems to suggest in *Serbia. The History Behind the Name*, (London: Hurst, 2002) that words were used in the context of Serbian protests at being beaten by the Albanian

police with truncheons, p. 192. Thomas, in *Serbia Under Milošević* is rather less charitable and goes as far as to argue that the demonstration was organised by Milošević in advance, pp. 44–5.

23. Pavlowitch, *Serbia*, pp. 194–5.

24. Stokes, 'The Devil's Finger', pp. 122–3.

25. V. Meier, *Yugoslavia. A History of its Demise*, trans. S. Ramet, (London: Routledge, 1995), pp. 35–6.

26. Meier, *Yugoslavia*, pp. 63–7; Gow, *Legitimacy and the Military*, pp. 80–1.

27. Stokes, 'The Devil's Finger', pp. 127–9.

28. Lampe, *Yugoslavia as History*, p. 246–7.

29. Meier, *Yugoslavia*, p. 123; Crnobrnja, *The Yugoslav Drama*, pp. 113–14.

9.   NEMESIS

1. A wealth of literature has appeared detailing the many aspects, domestic and international, to the violent dissolution of Yugoslavia. Much of this literature inclines towards partisanship towards one or other party to the dispute. Among those which avoid this pitfall are L. Silber and A. Little, *The Death of Yugoslavia*, (London: Penguin 1995), a reliable eyewitness account written in journalese and A. Pavkovic, *The Fragmentation of Yugoslavia: Nationalism and War in the Balkans*, 2nd edn, (Basingstoke: Macmillan, 2000). A wealth of detail on the international diplomacy is provided by J. Gow, *Triumph of the Lack of Will: International Diplomacy and the Yugoslav Question*, (London: Hurst & Co, 1997). Bennett, *Yugoslavia's Bloody Collapse*, is a useful summary but takes a hostile attitude towards the Serbs.

2. Schönflin, *Nation, Identity and Power*, pp. 324–69.

3. Stokes, 'The Devil's Finger', p. 132.

4. Gow, *Legitimacy and the Military*, pp. 54–5.

5. Bennett, *Yugoslavia's Bloody Collapse*, pp. 76–7. M. Vasic, 'The Yugoslav Army and the Post-Yugoslav Armies', in D. Dyker and I. Vejvoda, eds, *Yugoslavia and After: A Study of Fragmentation and Despair*, (London: Longman, 1996), pp. 116–37.

6. The most detailed analysis of the first post-communist elections is that by L.J. Cohen, *Broken Bonds. Yugoslavia's Disintegration and Balkan Politics in Transition*, 2nd edn, (Boulder, Co & Oxford: Westview Press, 1995).

7. L.J. Cohen, 'Embattled Democracy: Post-communist Croatia in Transition', in K. Dawisha and B. Parrott, eds, *Politics, Power and the Struggle for Democracy in South-East Europe*, (Cambridge: Cambridge University Press, 1977), pp. 69–121.

8. J. Teokarević, 'Neither War Nor Peace: Serbia and Montenegro in the first half of the 1990s', in Dyker and Vejvoda, eds, *Yugoslavia and After*, p. 184; Stokes, 'The Devil's Finger', pp. 134–5.

9. A. Pavkovic, *The Fragmentation of Yugoslavia*, p. 79.

10. Ibid., pp. 222–3.

11. Meier, *Yugoslavia*, pp. 179–95.

12. Bennett, *Yugoslavia's Bloody Collapse*, pp. 124–5.

13. Stokes, 'The Devil's Finger', p. 139.

14. Official figures recorded 13 Slovene deaths, with 112 wounded. On the JNA side, 39 killed, 163 wounded.

15. The most detailed single volume study of the diplomacy surrounding the Yugoslav wars of dissolution is that by J. Gow, *Triumph of the Lack of Will. International Diplomacy and the Yugoslav War*, (London: Hurst, 1977), pp. 50–3.

16. The author is grateful to Christopher Cviic for this convenient shorthand.

17. Bennett, *Yugoslavia's Bloody Collapse*, pp. 173–9

18. Pavkovic, *The Fragmentation of Yugoslavia*, pp. 147–53.

19. Bennett, *Yugoslavia's Bloody Collapse*, pp. 182–3.

20. G.F. Kennan, 'The Balkan Crises: 1913 and 1993', published originally in *New York Review of Books*, 15 July 1993 and reprinted in G.F. Kennan, *At a Century's Ending: Reflections 1982–1995*, (London: W.N. Norton & Co. 1996), pp. 191–208.

21. Cohen, *Broken Bonds*, p. 295.

22. Gow, *Triumph of the Lack of Will*, pp. 263–5.

23. D.N. Perry, 'The Republic of Macedonia Finding its Way', in Dawisha and Parrott, eds, *Politics, Power and the Struggle for Democracy*, pp. 226–85.

24. M. Weller, 'The Rambouillet Conference on Kosovo', *International Affairs*, vol. 75, no. 2, (April 1999), pp. 211–52; R. Caplan, 'International Diplomacy and the Crisis in Kosovo', *International Affairs*, vol. 74, no. 4, (October 1998), pp. 745–62.

25. Bennett, *Yugoslavia's Bloody Collapse*, p. 216.

Glossary

autocephalous	Church having administrative autonomy under its own 'head'
AVNOJ	Anti-Fascist Council of National Liberation
ban	Croatian head of state appointed by the Hungarian Crown
chetniks	Members of armed bands of insurgents (chetas) in Greater Serbia at the beginning of the twentieth century and in Yugoslavia during the Second World War
Cominform	Communist Information Bureau
Comintern	Communist International
CPP	Croat Peasant Party
IMRO	Internal Macedonian Revolutionary Organisation
JNA	Yugoslav Army of National Liberation
kulaks	Perjorative term employed in Sovietised states to describe wealthy peasants
millet	A population group under Ottoman rule defined by religious confession
OZNa	Department for the Protection of the People
Sabor	Parliament (Croatia)
SAWPY	Socialist Alliance of Working People of Yugoslavia
Skupština	Parliament (Serbia)
Sobranje	Parliament (Macedonia)
Sporazum	The agreement granting autonomous status to Croatia under the Yugoslav monarchy, August 1939
UDBa	State Security Service
Ustaša	Croatian Liberation Movement (Fascists)

Bibliographical Essay

Of the more general studies of Yugoslavia's place in the broader history of the Balkans, Stevan K. Pavlowitch's *A History of the Balkans 1804–1945* (London: Longman, 1999) provides both a shrewd analysis and a balanced source; the post-1945 period is covered in the same series by Richard Crampton, *The Balkans since the Second World War* (New York and London: Longman, 2002). For a more journalist account see Misha Glenny, *The Balkans 1804–1999: Nationalism, War and the Great Powers* (London: Granta Books, 1999) which is valuable not least for its fascinating insights into the key personalities.

Fred Singleton's *A Short History of the Yugoslav Peoples* (Cambridge: Cambridge University Press, 1985) is very accessible but is outdated since its analysis self-evidently does not allow for the de-legitimisation of communism. Cambridge have supplanted it with an excellent modern single volume study by John R. Lampe, *Yugoslavia as History: Twice there was a Country* (Cambridge: Cambridge University Press, 1996) which places particular emphasis on the economic background to Yugoslav history. Stevan Pavlowitch's *Yugoslavia* (London: Ernest Benn, 1971) remains possibly the best in-depth study of Yugoslavia's development up to the reactions to reform, while his later single volume of essays, *The Improbable Survivor: Yugoslavia and its Problems 1918–1988* (London: Hurst & Co, 1988) is an insightful volume drawing on key themes of the period.

The national identities of the Yugoslav peoples is examined in magisterial detail by Ivo Banac in *The National Question in Yugoslavia: Origins, History, Politics* (London: Cornell University Press, 1984); for an eclectic study of the Yugoslav idea as it developed during the First World War politics of the Yugoslav peoples see Dimitrije Djordjevic, *The Creation of Yugoslavia 1914–1918* (Santa Barbara: Clio Books, 1980). Alexa Djilas's monograph *The Contested Country: Yugoslav Unity and Communist Revolution 1919–1953* (Cambridge, MA: Harvard University Press, 1991) discusses the relationship between communism and nationalism in the context of the origins of communist Yugoslavia. This should be read in conjunction with F.W. Neal's *Yugoslavia and the New Communism* (New York: 1962) and Dennison Rusinow's *The Yugoslav Experiment 1948–1974* (London: Hurst, 1977).

Much of the best literature on the Second World War dates from the 1970s. The most balanced study of the civil war and allied politics is that by Walter Roberts, *Tito, Mihailovic and the Allies* (New Brunswick, NJ: Rutgers University Press, 1973). Matteo J. Milazzo, *The Chetnik Movement and Yugoslav Resistance* (Baltimore and London: Johns Hopkins University Press, 1975) and Jozo Tomasevich, *The Chetniks: War and Revolution in Yugoslavia 1941–45* (Stanford: Stanford University Press, 1975) also remain good accounts.

Biographies of Tito range from the hagiographical to the iconoclastic. Among the best still is Stevan K. Pavlowitch's short and highly readable study, *Tito: Yugoslavia's Great Dictator: A Reassessment* (C Hurst & Co: London, 1992). For an inside account, Milovan Djilas's memoir: *Tito: The Story from Inside* (London: Phoenix Press, 2000) published originally a year after Tito's death, has recently been reprinted.

Among the plethora of works published on the origins of Yugoslavia's wars of dissolution the most balanced are Aleksandar Pavkovic, *The Fragmentation of Yugoslavia: Nationalism and War in the Balkans* (London: Macmillan, 2000) and that by Viktor Meier, formerly Balkan Correspondent for the *Frankfurter Allgemein* entitled *Yugoslavia: A History of Its Demise* (London and New York: Routledge, 1999). The latter is particularly strong on the politics of the emergence of the new republics. For an account of the wars between 1991 and 1995 see *The Death of Yugoslavia* (Penguin Books, BBC Books, 1995) which accompanied the BBC series of the same name, written by Laura Silber and Allan Little who reported the conflict for the *Financial Times* and the BBC.

Index

Acheson, Dean   109
Agriculture   52–3, 67, 69, 84, 97, 107, 111
Albania   30, 40, 55, 62, 71, 76, 92, 105,
    134, 144, 156–7
Albanian language   137, 157
Alexander (Karadjordjević) King   48, 57,
    58–60, 63, 68, 74, 89–90, 95
Anschluss (1938)   68
Anti-Fascist Council of National
    Liberation (AVNOJ)   83, 88–91, 95,
    111
Apis *see* Dimitrijević
Aung San   110
Austria   8, 9, 10–11, 13–14, 16, 20–33,
    40, 52, 62, 68, 99, 100–2, 104, 121,
    150
Austria-Hungary   9, 24, 25, 30–1, 35, 38,
    40, 96
Axis   69, 71, 72, 76–7, 79, 82, 88, 91

Balkan Alliance   121
Balkan federation   87, 104
Balkan League   28
Balkan Pact (1931)   62–3, 68
Balkan Wars   27–8, 41, 43
Banat   17, 18, 19, 20, 76
Bandung Conference (1955)   126
Barthou, Louis   63
Belgrade   91, 102–5, 109, 117, 121–2,
    125, 127, 129, 132, 136–8, 140, 144,
    146–7, 151, 156, 161, 164, 165, 167,
    168, 174, 183, 185, 187, 192–3
Benkovac   181
Berchtold, Count   28
Berlin, Treaty (1878)   22–3, 29, 33
Bihać   83
Bilandžić, Dušan   146
Black Hand   29, 33
Bled   103
Borba   174

Bosnia-Herzegovina   8, 10, 14, 18, 20, 24,
    26–7, 29, 31, 41, 44, 50, 65–6, 69, 74,
    77, 79, 81, 83, 92, 96, 110, 117,
    130–1, 137, 141, 147, 155, 160, 166,
    174, 177–9, 182, 185, 186–92, 194
Bosnian crisis (1908)   26–7
Bosnian Muslims   8, 17–18, 22, 41, 65,
    66, 78, 81, 83, 96, 188
Bosnian Serbs   177, 188, 189
Bosnia War (1992–95)   189–90
Brajici   83
Brezhnev Doctrine   150, 162, 178
Brioni   117–18, 123, 135, 184
Brotherhood & Unity   174
Broz, Josip *see* Tito
Bucharest, Treaty (1913)   28
Bulatović, Momir   178
Bulgaria   21, 23–5, 27–8, 40–1, 47, 54,
    62, 68, 71, 76, 84, 90–1, 103–5, 122
Bulgarian Exarchate   23
bureaucratization   120–2
Burma   126
Byzantium   8, 23

Campbell, Sir Ronald   65
Carinthia   40, 102
Carniola   40
Carr, E H   74
Carrington, Lord   185
Cartwright, Sir Fairfax   28
Ceauçescu   150, 162
Cer, Battle of   30
Četniks   80–1, 83, 84, 87, 88, 91–2, 99,
    178
China   124, 151
Churchill, Winston S   72, 88–9, 90
Cincar-Marković, Alexander   72, 73, 96
Cold War   3, 94, 100, 102, 109, 110,
    113, 115, 116, 146, 148, 152, 162,
    172, 183, 184, 188

collaboration   45, 95, 99–100
COMECON   112, 133, 147
Cominform   104–6, 110, 123, 125
Comintern   47, 70–1, 81–2, 86, 87
Communism   71, 84, 87, 102, 104, 105,
     107, 115, 116, 122, 144, 150, 151,
     152, 154, 162–3, 167, 171–2, 176,
     183, 186–7, 195, 196
Communist Party of Yugoslavia (CPY)
   inter-war activities   46–7, 59, 70, 82,
     95, 98
   and coup of 1941   72–3
Constitutions
   1921   44–5, 56, 58
   1931   60
   1946   96–8
   1953   108–9
   1963   131–2
   1974   143–4, 156, 163, 173
Contact Group   188–90, 193–4
Corfu Declaration   32–3
Cošić, Dobrica   162
Coup d'état (1941)   72–3
Croat Peasant Party   42, 47, 56
Croatia   10–12, 14–15, 26, 31, 48, 52,
     59, 63, 96, 182, 183
   nationalism   11–13, 53, 76, 77, 160–70
Croatian Democratic Community   179
Croatian Democratic Union   177
Croatian Spring   139–43, 169
Crvenkovski, Krste,   135
Čvetković, Dragiša,   66, 71, 76
Čvetković-Maček Agreement 1939   69
Cvijić, Jovan   30
Czechoslovakia   53, 63, 110, 138–9,
     149–51, 175

Dabčević-Kučar, Savka   140
Dalmatia   15, 31, 69, 73, 96
D'Annunzio, Gabriele   39
Danube River   51
Davidović, Ljuba   46
Dapčević, Peko   103
Dayton Agreement   190–2
Deakin, F W (Bill)   87, 88
Dedijer, Vladimir   118–19, 155
DEMOS   176
Dimitrijević, Colonel Dragutin   29, 33

Dimitrov, Georgi   86, 105, 107
Djilas, Milovan   97, 105, 106, 107,
     117–19, 120, 122, 136, 142
Domobranci   79
Donovan, William   72
Drasković, Milorad   47
Drašković, Vuk   155, 178
Dubček, Alexander   149–50
Dumba, Constantine   25

EAM   103
Eastern Question   9, 17
economy   3, 5, 16–17, 22–4, 36, 51–3,
     65–9, 79, 97, 110–13, 121, 125–7,
     128, 132–3, 145–7, 149, 156, 159–60
   aid to underdeveloped regions   147–8,
     169
   Five Year Plans   112–13, 125–6, 127
   reform   16, 59–61, 129, 130–1, 160–2,
     174
Eden, Anthony   64, 89
education   8, 9, 11–12, 15, 48, 50, 64,
     67, 69, 117, 135, 137
Egypt   133
Enlightenment   10, 11
European Union (EC, EEC)   147, 150,
     182, 183, 186

fascism   61–3
First World War   30, 37–8, 45, 52, 80
Fiume, see Rijeka   67
Foča   83
France   9, 11, 19, 25, 36, 42, 52, 54–5,
     62–4, 67, 69–70, 104, 132, 138, 142,
     149, 186, 189
Frank, Josip   31
Franz Ferdinand, Archduke   1, 27, 29
French Revolution   10, 11, 12

Gaj, Ludjevit   13
Garašanin, Ilija   13, 19–20
genocide   78, 92
George VI, King   72
Germany   4, 9, 27, 59, 64, 73, 75, 79,
     83, 87, 97, 126–7, 186
Gligorov, Kovo   180, 191
Goražde   188
Gorbachev, Mikhail   162

Gorizia 15
Gospić 78
Government-in Exile 83, 86, 89
Grand Alliance 88
Great Britain 21, 25, 37, 52, 54, 61, 68,
  71, 72, 97, 86, 88, 132
Greece 23, 28, 62–3, 71, 73, 85,
  90, 102–3, 105, 113, 121, 123,
  190
Grol, Milan 91, 95

Habsburg Slavs 10–13, 31
Hebrang, Andrija 97, 106, 111
Helsinki Agreement 151
Henderson, Neville 65
Hitler, Adolf 62, 68, 70, 72–3, 76, 79,
  83, 196
Hobsbawn, Eric 1
Holy Roman Empire 8
Horstenau, Edmund von 78
Hoxha, Enver 105
Hudson, D T (Bill) 86, 87
Hungary 9–12, 21, 22, 25–7, 30–2, 34,
  40, 43, 47, 53, 59, 63–4, 68, 76–7,
  90–1, 96, 97, 104, 123

Illinden Uprising 24
Illyrian idea 12–13
Illyrian Provinces 12
IMF 132, 146
IMRO 24, 54–5, 180
Independent Radical Party 72
Independent State of Croatia 76
India 125, 133
Industrialization 9
Istanbul
Italy 27, 34, 40, 54, 55, 59, 63–4, 68,
  85, 89, 99, 104, 121, 131, 132, 150,
  184
  frontier with 38, 100, 121, 150
Izetbegović, Alija 120, 186

Jajce 88, 101
Janković, Radivoje 73
Jasenovac 78
Jevtić, Bogoljub 65
Jovanović, Dragoljub 96
Jovanović, Slobodan 73

Kadijević, Gen Veljko 176
Kalman 12
Karadjordjević dynasty 33
Karadžić, Vuk 15, 19
Karadžić, Radovan 177
Kardelj, Edvard 97, 105, 106, 109, 131,
  142, 145, 157–8
Karl IV, King 53
Kasche, Siegfried 78
Khrushchev, Nikita 122–3, 124
Khuen-Hedérvary, Count Karoly 14
Kidrić, Boris 97, 111
Klagenfurt 102
Kljvić, Stejpan 179
Knin 81
Korean War 109–10
Korošec, Anton 32, 38, 58, 65
Kosovo 17, 41, 53, 96, 127, 131, 134–5,
  137, 143, 146–7, 156, 160, 162–6,
  169, 174, 191–4
Kosovo Liberation Army 192–3
Krajina 10, 181, 183, 185, 186–8, 189
Krleža, Miroslav 137
Kučan, Milan 176
Kun, Bela 47

Lalatović, Maj 86
Lansing, Robert 36–8
Laval, Pierre 64
League of Communists of Yugoslavia
  107, 108, 115, 117–19, 120, 124,
  127, 129, 130, 132, 134–5, 137–9,
  143–4, 149, 154–5, 174, 176, 180
  6h Congress (1953) 117
  7th Congress (1958) 117–20
  8th Congress (1964) 131–2
  12th Congress (1982) 156
  14th Congress (1990) 176
League of Nations 40, 54, 63–4
Linhart, Tomas 15
Little Entente 52, 53, 63–4, 68, 150
Ljotić, Dimitrije 76
Ljubljana (Laibach) 16, 50, 120, 124,
  150, 158, 169, 176
London
  Agreement 1954 121
  Treaty (1913) 28, 37
  Treaty (1915) 32, 39

Macedonia   7, 20, 22, 23–4, 26, 27, 31,
    38, 41, 44, 54–5, 68, 73, 76, 81, 84,
    96, 103, 131, 137, 147, 156, 158, 179
Maček, Vladko   59, 63, 65, 66, 73, 78,
    89
Maclean, Fitzroy   88
magyarisation   12–15
Marković, Ante   160–2, 169, 174, 176,
    180, 184, 191
Marshall Aid   104, 113
Marx, Karl   89
Masaryck, Thomas,   33, 59
Matica Hrvatska   140
Medjumurje   96
Mešic, Stipe   181
Mestrovich, Ivan   31
Metternich   13
Middle East Defence Committee
    88
Mihailov, Mihailo   136–7
Mihailović, Draža   80, 83, 84, 86, 88, 92,
    99
Mikoyan, Anastasi   122
Mikulić, Branko   160–2
military border   15, 17
millet   18
Milosević, Slobodan   160–2, 164–5, 169,
    170, 176, 177–8, 179
Mirković, Bora   72
Mitterand, François   1
Montenegro   7, 20–2, 24–6, 28–32, 44,
    51, 53, 76, 79, 84, 96, 117, 130,
    132–48, 147, 159, 166, 178, 180,
    188, 191
Moscow   90, 103–5, 106, 123,
    150
    Percentage Agreement (1944)   90, 123
Mussolini, Benito   39, 69, 70–1, 196

Narodna Odbrana   29
Nasser, Gamal   125
nationalism   2, 4, 7, 10, 27, 29, 30, 31,
    37, 45–6, 74, 108, 124, 128, 129,
    136, 141, 152, 154, 156, 162, 165,
    167, 170, 171, 196
NATO   121, 150, 189, 183, 191, 193–4
Nazi-Soviet Pact   70
Nedić, Milan   76, 80, 99

Nehru, Pandit   125
Neuilly-sur-Seine, Treaty   40
Nicholas I, Tsar   20
Niš Declaration   30
nomenklatura   108, 158
non-alignment   124–5, 148–9, 150–1
Novi Sad Agreement   117, 136
Novotny, Jan   149

Obrenović, Milos   17, 18, 19, 24
OECD   133
Omar Pasha   24
Orthodox Church   11, 100
Ottoman Empire   8, 10, 16–17
Owen, David   188–90
OZNA   98

Paris   40–1, 54, 64, 71
    Peace Conference (1946)   101–2
Partisans   76, 79, 82–4, 86, 87, 91, 101
Pašić, Nikola   25, 26, 27, 31, 33, 38, 43,
    45, 51, 56
Paul, Prince   64–5, 66, 68, 70, 72–3, 75
Pavelić, Ante   63, 77, 78, 99
Perestroika   160
Perović, Ivan   64
Peter Karadjeordje   24–5
Peter II, King   64, 72, 89, 91
Petrović, Djorde (Karadjordje)   17–18
Poland   123
polycentrism   124, 134
Popular Front   70, 95
Pozderac, Hamidja   178
Praxis Group   138
Pribičević, Svetozar   46, 48, 56, 50
Princip, Gavrilo   29
Priština   156–8

Radić, Stepjan   42, 43, 47–8, 49, 56, 65
Ranković, Alexander   97, 98, 105, 134,
    141
Rapallo, Treaty of   39
Rašković, Jovan   177
Ravna Gora   83, 86
Ribar, Ivan   83, 96
Ribbentrop, Baron Von   71
Rijeka (Fiume)   39, 40
Roosevelt, Franklin D   72, 88

Rumania 51, 62, 63, 71, 77, 91, 104, 112, 150, 169
Russia 9, 11, 17, 20–1, 25–6, 28, 36, 189, 191, 194

Saddam Hussein 184
Saint-Germain-en-Laye, Treaty 40
Sandzak of Novi Pazar 22, 92
San Stefano, Treaty 21, 23–4
Sarajevo 1, 46, 129, 188
SAWPY 87
Second World War 58, 74, 94, 108, 115, 132, 164, 172, 179, 180–1
self-management 116, 118, 120, 125–6, 130–2, 146, 154, 158, 161, 196
Serb Peasant Party 72, 96
Serbia 16, 18–19, 21, 22–3, 24–8, 30–1, 34–5, 41, 44, 47, 49, 54, 58, 66, 69, 73, 76, 77, 79, 80–3, 91–2, 96, 117, 130, 132, 142, 146–7, 152, 161, 163–6, 170, 177, 180–3, 191–3
   nationalism 18–20, 28, 45, 96, 163–7
Serbian Democratic Party 46, 177
Serbian Independence Party 46
Serbian Radical Party 44, 46
Serbian Renewal Movement 178
Serbian Orthodox Church 7, 11, 18, 66
Serbo Croat language 138, 175
Seton-Watson, H 95
Seton Watson, R W 42
Simović, General Dusan 72, 73
Sinn Fein 43
Sino-Soviet relations 124
Skarleska Poreba 104
Skopje 23, 27, 158, 179
Slavonia 11, 17
Slovenia 15–16, 40, 49, 52, 73, 76, 81, 96, 127, 142, 176
society 2, 5, 16, 17–19, 50, 55, 67, 71, 77, 82, 92, 100, 108, 115–16, 119, 120, 133, 134, 140, 141, 144, 154–5, 164, 167, 169, 180, 187, 197
South Slavs 7, 8
Soviet bloc 124
Soviet Union 70, 79, 85–7, 91, 100–1, 104
Soviet-Yugoslav dispute 103–6, 121–4
Spaho, Mehemet 65

Spanish Civil War 71, 87
Srebrenica 188
Sremski Karlovci, Treaty 11
Stalin, Josef 70, 86, 88, 94, 101, 103, 113, 136
Stambolić, Ivan 164–5
Stanković, Radenko 64
Stara gradiska 78
Starčević, Ante 14, 31
Stepinac, Archbishop 78
Stojadinović, Milan 65, 66, 76
Strossmayer, Bishop Josip Juraj 13
Styria 40
Šubašić, Ivan 89–90, 91, 95
Sujetska 87
Supilo, Frano 31–2, 46
Sutej, Dr Juraj 72
Šuvar, Stipe 169

Teheran conference 1943 89
Territorial Defence Units 139, 182, 187
Tirana 41, 138, 157, 158
Tito, Josip Broz 47, 70–1, 59, 81, 82, 83, 86, 88, 91, 92, 93, 96–7, 105, 107–8, 112, 117, 131, 134, 138–9, 142–3, 148, 170
   cult 119, 154
   death & legacy 114, 151–2, 155, 158
   foreign policy 120, 125–6, 148–51
Titoism 115–16, 123–4, 128, 152–3, 164
Tito-Šubašić Agreement (1944) 98, 89–90
Tolbukhin, F I 91
tourism 133, 152, 160
Trepča 165
trialism 27
Trianon, Treaty 40
Trieste 40, 51, 68
Tripalo, Mihailo 140
Tripartite Pact 71–2
Triple Alliance 27
Triple Entente 27
Truman, Harry 102
Trumbić, Ante 31–2, 38
Tudjman, Franjo 137, 140, 144, 170, 177, 178, 181, 182, 183, 189
Turkey 62, 103, 121

UDBA 91, 95, 135, 136
'Unification or Death' 98, 134, 135
United Nations 110, 125, 150, 183, 85–6, 188–90, 193–4
United Provisional Government 91, 95, 98
United States of America 26, 54, 60–1, 72, 87, 102, 104, 109, 110, 127, 132, 183, 184, 186, 189, 191
UNRRA 110
Ustaša 63, 76, 78, 81
Užice 82, 86

Valona 39
Vardar 53
Venezia Giulia *see* Trieste
Versailles, Treaty *see also* Paris Peace Treaty
Viafides, Markos 103
Vienna, Treaty (1815) 16, 23
Villach 103
Vojvodina 11–12, 17, 34, 40, 65, 76, 95, 119, 131, 135
Vukmanović-Tempo, Svetozar 103

war crimes 99
Warsaw Pact 103, 175
White Hand 50, 58

Wickham Steed, Henry 42
Wilson, President Woodrow 36, 39, 43, 89

Yalta Conference 104, 123
Young Bosnia 29
Yugoslav Army 50, 58, 64, 140, 144, 173–5, 182, 184
Yugoslav Committee 31–35
Yugoslav Philosophical Association 138
Yugoslav Radical Union 65
Yugoslavia
  'ancient hatreds' 3
  concept 2, 36, 94, 108–9, 117, 119
  demography 41, 60, 100, 172–3
  foreign aid 121, 128
  foreign policy objectives 63, 68, 69–70, 148–9
  foundation 2, 4, 33–4, 36–7, 42
  sovietisation 95, 103–4
Yugoslavism 116–17, 131, 137, 154, 162

Zadar (Zara) 39
Zagreb 77, 92, 107, 37, 142
Zepa 178
Živković, Peter 58–9, 64, 65
Zujović, Sretan 106